Mary's Message for a New Day

Mary's Message for a New Day

Mark L. Prophet
Elizabeth Clare Prophet

SUMMIT UNIVERSITY PRESS®

*To all devotees
of the Blessed Mother
and of her Son
Jesus Christ*

MARY'S MESSAGE FOR A NEW DAY
by Mark L. Prophet and Elizabeth Clare Prophet
Copyright © 2004 by Summit University Press
All rights reserved

No part of this book may be reproduced, translated, or electronically stored, posted or transmitted, or used in any format or medium whatsoever without prior written permission, except by a reviewer who may quote brief passages in a review. For information, contact Summit University Press, PO Box 5000, Corwin Springs, MT 59030-5000.
Tel: 1-800-245-5445 or 406-848-9500.
Web site: www.summituniversitypress.com

Previously published as *My Soul Doth Magnify the Lord!*
by Summit University Press, Copyright © 1974, 1979, 1986
All rights reserved

Design and layout: Brad Davis

Library of Congress Control Number: 2003104588
ISBN: 0-922729-88-3

SUMMIT UNIVERSITY ꩜ PRESS

The Summit Lighthouse, ꩜, *Pearls of Wisdom,* Keepers of the Flame, Church Universal and Triumphant, and Science of the Spoken Word are trademarks registered in the U.S. Patent and Trademark Office and in other countries. All rights reserved

Contents

Preface 1

Foreword 23

Introduction: The Soul of Mary on Earth 33

PART ONE
The Wisdom Aspect of the Christ Flame
Fourteen Letters from a Mother to Her Children

THE TEMPLE OF UNDERSTANDING
An Exposé of the Abuses of Doctrine and Dogma
by Mother Mary

1 Darkness Shall Be Overcome by Light! 51
2 A Secret Covenant with God through Total Surrender . .56
3 Peace, Be Still! 59
4 It Is the Sense of Struggle That Makes the Struggle 65
5 O Mankind, How Lovely You Are
    in Your God-Identity! 70
6 My God Shall Supply All Your Need 75
7 He Was Made Man That We Might Be Made God! 80
8 The Son Shall Also Be Subject unto Him That Put
    All Things under Him 84
9 As Men Sow, So Shall They Reap 88
10 Let Us Not Be Weary in Well Doing 91
11 For the Letter Killeth but the Spirit Giveth Life 95
12 Father, into Thy Hands I Commend My Spirit 101

13 I and My Father Are One 108
14 The Correct Understanding of Universal Purpose 112

PART TWO
The Love Aspect of the Christ Flame
Eight Mysteries of the Rosary by the
  Mother for Her Children

Christian Prayer Forms
  and the Evolution of the Rosary 119

Adorations of the Rosary 143

Mary's Ritual of the Rosary
  for Sons and Daughters of Dominion 151

MARY'S SCRIPTURAL ROSARY
FOR THE NEW AGE

The Teaching Mysteries
Sunday Morning - The Second Ray
  First Teaching Mystery:
    The Beatitudes 157
  Second Teaching Mystery:
    *The Marriage Feast
    and the Wedding Garment* 158
  Third Teaching Mystery:
    The Unmerciful Servant 160
  Fourth Teaching Mystery:
    The Ten Virgins 161
  Fifth Teaching Mystery:
    The Tares among the Wheat 163

The Masterful Mysteries
Sunday Evening - The Eighth Ray
  First Masterful Mystery:
    The Temptation in the Wilderness 165
  Second Masterful Mystery:
    *Raising of Jairus' Daughter
    and the Woman Who Touched Christ's Garment* 167

Contents

- Third Masterful Mystery:
  Jesus Walking on the Water 168
- Fourth Masterful Mystery:
  The Transfiguration 170
- Fifth Masterful Mystery:
  The Raising of Lazarus 171

The Love Mysteries
Monday Morning - The Third Ray

- First Love Mystery:
  The Love of John the Baptist and Jesus 173
- Second Love Mystery:
  The Love of the Disciples for the Master 175
- Third Love Mystery:
  The Love of Christ and His Members 176
- Fourth Love Mystery:
  The Love of the Master for His Disciples 178
- Fifth Love Mystery:
  The Love of the Father 180

The Joyful Mysteries
Tuesday Morning - The First Ray

- First Joyful Mystery:
  The Annunciation 182
- Second Joyful Mystery:
  The Visitation 183
- Third Joyful Mystery:
  The Nativity 185
- Fourth Joyful Mystery:
  The Presentation 187
- Fifth Joyful Mystery:
  The Finding of Jesus in the Temple 189

The Healing Mysteries
Wednesday Morning - The Fifth Ray

- First Healing Mystery:
  Christ the Light of the World 191

Second Healing Mystery:
   At the Pool of Bethesda 192
Third Healing Mystery:
   One Born Blind 194
Fourth Healing Mystery:
   The Ten Lepers 195
Fifth Healing Mystery:
   The Two Witnesses 197

The Initiatic Mysteries
Thursday Morning - The Sixth Ray
   First Initiatic Mystery:
      The Last Supper 199
   Second Initiatic Mystery:
      The Vigil in the Garden 201
   Third Initiatic Mystery:
      The Trial 203
   Fourth Initiatic Mystery:
      The Carrying of the Cross 204
   Fifth Initiatic Mystery:
      The Crucifixion 206

The Glorious Mysteries
Friday Morning - The Fourth Ray
   First Glorious Mystery:
      The Resurrection 208
   Second Glorious Mystery:
      The Ascension 210
   Third Glorious Mystery:
      The Descent of the Holy Spirit 211
   Fourth Glorious Mystery:
      The Glory of the Woman and the Man Child 213
   Fifth Glorious Mystery:
      The Triumph of the Divine Mother 214

Contents

The Miracle Mysteries
Saturday Morning - The Seventh Ray
  First Miracle Mystery:
    The Marriage at Cana 217
  Second Miracle Mystery:
    Jesus Stills the Tempest and Heals the Gadarene Demoniac ..218
  Third Miracle Mystery:
    The Feeding of the Five Thousand 220
  Fourth Miracle Mystery:
    Christ Forgives the Adulterous Woman 222
  Fifth Miracle Mystery:
    Christ the Bread of Life 223

PART THREE
The Power Aspect of the Christ Flame
Fourteen Messages of the Word of Life
  to the Children of the Mother

 1 A Perpetual Vigil Is the Requirement of the Hour 228
 2 A Cup of Freedom in His Name 238
 3 The Chalice of My Heart 245
 4 Create the World Without That Is Your World Within ..250
 5 The Prayer and the Warning of the Universal Mother .256
 6 The Law of the Transposition of Energy 265
 7 Sons and Daughters of the Dominion
    of the Water Element 276
 8 The Beckoning and the Call of the Cosmic Mother ...282
 9 It Is the Father's Good Pleasure
    to Give You the Kingdom 289
10 The Light That Shines in the Dark Streets
    of Jerusalem 297
11 Hail, Thou That Art Highly Favored! 303
12 Go Forth to Challenge the Night! 310
13 The Key to Opportunity 317
14 Come into the Arms of the Divine Mother 328

The Chart of Your Divine Self 337

Notes 341

Illustrations
Chart of the Rosary 137
Chart of Your Divine Self 338

Preface

Beloved Who Love Life,

    I must tell you the story of my conversion to the Spirit of the age of Aquarius. The Mother. The Great Goddess. "A woman clothed with the sun, and the moon under her feet, and upon her head a crown of twelve stars."

    My conversion to God as Mother, the counterpart of the God I had always known as Father, was through the blessed, the beautiful Mother Mary. Strange that our Judeo-Christian tradition has not given to us the sense of God in the feminine gender. Yet she is there with him when Elohim (the plural noun for God expressing plurality, polarity, in the unity of the One) create us, male and female, after the image of the Divine Us.

    When I found Mother Mary, or rather when she found me, I realized the great canyon of aloneness that I and others experience without Mother. And Mary taught me how we all desperately yearn to know our Cosmic Mother and our soul's aborning in the cosmic womb—how we fill the vacuum with the frenzied pursuits of the pleasure cult, so much noise and running here and there, escaping from the aloneness, her laughter silenced to our soul senses, deadened by drugs. Her footsteps on the threshold of consciousness buried in the beat of rock, hard rock and more rock, rocking to a deep hypnotic sleep the generation she is calling to come home. With our cults of death and dying, we cover over and over the gnawing aching to find Mother.

    The pain has been there so long that we no longer recognize it—its cause or its cure. We just get more and more self-sufficient. We're all grown up. We don't need Mother any more. But we keep on looking for mothering. The TV is Mother—the violence, loud commercials, soap operas, personality parades, talk and more talk never arriving at the truth, and sex of every conceivable configuration. Is this our escape as we sit hour by hour in our silent screaming for Mother? "Mother, look at me, talk to me! Do something! Anything! If you won't praise me when I'm good, then at least spank me when I'm bad. But don't hate me. Mother, please don't leave me alone."

Affair after affair, unfulfilled love, preoccupations with sex, her body, her sacred force in both man and woman—all of these are abortive attempts to get to, and even control, the elusive goddess. And what of abortion? And who is really aborted—child or mother? Is it the anticlimax of the love-hate relationship with the one we really love, who, no matter what we do, won't love us, won't need us, won't notice us—or so it seems.

The computer is Mother, but the alien is also Mother. And fascination with horror, cataclysm and the superhuman, supermaddening intergalactic wars between the personae of good and evil becomes the inversion of our quest for Mother. And when she doesn't come and doesn't come, or so it seems, we see a nation in the act of national suicide, in utter despondence. Or is it in ultimate revenge against her?

Yes, we need the Divine Mother. Oh, how we need her! We need her as much if not more than we need the Divine Father because we know that she is the one who will teach us all about him. Without her, we fear to approach his throne. But approach it we must. Where is Mother!

When Mother comes—and when she does, she tells us she's been there always in love—she is teacher. Preeminently, eminently, Mother is the Knower and the known.

First she reassures us in the deepest levels of our psyche that our Father-Mother is one and that our souls were created out of the union of the sacred fire, Alpha and Omega, in the Great Central Sun. She soothes us and dissolves our disquietude with the assurance that our Father and our Mother are indeed one and in love.

She shows us their love in a cosmic panorama—the turning of worlds within and without, and everywhere the multiplication of life by their Word that went forth. This love interchange of the cosmic lovers is light, scintillating light, that ripples across the warp and woof of the whole creation and seals our souls in the Cosmic Egg. Mother gives us the peace that passeth all understanding by sharing with us our origin and the experience of our soul's immaculate conception in the fiery core of universal being.

She teaches us that long, long ago by free will we spiraled far, far away from the hub of life and that we decelerated into time and space dimensions worlds apart, suspended in random freedom in the cosmic womb. In our experiments with energy, we crystallized universes and compartments of consciousness—until the memory of their love and of our souls cradled in its sacred fires became distorted, distended and finally disintegrated.

In the midst of outer oblivion, our only clue is the inner longing quickened by the inner soul memory that once we were one in love.

It is Mother Mary, bright beatific daughter of God, who reconnects our souls to the umbilical cord of the Cosmic Virgin. And the rhythm of her life, pulsing life, is once more our own. Mother Mary is the nearest and most dear incarnation of the Virgin that we know. Through her, we get to her. She is her messenger, the form of her formlessness, the presence of her elusive all-pervasiveness.

Mother Mary, by the grace of her soul's initiations under the Cosmic Virgin, is the one anointed by God to bear to us the Christ in the person of Jesus, the Son. She comes today to teach us how we, too, can receive him into our hearts as the Real Person of our soul. She teaches us how to listen to the still small voice of the Word as he speaks to us in our hearts. And by and by, she explains the mystery of the indwelling Christ.

It is she who tells us of the Son and his redemptive spirit. She teaches us that we are God's beloved children and that through our love of his Son, whom he made her own, we can become the sons and daughters of God and that when we obey his commandments, the Father and the Son will love us tenderly and come unto us and make their abode with us. She is our teacher until we know him as the teacher. But even then, she keeps the vigil of our communion with the Father and the Son and the Holy Spirit.

She is the guardian of our enlightenment. She knows us better than we know ourselves. She knows our weaknesses and our worries. She listens as we recount our problems. She helps us measure them against the mountains and the stars. She shows us the nonpermanence of time and space and all that's in it. She makes life beautiful, full and joyous—here and now.

She is priestess at the altar of our heart, tending the sacred fires of the Trinity. She shows us how to bow before the Lord's Spirit, the Comforter sent by the Father and the Son to teach us of a practical self-giving love. Through her we recognize the person who will make us remember all the things the Son taught us when he was with us on earth and when we were with him in heaven.

Even before Abraham was born, he taught us the name I AM and revealed our true being in him. And just before our last parting at Golgotha and then at Bethany, he told us again the name of the Father, I AM THAT I AM, even the name behind that name. And he revealed to us the Word and the great mystery of its incarnation in him. Then he unveiled the truth that "where I AM—in consciousness, in attainment, in love—there ye may be also."

The Mother reminds us that we might do the works that he did and greater works. She, the bride of the Holy Spirit, stands with the Comforter as he explains that through loving obedience to the Father and the wise living of our lives and the giving of ourselves to the Son in one another, the promise of our inheritance will be fulfilled.

Sometimes when we've disobeyed him and we want to run and hide, she takes us by the hand and assures us that we can face him, receive his chastening love and bravely accept the discipline our souls really need and want. Then by and by when we pass the many testings of our love by their love, she promises us that the Son will ignite the flame of his Christ consciousness in our hearts, making it our very own.

We will then no more be children, but we will be Sons of God and heirs with him of the inner light. And it is Mother who teaches us the path, step-by-step, which leads to this reunion of our soul first with the Father through the Son, second with the Holy Spirit through the Son, and third with the company of saints who have already achieved that union, whether in heaven or on earth.

Our Mother will not leave us—no, she will not leave us alone—until our course is set, the lines of victory crystal clear and we are strong enough, wearing the mantle of her, of him, to meet the challenge of life and win.

John bore record of her appearance, the Woman clothed with the Sun, along with the "great red dragon" in the twelfth chapter of the Book of Revelation. According to the cosmic clock, she emerges at the threshold of consciousness at the hour of Aquarius. At the end of the two-thousand-year Piscean dispensation of Jesus Christ, she comes to give birth to the Manchild within us all. Her defender is Michael the archangel, who defeats the dragon, the Fallen One, and casts him and his angels out of heaven into the earth. There they continue "to make war with the remnant of her seed, which keep the commandments of God and have the testimony of Jesus Christ."

The Manchild, O children of the Woman, is the individual Christ consciousness. And she is in the process of giving birth to this Christ Child within your soul. Being with this Child, she cries, travailing in birth, and is in pain to be delivered. We are living in the moment of her birthing, our birthing. And it is we who are being born into our Higher Self.

The dragon is standing by, ready to devour her Child as soon as it is born within us. His seed who inhabit the earth today are the tares which the enemy has sown among the wheat. They are the children of the wicked one. They vehemently oppose on every frontier of consciousness the coming of age of the Woman in both male and female and the coming of age of her Manchild within every soul born of God. This opposition is manifesting as the subtle serpent with his false logic of the sufficiency of human solutions to human problems without the Presence or the Person of the Son of God.

Today our conceptions of life are so colored by this force of Antichrist, this force that is "anti" the light in you and me, that we are quite often outraged by the truth which the Mother brings, until she exorcises the rage implanted in the recesses of the collective unconscious by the offspring of the wicked one.

They are the raging rebels against life who dance their do-it-yourself death dance, entrancing our youth into deeper and deeper levels of a self-hypnotized death. Their death is so insidious because it is so gradual, a slipping away from selfhood while the body and the surface senses are still in motion. It is a death of awareness, of sensitivity to life—of the will to be. Their hatred of the Virgin is so virulent that they daily make a spectacle of sweet death, sugarcoated death. No more the free choice—life or death. Life is no longer real. The only choice is what color, what flavor death.

We watch as little children are lured to drugs, to violence, horror, hatred, war, murder and suicide. These fill the vacuum of boredom that a sort of existence has become without the personal equation of the Mother. Now we see the imagination of some men's hearts as it was in the days of Noah is "only evil continually." We watch as even the educated are magnetized into the glamour of the self-destructive subculture of the seed of the wicked as they march single file, like robot ants, to the Last Judgment and the second death.

They know their time is short. They seek whom they may devour. They sing their songs about coming from hell and going to hell and taking America with them by revolution, rock and drugs. So goes the madness of their lurid logic. And no one seems to know it is they who are the unreal.

They are the loud illusion, ghosts of their former time and space, spending their last energy on radical inverse, perverse, obsessive departures from the rhythm of life that is the order and geometry of a cosmos—the cosmos that is us, that we make up, that we're made out of. And so their violations of the law of love are against us personally, not just against the impersonal "them."

"He that is not for me—the cosmos that I AM—is against me. When any part of the One suffers, it is I who suffer." So says our Mother. So say we, when we are a part of her, no longer apart. Therefore we mobilize to exorcise the cancer of self-apartness that is eating away at the body of God—of us children.

But, alarmingly, a larger and larger segment of our society is anesthetized by the subliminal permeation of noise and nihilism and perhaps psychopolitical as well as chemical warfare where perceptions of the Real and the unreal in good and evil are altered drastically and people fear the enemy without, not knowing he is within. And anxiety itself becomes the syndrome of a society in inertia, afraid to grow—though well aware that that which ceases to grow ceases to be—afraid to live and afraid to die.

She comes, the Saviouress, to rescue us from the downward spiral of the degradation of the age. Let us hear her call and give answer before it is too late! Too late and the eyes of our souls can no longer meet her tender eyes.

Mother Mary, archetype of the Woman, has taught me this and much more concerning her Fátima prophecy, but her message is terribly hard to bear and very unpopular. It is nevertheless true.

Mother Mary could not teach me until I would recognize her as teacher—and listen. But how could I recognize her, seeing I did not know her—seeing all my life I heard only hatred of her name and ignorance or a malicious neglect of her office both human and divine. With all of the anti-Catholic, anti-Mary prejudice drilled into me since childhood by a fanatical fear, unbelievable, how would I recognize the one who was the key to Mother?

There was only one way it could have happened, and it did—by conversion. I was converted to the Mother by Mary.

I was in Boston finishing my degree in political science at Boston University and preparing to go to Washington, D.C., to serve the ascended masters. But before I left that city, I was to have one of the most important experiences—if not the most important—on the Path. It taught me more about myself than years of philosophy or logic or psychology and the best instructors.

I realized that I had had a prejudice imposed upon me since childhood that I had never challenged and never reasoned through for myself. Like anything that we are taught and we accept early in life, it was just there growing inside of me. Childhood indoctrinations can become such a blindness, such a blight on the natural unfoldment of our souls! Sometimes they are so entrenched that often we do not break the stranglehold of our prejudices for decades or even in a given lifetime.

I had always received much comfort in Catholic churches. While I was studying in Europe, I made a pilgrimage to the Catholic cathedrals. But I still believed, as I had been told, that Catholics worshiped idols, that Mother Mary was some sort of a goddess that allowed herself to be called the "Mother of God" and other such things. I thought people worshiped her person in place of God. I didn't understand why you needed to go through

Mary to get to Jesus to get to God. And I was taught that people made her equal with or even greater than Jesus Christ or Almighty God himself.

I found myself reacting with intense feelings to the images and icons of Mother Mary all over Boston. One in particular was a huge mural which covered the wall of the subway I took to BU every day, bearing the title "Queen of the Universe." If she was so great, why did she allow this blasphemy! I was angry with her. With all of the other problems that made for division and confusion in Christendom, why didn't she come down and straighten this one out! I guess I was disturbed only because deep down inside of me I really loved her, and I wanted to know her as she was, as she is and not as others had portrayed her to me.

But even in my willfulness and independence, God had been showing me little by little how utterly and totally inadequate my subjective awareness was, that I really could not in any way expect to be found acceptable as an offering to him or even be found in his likeness without someone else who had already come into that close relationship.

In other words, I was being shown and I was coming to accept, with a newfound humility and patience, that I desperately needed a teacher. The Path has cardinal principles, it has initiations, it has teachings, and these we put on and wear like a garment, cycle by cycle. We can go only so far in preparing ourselves for the coming of the King. Then, because we do not see ourselves as we are, we need another, wiser than ourselves, to tell us how to trim our lamps.

So God had answered my call and sent Mark to me, the teacher who was to become my husband and beloved co-worker on the Path. He was the visible sign of the heretofore invisible ascended masters. Through him I first heard the Word of the Lord delivered by Archangel Michael in the full fire of the Holy Spirit. Through him I found El Morya (the beloved Saint Thomas More).

A truer friend no soul has ever known. Even my search for Saint Germain (Saint Joseph) was ended.

That sunny day in Boston I was in the joy of the Presence of God, the hosts of the Lord, the holy angels! They were real. They were moving among us to help us in this "time of trouble" that Daniel foresaw. There was hope, much hope in my heart for the world. Confident in the Lord, I was walking, fairly skipping, along the sidewalk in the middle of crowds and traffic on a lunch hour, praying and talking to God in joyous realization of his servant sons and daughters, the ascended masters. I had found what I had been looking for. Yet, though I really didn't know it fully, one thing was lacking—one area of my life was still a void. It was in this state of my unawareness, my ignorance and, yes, I do confess, my conscious/unconscious programmed hostility toward Mary that she found me.

All of a sudden I looked up—and there she was! I was face-to-face with the Blessed Mother. I saw very clearly, for the first time in my life, the beautiful Mary, a being of great light. A charge of light and indescribable joy passed through my body, traveling like a loop of electricity from my head to my feet and back again.

I remember the exact place in the pavement where I was stopped—transfixed, transformed. She had the face of a young maiden, a daughter of God. She was Michelangelo's La Pietà—alive and well and glorious. I saw her at once as Mary, the Woman of the age, and as the light emanation of a greater light. She was clothed with the Sun behind the sun. Her immaculate heart was on fire with an energy that she transmitted at will to me, to anyone. It was clear that she was the one whose pure devotion to the Father was a crystal stream whose issue was the Son, Jesus Christ.

There she was before me, the most transcendent and lovely young woman, full of grace and truth and beauty and integrity. She looked like a young girl you would see in this century, suspended above and before me, as real as you are, as real as I am.

She was someone you could invite into your kitchen to have a cup of tea, someone you could talk to about anything. She was someone just like me except in another dimension. Except she really wasn't quite like me. She was something much much more. Her Presence was resplendent with the light she had adored and become. It was evident that by her meditation upon the macrocosm, she had become something of a cosmos all her own. She had entered into and consciously become a part of life, infinity, that I had not. She had realized a greater portion of the Self than most of earth's evolutions had any idea was there to be realized.

There was enough of her (the divine part) in me and enough of me (the human part) in her that I knew that whatever she had done to become what she was, I could do it too—if she would show me the way. I knew this truth because her Presence communicated it to me. Her Presence was one of possibilities, infinite possibilities, not just for me but for all women—and for men as well. Her very person said, "I AM what I AM because the Son of God is born in me. He can be born in you physically/spiritually, symbolically/actually. And when he is, you will know the same I AM Presence where you are…the works that I do shall ye do also, and greater works."

I wanted to be like her, and I knew that I could if I embraced her and her path. Mother Mary was not just Mother Mary! She was Mother Mary *and* the Spirit of the Lord, who was with her and in her. What's more, she was the teacher—someone who had walked the earth and successfully overcome the trials and tribulations of her time and her space and ascended (accelerated the light of her soul) unto her Father and my Father, her God and my God. She was someone who had understood God as Mother uniquely as no other woman had ever done. She was someone who could teach me how to be me, how to be woman, how to be one with God, as Mother.

Today Mother Mary represents to me one among many of the

hosts of the Lord who are feminine beings—personifications, exemplifications of God as Mother. She is one of the ascended masters who has realized the self as Mother, who has taken that Mother energy to its logical conclusion, who has reunited with the Trinity and, by her own consciousness of God, brought forth the avatar of the age, Jesus Christ.

The love of her heart poured out to me. It melted my soul, my self. In the presence of her immense compassion, I was being wrapped in the swaddling garment of her understanding. She knew my sin and understood it. There was an exchange. She took my sin and consumed it in the sacred fire of her heart. She gave me her understanding. By her wisdom I was made whole. In that instant I realized that I had loved her, the real Mother Mary, forever.

Mother Mary was my friend. In my inner soul, I had always loved her, but my outer mind had been programmed. How could such a dichotomy exist in one person? I realized that I had accepted into my being, if for a moment or for an hour, the same hatred that was abroad in the world for the Mother of Christ. As it is the power of 'anti-Christ' that denies the Son of God within us, Mother Mary explains that it is the hatred of Mother, or 'anti-Mother', that denies the source of that Christ consciousness in all. That denial effectively closes off to the children of this generation the rising fountain of purity that is the Mother light within their own temples.

All of that unreal overlay from earlier years dropped from me, and I saw her in all of her beauty and radiance and love and utter humility before God and before his light burning in my own being, however imperfect. I felt ashamed that I had allowed myself to be shrouded in the world's death consciousness covering the Mother. And I thought, what other brainwashing have you accepted because it is the way of the world? Think of it! All of this you have taken in from other people, contrary to your truest feelings, and from people who have set themselves up as authorities in matters of the soul in the sanctity of its communion with the Spirit. This you were willing to accept without literally going to the fount of life and demanding your own empirical, scientifically spiritual proof when life as God, as Mother was so ready and willing to reveal itself to you!

I became so enamored with Mother Mary that I didn't walk, I *ran* to the nearest Catholic church! I went down the aisle. I knelt before her statue in full awareness that I was kneeling before a representation of the Divine Mother. I was worshiping neither the statue nor Mother Mary. I was bowing to the light within her, the light of the one God that had manifest itself to me in the Person of that Mother whom Mary had become. I acknowledged her as teacher because she was the example.

I called to her and to God the Father, whose daughter she is, for forgiveness. I called to God the Son, whose Mother she was, for forgiveness. And I called to God the Holy Spirit, whose bride her soul had become, for forgiveness. It was all too clear—to offend the Mother was to offend the Trinity. No wonder the world was in such a shambles! No wonder the Antichrist and the Dragon were in such prominence!

I could feel her love flowing to me and her forgiveness dissolving all misunderstanding. In that moment, I gave her my life. And I knew I was giving myself to God in her, to the God she adored, who has assumed her soul into his Spirit in the blessed initiation of the assumption.

I gave my life to the light in her heart—"that was the true Light, which lighteth every man that cometh into the world." I reconsecrated my life to the one God in manifold expressions in his sons and daughters. Now I knew another magnificent expression, one who by free will had made his image her own. It was perfectly clear that in the being whom I saw, the image of Christ had been magnified in her heart until his image was reflected not only in her Son but also in her radiant soul.

And I said, "Mother Mary, forgive me! forgive me! forgive me! and let me be your instrument. Let me go where you lead and let me nourish your children. Let me mother life and set life free. Let me be your hands and feet. Let me be your heart and your temple. And let me serve your children, minister to them and bring comfort to life. Here, take my temple! Let me go and find your children and give to them your love and light and your understanding. Use me. I am your daughter. My life is yours and I will go forth to defend your children." I felt her love, I felt her forgiveness, and I had a newfound Mother.

Mother Mary has been a part of my desiring God and seeking God all these years. I felt that, like Saul, I had been blinded by the deadly beast of religious bigotry, which allowed me to despise another part of God, a most sacred part of God, through an educated self-righteousness. My conversion was, through her blessed intercession, the healing of my soul by the Father, the Son and the Holy Spirit. Through her, the 'blinding' light transmuted my other blindness and I was reconciled to all three.

To see her was to love her. She held up no barriers to herself. She allowed me to love her. She gave herself to me. She beckoned me to enter her meditation upon the Son. In so doing, I entered the upper room of her consciousness. I became one with her.

As she offered her exalted state to me, I offered my lowly estate to her. I knew I had something to give her, the one thing she did not have—a physical body, a mind, a heart, a soul to magnify the Lord on earth and to magnify her heavenly presence. I would witness. I would tell her story. I would challenge the ignorance and the malice heaped upon her blessed name and person. And whatever she told me to do, I would do it gladly.

How else than by just words and deeds does one right the wrong of so grave an injustice? Though God forgave me fully in that hour, I had to go and search out the people I had erroneously influenced by my error. And what of other millions yet suffering from the fraudulent claims of the false ones? Denying the children of God access to the Mother, they had cleverly denied them access to her Son. The hatred of Mother Mary was the hatred of the womb that bore him to us. If the Father had so venerated her, surely our failure to do the same was an offense to him.

Yes, I became one with Mother Mary. And in the years since then, I have communed with her heart and her soul. She is immense—as immense as the universe her consciousness fills. Yes, to me she is my Queen of queens and the Queen of the Universe, gladly. Her power is the power God gives her. And she gives it freely to all who acknowledge her service in love, to all who give adoration to the Mother, God as Mother, through her sacred name. It was a conversion complete that has never left me, nor has the intensity of the moment of her love to me and my promise to her.

When I speak of conversion, I speak of entering into communion with God, perhaps with one of his saints, East or West, or a communion with his light, his Presence. Conversion is more than an intellectual apprehension or an emotional experience. It is entering into a spiral of energy, of being and then becoming that spiral, that energy, that being. In a real conversion experience, we find that all of our own consciousness and energy has been truly converted, or "turned around," to flow with the movement, with the direction of that consciousness of God, whom we have contacted in one of his emissaries.

So many of us have taken our inspiration from people who have lived among us or from those who have lived in the past and not necessarily from those who have entered into God consciousness. Today, as never before, there is a door that is opened in heaven and we can take our inspiration from the true saints of the inner Church, East and West. I call them, and they call themselves, ascended masters. Because they have passed their tests in earth's schoolroom under the master teacher Christ Jesus. Because they have become one with him. Because he has given to them the mantle of his soul's mastery. Because, by his grace, they have ascended to his Presence. Because he has fulfilled his promise to them:

> If a man love me, he will keep my words: and my Father will love him, and we will come unto him, and make our abode with him....
>
> Father, the hour is come; glorify thy Son, that thy Son also may glorify thee: as thou hast given him power over all flesh, that he should give eternal life to as many as thou hast given him....
>
> That they all may be one; as thou, Father, art in me, and I in thee, that they also may be one in us....That they may be one, even as we are one: I in them, and thou in me, that they may be made perfect in one....
>
> Yes, the ascended masters are the saints who have kept the sayings of Jesus Christ. In them his Word is fulfilled: "If a man keep my saying, he shall never see death."

And so I was liberated, by the intercession of the Mother, from one of those pockets of hatred. And a freeing of my energy came about through the freeing of my thoughts and feelings, both conscious and subconscious. Ever since that moment, I have felt the Presence of Mother Mary with me, teaching me what it means to be Mother, to be willing to take up the responsibility that is upon all women to be guardians of the flame of the Trinity in our husbands and our children, in our communities and our nations.

I believe there is no liberation for any woman without the confession that Mary became one with God as Mother and, because she did and she is showing us how, we can also. If I can't see the Mother light in her and in her Son, how can I expect to see it in myself or in my family?

Mary tells us, "This is the age of the liberation of woman. This is the age of the coming into awareness of God the Mother. I am simply a pioneer, a wayshower going before you to show you that what I have become, you also can become. Whatever you see in me of God, I have realized so that every son and daughter, through this Mother light, this Mother energy, can own the full potential of God-awareness. As I have been called the Mother of God, the one who gives birth to his Son on earth, it is that you also might do the same."

To 'mother' God is to nourish the life of God on earth in Matter, in embodiment, here in time and space. And this is our calling as sons and daughters of God. And when we realize the Self as Mother, we too will mother the flame of life—first on the altar of the temple of being and then in one another—to give succor and teaching and service and help to other parts of life who are in need, greatly in need of Mother.

We can't go any further on the spiritual path unless we have a reconciliation with our own Inner Self as Mother, God as Mother within us, the World Mother, and then God as Mother in many saints who have gone on to realize the Self through that Mother flame, not the least of whom is Mother Mary. The understanding of Mother is the liberation of the creative feminine beauty, the aspiration, the energy within us that is a white light of purity. It is a moving stream of consciousness.

The Hindus have meditated upon Mother and called her the Goddess Kundalini, describing her as the white light, or the coiled serpent, that rises from the base of the spine to the crown, activating levels of cosmic consciousness in each of the chakras (spiritual centers) through which it passes along the way. In this world, the souls of men and women alike are intended to realize the Self as Mother by raising up this sacred fire, called the 'Kundalini'— after the Goddess.

In the caduceus, its threefold energies are seen as a staff with two entwined snakes. It is a spiritual energy which, impelled by our adoration of the light who is God, travels from the spiritual center that corresponds with the base of the spine (Muladhara) to the spiritual center that corresponds with the top of the head, or crown (Sahasrara). The key to unlock this energy, which we all need for the consummation of wholeness within ourselves, is the adoration of the Mother, God as Mother—that portion of himself that is feminine which he has placed in every part of life. The Hindus have called her the divine Shakti—the Great Counterpart, the Conscious Force, of the Trinity. She is known by several names denoting her several offices, functions, aspects, in relation to the Persons of the Godhead: Maheshwari, Mahakali, Mahalakshmi, Mahasarasvati—Wisdom, Strength, Harmony, Perfection.

Nature (Prakriti) is Mother, a manifestation of the Motherhood of God, mothering every creature through the extensions of herself in the beings of the elements, fire, air, water and earth. Even the entire Matter universe is Mother—a womb of time and space and energy where we are in gestation until the fullness of our cycle is come and we enter 'cosmic consciousness'.

And so when we say, "Hail Mary!" it means "Hail, Mother ray!" We are greeting the Woman clothed with the Sun, the feminine principle of the Godhead, whom we know and love surely and above all in the beautiful Mother of Christ but who is also resident, though dormant, in man, in woman and as the light in our innermost being. The white sphere of the Mother is sealed in the sacral, or sacred, base chakra until we love her enough to magnetize her—to actually coax her to mount the spiral staircase and rendezvous with our souls in our very heart of hearts. Here in the Holy of holies, we recite with her,

> Hail, Mary, full of grace. The Lord is with thee. Blessed art thou among women and blessed is the fruit of thy womb, Jesus.
>
> Holy Mary, Mother of God, pray for us, sons and daughters of God, now and at the hour of our victory over sin, disease, and death.

We enthrone her as our beloved Mother and she reunites us with the Trinity, the threefold flame of life. She takes us by the hand and leads us all the way to the summit of Being, the crown of crowns where God is All-in-all.

Mother Mary has assured me that the path of Kundalini yoga is indeed a part of Western tradition. And this is why she appeared to several of the saints with the safe and sound method of raising the Mother light through the rosary. This is why the saints have been portrayed with a white light upon their heads—because they have opened their crown chakras and entered into direct oneness with the I AM Presence. They have entered into the bliss of God.

The great mystics of the Western church have written down their experiences with this beloved God and their souls' 'coming in' and 'going out' of that Presence. We know that the great lights such as Saint John of the Cross and Saint Thérèse of Lisieux and Padre Pio have all had this inner experience, so filled with the divine passion, the bliss of the beloved as to defy comprehension by those who interpret the signs of the cross as mere martyrdom.

In the ritual of the rosary, wherein we always contemplate the mission of the Son in sacred scripture, we are guarded from the abuses of 'forcing' the chakras (in the violent taking of heaven by force about which Jesus warned) by the angels of the Trinity and the Mother. Only pure motive for the very love of God and our service to his children, not self-glory, should impel the love of Mother upward, onward, carrying our soul to the bliss of reunion.

Some false teachers have gone forth to wreak havoc among the children of this generation with their false teachings on the Mother light. They have presumed to teach Kundalini yoga without the anointing of the Trinity without the aegis of the Mother. They have taught it as a psychic phenomenon and left their all-too-trusting victims vulnerable to the dangers of the premature and uncontrolled release of this all-power of the Mother. Insanity, sexual obsession, demon possession and serious emotional and psychological disorders have left many frightened and turned off to the real path of Mother through their encounters with the self-styled gurus.

But after all of this, the Mother still reminds us of the words of her Son, "I will not leave you comfortless," and she comes to us with the Person of the Comforter to teach us the right way, the light way, that both Jesus and Gautama used to attain the victory that is ours to win—divine Selfhood through the adoration of the Mother flame.

So I have become a student of this Mother ray and this Mother energy. I have identified with it so much that some people have called me "Mother." It's a simple title, one of respectful regard, as you would call a Catholic priest "Father" or the head of a convent the "Mother Superior." It doesn't mean anything more than that. It doesn't mean that I'm exalted. It means that I am exalting God within me as Mother every hour. That is the path of my devotion.

The devotion to the Mother is the understanding that in the Aquarian age, when we raise up this light by pure love to the Mother—(1) as person (in God and in his emissaries) and (2) as principle (the mathematics, the science and the energy of the Kundalini)—then we will experience the quickening of our own Real Selfhood.

Then we will have the answers to the fundamental questions of who is this God the Father? And who are we as his sons and daughters? Who is this God the Son? And who are we, male and female, as his father and his mother? Who is this God the Holy Spirit? And what is this soul within us, man or woman, who longs to be his bride?

This book is a compelling message to all who, having been through these turbulent soul-searching decades, still have the courage to seek her and to know her as she is. Mother Mary reveals the Mother in her New Age teaching and in her New Age rosary. First she teaches the path of wisdom through the enlightened self-knowledge of the Son, and second she teaches the path of love through devotion to the Trinity by way of the Sacred Heart of Mother in the daily giving of the rosary.

Try it. It worked for me. And she tells me, with faith it won't fail to work for you.

Elizabeth Clare Prophet

And I will give power unto my two witnesses, and they shall prophesy a thousand two hundred and threescore days, clothed in sackcloth.

These are the two olive trees, and the two candlesticks standing before the God of the earth. —Revelation

Foreword

This work is a tribute to the World Mother and to Mary, who, as the Mother of Jesus, was her foremost representative in the Piscean age. It is a trilogy of wisdom, love and power that flows from the heart of the Mother to her children. It contains not only the worded revelations of Mary through our messengership but also the light emanations of her Presence made manifest to us. Thus we would bear witness to her immortal soul that does continually magnify the Lord.

The three parts of each of the three books of the Golden Word of Mary series fulfill the words of Jesus "The kingdom of heaven is like unto leaven which a woman took and hid in three measures of meal, till the whole was leavened."[1] The leaven is the Christ consciousness, the woman is the Divine Mother, and the three measures of meal are the three aspects of God made manifest in man as the holy Trinity. We have endeavored to make a measure of the Trinity understandable in each book. Book One* shows forth the glorious wisdom of the Son, Book Two reflects the comforting love of the Holy Spirit, and Book Three defines the perfection of the Father's goodwill.

The whole of humanity's consciousness will ultimately be leavened by the wisdom of the Mother as she raises her children to the true awareness of Father, Son and Holy Spirit. The Mother teaches the law of the great Three-in-One through the understanding she imparts of the Holy of holies and the Christ flame that burns upon the altar of the heart. This threefold flame is the spark of his Spirit, the flame of his flame, that is God's gift of life to every one of his sons and daughters.

Part One of this book, composed of "Fourteen Letters from a

---

* *Mary's Message for a New Day.* Books Two and Three are forthcoming.

Mother to Her Children," is intended to anchor the wisdom aspect of the Christ flame within the self-awareness of the disciple. These letters were dictated by Mother Mary to us as messengers for the heavenly hierarchy in the hope that her children might "stay with the dream of God, shut out the clamoring wakefulness of the outer mind, and never lose touch with the components of reality in all parts of life." The instruction in the fourteen letters also introduces the devotee of Mary to an illumined awareness of the fourteen stations of the cross, whose challenge each soul destined for the immortal reunion with the Spirit of God must one day meet.

Originally distributed as *Pearls of Wisdom* to disciples of Mary's Son throughout the world, these letters are the gift of the Cosmic Mother for the tutoring of the heart in her wisdom and in the immaculate concept she holds for all of her children. Entrusted to her by the Father, this image pure and undefiled of the perfection of each one, immaculately held in heart and mind, is the hope, the faith, the charity of the Godhead toward an evolving humanity.

Part Two of this book, "Eight Mysteries of the Rosary by the Mother for Her Children," shows forth the love aspect of the Christ flame. These mysteries were dictated by Mother Mary to me as the Mother of the Flame. The seven rosaries for the seven mornings of the week correspond to the seven rays of the Christic light that emerge from the prism of the Holy Spirit. The eighth mystery, given Sunday evening, focuses the power of the eighth ray. By daily giving the rosary in this format, Sons and Daughters of Dominion* anchor the love of Mother Mary within their heart's chalice, thereby consecrating their life's energies to the expansion

---

* The Sons and Daughters of Dominion is a spiritual order of men and women pledged to the service of the Mother through their vows to take dominion over earth, air, fire and water and gain self-mastery in the planes of Matter through the example of Jesus the Christ. (See Message VII.)

of the Mother's light throughout the planetary body.

When Mother Mary came to me and told me of her desire to have devotees throughout the world give a Scriptural Rosary for the New Age, she first announced the seven mysteries for the seven rays, together with the prayer format that was to be used. These mysteries are: The First Ray: The Joyful Mysteries, which amplify the will of God; The Second Ray: The Teaching Mysteries, which extol the wisdom of God; The Third Ray: The Love Mysteries, which magnetize the love of God; The Fourth Ray: The Glorious Mysteries, which show forth the purity of God; The Fifth Ray: The Healing Mysteries, which demonstrate the truth and the science of God; The Sixth Ray: The Initiatic Mysteries, which exemplify the ministration and service of God; and The Seventh Ray: The Miracle Mysteries, which bear witness to the transmutation, the freedom and the forgiveness of God.

When these rosaries were completed under her direction, the Blessed Mother released The Masterful Mysteries for the eighth ray, which focalize the majesty and the mastery of God. In her third appearance, the Holy Virgin presented the mysteries and the prayer format for the five secret rays, which she said were to be given at eventide Monday through Friday. This set of rosaries, which will be released in Book Two, are: The First Secret Ray: The Inspiration Mysteries; The Second Secret Ray: The Action Mysteries; The Third Secret Ray: The Revelation Mysteries; The Fourth Secret Ray: The Declaration Mysteries; and The Fifth Secret Ray: The Exhortation Mysteries. Mother Mary said that when a sufficient number of people would have established their daily ritual of reciting these rosaries, she would dictate the Fourteenth Rosary, which is to be released in Book Three.

Mary's Scriptural Rosary for the New Age teaches the disciple the devotional aspect of the love of Mother and Son—their love for him and his love for them—while reinforcing the pattern of the life and works of Mary and Jesus as they set forth for all the highest and best example of the Christian way of life and laid the foundation for the Christian dispensation.

The giving of this rosary, formulated by our spiritual Mother to meet the needs of the hour, affords a universally Christic experience calculated by heaven to awaken the soul to the realities of the Divine Woman and the Manchild. For it is their light that goes forth from each one who elects to be a part of the rosary of life that garlands the earth. This living rosary is composed of every son and daughter of the flame who daily consecrates his energies both in heaven and on earth in the ongoing service of Jesus and Mary.

The rosary of souls is an endless chain of floral offerings to the Mother which she receives, blesses and returns to her children to make them one—heart, soul and mind—as the great body of Christ[2] on earth, the living Church Universal and Triumphant. These prayers are the true and lasting praise of the saints who shall overcome the accuser of our brethren by the blood (the essence of the sacred fire) of the Lamb (of the Christ). This is the word (the spoken Word) of their testimony—of them that loved not their lives unto the death.[3]

And when the oneness of the children of the light is made manifest in the flow of their communion with the Father and the Mother—affirming "I and my Father are One; I and my Mother are One"—then shall they be found with one accord in one place.[4] And they shall hear "a great voice out of heaven saying, Behold, the tabernacle of God is with men, and he will dwell with them, and they shall be his people, and God himself shall be with them and be their God."[5]

The "Christian Prayer Forms and the Evolution of the Rosary" included in Part Two will show how Christians have prayed to God through Jesus and Mary and how prayer forms have evolved from the founding of the early Church to the present. Thus it will be seen that the giving of the rosary is the exaltation of the Motherhood of God and of the Divine Sonship, which can never be confined to one church or one dogma. Just as the theme of the Son of God conceived of the Cosmic Virgin is heard over and again in many of the world's religions, so all mankind will one day revere the Mother as the source of life and the Son of God as the Saviour of the Christic light within all.

The "Adorations of the Rosary" which precede the mysteries in Part Two consist of the prayers outlined by Mother Mary for the seven rays and the eighth ray. And in "Mary's Ritual of the Rosary," the giving of the rosary is explained in fourteen steps so that all who read and feel the love of the Mother may return that love by immediately offering these meditations, salutations and affirmations even while they recall the sacred events in the life of our Lord, whose grace is sufficient for us and whose hope is our eternal salvation.

Part Three of this book is a collection of "Fourteen Messages of the Word of Life" dictated by Mother Mary to us as we have journeyed throughout the world preaching the gospel of the kingdom.[6] As a part of the mission of the heavenly hierarchy to the age, the spoken Word of God has been delivered through our twin flames from the body of saints whom we know as ascended masters. In this giving of the testimony of the sacred fire and of the law of the Logos, hierarchy has proclaimed that the work of the two witnesses[7] has been accomplished.

The Word of Mary set forth in these fourteen messages also prepares the individual consciousness for the initiatic experiences of Jesus' last days on earth. As the disciple assimilates Mother Mary's own awareness of the perfect will of God for every son and daughter, he is blessed by Jesus' momentum of overcoming at each of the fourteen stations (initiations) on the *via dolorosa*.

To know Mary the Mother, we must become aware of the appearance of the individualization of her God flame during the centuries of her service to the Father, to the Son and to the Holy Spirit. Therefore in our introduction on The Soul of Mary on

Earth, we have provided the reader with an appreciation of the triumphs of Mary the Mother in several of her many incarnations of devotion to the flame of truth upon earth.

We have also desired to acquaint the children of the Mother, those who have known and acknowledged her flame and those who have not, with new insight and a better understanding of the functions of this ascended lady master. For as the patroness of the youth of the world, she holds a key position in the hierarchy of ascended masters who have set forth the scriptures for the golden age in the teachings and publications of The Summit Lighthouse. Accordingly, our introduction to Book Two is on "The Soul of Mary in Heaven."

Mother Mary has bequeathed to humanity the archetype of the New Age woman. By her example and constancy, she calls forth the Divine Woman in us all. She not only shows us *how* the feminine principle can be redeemed but *why* it must be redeemed in order that the Divine Manchild as the unfolding Christed man and Christed woman might appear within every son and daughter beloved of God.

This is the Divine Manchild who must go forth to rule all nations—every aspect of the human consciousness—with the rod of iron.[8] The meaning of *rod* is "radiance of divinity." The meaning of *iron* is "I," or the I AM, "rules over nature." And nature includes the four planes of God's consciousness designated as fire, air, water and earth, which correspond to the four lower bodies of man and of the planet.

The ruling of the nations with the rod of iron is the "radiance of divinity in the I AM rule over nations." The establishment of this rule is the goal of the incarnation of the feminine ray in this and every age. The culmination of the mission of the divine feminine, the energy spiral of Omega in both man and woman, is the realization of the Christ consciousness.

Until the feminine principle of the Godhead is ennobled in

each man and each woman, the Christ cannot be born. And until Christ is born in the individual, the evolving identity of man and woman cannot experience the new birth. Thus the rebirth of the Christ in man and woman, often referred to as the Second Coming, is necessary for the salvation of the soul. Indeed the individual Christ Self is the Saviour of the world of the individual.

When the Christ is born in the heart of man and woman, his consciousness dethrones the Antichrist, whom Paul referred to as the carnal mind that is enmity against God.[9] For the Son of God comes forth to slay the dragon of the lower self, the human ego, which must be put down that the Divine Ego may appear.

Without the Mother, there can be no Son. Therefore this trilogy is dedicated to all devotees of the Blessed Mother and of her Son, Jesus Christ, who personified the glory of the only begotten Son of God that we might behold his light—"the true Light which lighteth every man that cometh into the world"[10]—thus be molded in his image.

It is the fond hope of the Mother and her fervent faith that her children, following the precepts of the Father, shall succeed beyond their farthest dreams. Thus she beckons with a poem and a smile:

> The house of divine Sonship
> Holds open still the door.
> The darkness of the mortal mind
> Cannot, shall not, be anymore.

> For just beyond the mortal sunset
> Lies the light's immortal dawn,
> Trembling on the face of morning,
> Shining promise from now on.

> Day of life's immortal gladness
> Echoes from the dim-lit past,
> Shimmering freshness of the Daystar,

Crystal diamonds in the grass.

Like a dewdrop ever fairer
You reveal the bright new day;
In the fervor ever nearer
Christ's own face is seen today.

Like a gossamer veil atremble
With the thunder of the sun,
Beauteous doorway of forever
Swings wide open for each one!

In Her service I remain,

Elizabeth Clare Prophet

But Mary kept all these things and pondered them in her heart. —Luke

Introduction
The Soul of Mary on Earth

In the early days of Atlantis, Mary, the embodiment of the Mother ray, served in the Temple of Truth where, as priestess of the Most High God, she tended the emerald fires of the fifth ray. Serving under the masters of truth, Mary, together with other temple virgins, studied the healing arts and submitted to the disciplines required of every soul who desires to magnify the consciousness of the Lord.

Working with the laws governing the flow of God's energy from the planes of Spirit to the planes of Matter, she learned that all disease, decay and death are caused by an arresting of the flow of light at some point in the four lower bodies of man and that this clogging of energy results from his misuse of the sacred fire with its attendant karma.

She learned that the cure for disease is the harmonization of the flow through the light-centers in the lower bodies, whereas the reversal of the processes of death and decay is effected by the initiation of spirals of the resurrection flame within the chalice of the heart. Her mentors showed her how, once ignited, these spirals are expanded to include the entire being and consciousness until man becomes a pulsating sphere of white fire, the victor over hell and death, the Incorruptible One.

Thus long ago in the Temple of Truth, where religion and science stood as pillars of Alpha and Omega, Mary experimented with the laws of flow that also govern the science of precipitation. Did she then know that in another life she would be chosen to bear the Son of God who would demonstrate these laws in the changing of the water into wine, the healing of the withered hand, the multiplication of the loaves and fishes, and many other so-called miracles by which he would introduce to the world the supreme methodology of the sacred science?

In all of her incarnations, Mary worked closely with her twin flame, the archangel Raphael. He remained in heaven, the plane of Spirit, to focus the energies of Alpha while she made her abode on earth, the plane of Matter, there to focus the energies of Omega. Thus together they fulfilled the law of their God-identity, their sphere of Being, proving that "as Above, so below" God is omnipotent, omniscient and omnipresent.

With each life opportunity, Mary developed greater concentration upon the Image Most Holy of the Father, who appeared to her as the I AM Presence. Her consecration to the immaculate concept of the Son became intensified with each passing day while she perfected her four lower bodies as vehicles for her soul's expression of the Holy Spirit.

Her face shone with its inner light and her garments flowed to the rhythm of the flame. It was her magnification of the Christ light and of the Mother flame that actually sustained the healing focus in the Temple of Truth, and it was through her daily devotions that its emanations were expanded throughout Atlantis. One with the Cosmic Virgin, she remained a temple virgin during her entire embodiment and left a focus and a flame that shall rise again in the New Atlantis to enshrine the fundamentals of healing mastery in the hearts of those who, under the aegis of the Law, would be the true healers of the race.

In the days of the prophet Samuel, Mary was called of the Lord to be the wife of Jesse and the mother of his eight sons. And it happened that the Lord said unto Samuel: "How long wilt thou mourn for Saul, seeing I have rejected him from reigning over Israel? fill thine horn with oil, and go, I will send thee to Jesse the Bethlehemite: for I have provided Me a king among his sons."[1]

After Samuel had reviewed seven of his sons and had not found the Lord's anointed, the prophet said unto Jesse, "Are here all thy children?" And the father said, "There remaineth yet the youngest, and behold, he keepeth the sheep." And Samuel said unto Jesse, "Send and fetch him: for we will not sit down till he come hither." Thus the eighth son was sent for and brought before the man of God. And it is recorded in the Old Testament that he was "ruddy and withal of a beautiful countenance and goodly to look to." And the Lord spoke to Samuel and said, "Arise, anoint him: for this is he." It is written that "Samuel took the horn of oil and anointed him in the midst of his brethren: and the Spirit of the Lord came upon David from that day forward."[2]

Ever fulfilling her role as the Mother ray, Mary, in this incarnation of her soul on earth, magnified the light of the seven rays of the Christ in the first seven sons of Jesse. But in the youngest, David, she glorified not only the full complement of virtues from the prism of the Lord but also the majesty and mastery of the eighth ray, which David exemplified in his reign and extolled in his psalms.

The reincarnation of David as Jesus was prophesied by one of the greatest prophets of Israel, who wrote: "And there shall come forth a rod [a scepter of authority] out of the stem of Jesse [out of the Son, or the Christ flame of Jesse] and a Branch [the Christ consciousness of David] shall grow out of his roots [shall evolve out of his communion with the Lord]: and the Spirit of the Lord shall rest upon him, the spirit of wisdom and understanding, the spirit of counsel and might, the spirit of knowledge and of the fear of the LORD."[3]

David himself knew that he would be born again to perform a mighty work for the Lord. Therefore he exclaimed: "My heart is glad and my glory rejoiceth: my flesh also shall rest in hope. For thou wilt not leave my soul in hell; neither wilt thou suffer thine Holy One to see corruption. Thou wilt shew me the path of life: in thy presence is fulness of joy."[4] David longed for the day when he would see God face-to-face, prove his laws and be found in his image. He would not be satisfied with less. Thus he declared, "As for me, I will behold Thy face in righteousness: I shall be satisfied when I awake with Thy likeness."[5]

The Book of Psalms is David's tribute to his Maker. It shows forth the love, the wisdom and the power of a soul determined to become the Christ. It shows how faith, hope and charity, as seeds of light implanted within body, mind and soul, compel the totality of selfhood to engage its energies in the daily striving to be acceptable in the sight of God. The cry of David, the shepherd-king, was answered in the life of the carpenter of Nazareth: "Let the words of my mouth and the meditation of my heart be acceptable in thy sight, O LORD, my strength and my redeemer."[6]

Thus in the Psalms the Israelites have recourse to the teachings of one who has attained Christ-mastery while gentiles also reflect upon the meditations of the Saviour, all striving for the same goal set forth by him who is known as both the king of Israel and of the New Jerusalem. And so it is not surprising that today in the cenacle overlooking the city of Jerusalem, Christians pray in the Upper Room on the site where Jesus and the disciples celebrated the Last Supper, where Christ appeared after his resurrection and where the descent of the Holy Spirit took place. And in the lower level of the same house, there is a temple where Jews worship at the Tomb of David—"Hear, O Israel: The LORD our God is one LORD."[7] Nor is it surprising to those who offer praise to her name that Mary is the Mother of both the Judaic and the Christian dispensations.

In her final embodiment, "the Blessed and Ever Glorious Virgin Mary, sprung from the royal race and family of David, was born in the city of Nazareth and educated at Jerusalem in the temple of the Lord. Her father's name was Joachim and her mother's Anna. The family of her father was of Galilee and the city of Nazareth. The family of her mother was of Bethlehem. Their lives were plain and right in the sight of the Lord, pious and faultless before men."[8] So reads the Gospel of the Birth of Mary attributed to Saint Matthew, a work received as authentic by early Christians and included in the library of Jerome.

Anna and Joachim were initiates of the Brotherhood and followed many of the teachings of the Essene community. Among other spiritual disciplines, they followed a strict dietary regime and practiced certain temple rituals corresponding to the mystical teachings of Christ given in the retreats of the masters. To them prayer and fasting was a way of life.

The grandfather and grandmother of our Lord were humble and pious before God. They lived in obedience to the code of conduct taught in the retreats of the hierarchy and set forth by Jesus to meet the needs of disciples in every age who desire to learn the law of the conservation of Christic energies for the glory of the Law: "Let your communication be, Yea, yea; Nay, nay: for whatsoever is more than these cometh of evil."[9]

Jesus explained to us that when the disciple is on the homeward path, he encounters hourly and momentarily the cycles of his past uses and misuses of energy. If the effects of causes set in motion are good, then he must reaffirm that goodness and expand it for God and man. But if the effects of past actions be harmful or out of harmony with cosmic law, then he must be quick to deny and denounce their energy coils and to divest them of all negative influence through the transmutative fires of the Holy Spirit.

John the Beloved commented on this teaching in a recent dictation, saying that Jesus had in this manner counseled the disciples as they served their novitiate under him. John explained that Jesus taught them to say, "Yes!" to the light, affirming all good, and "No!" to the darkness, denying all evil, and then "Peace, be still!" "For then," he said, "all energy flows from God to man, from man to God, and you begin your ascension process right now."[10]

This teaching of the Brotherhood was strictly adhered to by

Anna and Joachim as they prepared themselves to be the vehicles for the virgin consciousness of Mary. For twenty years they lived "chastely, in the favour of God and the esteem of men, without any children. But they vowed, if God should favour them with any issue, they would devote it to the service of the Lord; on which account they went at every feast in the year to the temple of the Lord."[11] With this promise in heart and this purpose in mind, they diligently employed the Science of the Spoken Word, offering prayers and invocations to the Elohim, the archangels and the masterful Presence of life revealed to Moses as the I AM that I AM.[12]

Mary was born to Anna and Joachim because they gave their lives to the fulfillment of the plan of God. They were chosen to serve because they chose to serve, and their commitment was one which spanned the centuries of their previous existence both on earth and in heaven. Therefore, in keeping with heavenly protocol, the angel of the Lord appeared to them to announce the birth of the Virgin and told them that their daughter as a virgin would bear the Son of God, who would prove before the multitudes of Judaea the laws of the divine alchemy and the ability of the Christed man or woman to become the master of sin, disease and death.

In his discourse on the birth of the Virgin Mary, Saint John Damascene offers this fitting tribute to the ones who focused the spirals of Alpha and Omega, the Father-Mother God, on behalf of the soul of Mary:

"O blessed couple, Joachim and Anne! To you is every creature indebted. For through you, every creature has offered to the Creator this gift, the noblest of gifts, namely, that chaste mother who alone was worthy of the Creator. Rejoice Joachim, for from thy daughter a Son is born to us; and his name is called the angel of great counsel, that is, of the salvation of the whole world....

"O blessed couple, Joachim and Anne! And indeed you are known to be pure by the fruit of your bodies, as Christ said in a certain place: By their fruits you shall know them. You ordered your lives by rule, as was pleasing to God and worthy of her who was sprung from you. For the chaste and holy exercise of your office, you brought forth the treasure of virginity."[13]

In Matthew's Gospel of the Birth of Mary, we read of Issachar, the high priest of the temple of Jerusalem, who reproached Joachim at the feast of the dedication because "his offerings could never be acceptable to God who was judged by him unworthy to have children, the scripture having said, Cursed is every one who shall not beget a male in Israel. He further said that he ought first to be free from that curse by begetting some issue and then come with his offerings into the presence of God." Burdened by the harsh words of the priest who had thus publicly condemned him and "being much confounded with the shame of such reproach, [Joachim] retired to the shepherds who were with the cattle in their pastures."[14]

Matthew's account of the visitation of the angel to Joachim and Anna is noteworthy for the authenticity of the teachings of the Brotherhood it contains. It also provides us with another vivid scene of the free association of devout men and women with the angels of the Lord. "But when he had been there for some time," the apostle writes, "on a certain day when he was alone, the angel of the Lord stood by him with a prodigious light. To whom, being troubled at the appearance, the angel who had appeared to him, endeavoring to compose him, said: Be not afraid, Joachim, nor troubled at the sight of me, for I am an angel of the Lord sent by him to you, that I might inform you that your prayers are heard and your alms ascended in the sight of God. For he hath surely seen your shame and heard you unjustly reproached for not having children: for God is the avenger of sin, and not of nature; and so when He shuts the womb of any person, He does it for this reason, that He may in a more wonderful manner again open it and that which is born appear to be not the product of lust, but the gift of God.[15]

"'...Therefore Anna your wife shall bring you a daughter, and you shall call her name Mary; she shall, according to your vow, be devoted to the Lord from her infancy and be filled with the Holy Ghost from her mother's womb; she shall neither eat nor drink anything which is unclean, nor shall her conversation be without among the common people, but in the temple of the Lord, that so she may not fall under any slander or suspicion of what is bad. So in the process of her years, as she shall be in a miraculous manner born of one that was barren, so she shall while yet a virgin, in a way unparalleled, bring forth the Son of the Most High God who shall be called Jesus and, according to the signification of his name, be the Saviour of all nations.'[16]

"Afterwards the angel appeared to Anna his wife, saying: Fear not, neither think that which you see is a spirit. For I am that angel who hath offered up your prayers and alms before God and am now sent to you that I may inform you that a daughter will be born unto you who shall be called Mary and shall be blessed above all women. She shall be, immediately upon her birth, full of the grace of the Lord and shall continue during the three years of her weaning in her father's house, and afterwards, being devoted to the service of the Lord, shall not depart from the temple till she arrives to years of discretion.

"In a word, she shall there serve the Lord night and day in fasting and prayer, shall abstain from every unclean thing and never know any man; but, being an unparalleled instance without any pollution or defilement and a virgin not knowing any man, shall bring forth a son, and a maid shall bring forth the Lord, who, both by his grace and name and works, shall be the Saviour of the world....So Anna conceived and brought forth a daughter, and, according to the angel's command, the parents did call her name Mary."[17]

The account of the childhood of Mary is one of the tenderness of God enfolding the Queen of Angels incarnate. She who was to become the bride of the Holy Spirit was presented at the temple at the age of three. It is said that her parents placed her upon the first of the fifteen stairs symbolizing the initiations of the psalms of degrees (Psalms 120 through 134). The child ascended the stairs one after another "without the help of any to lead or lift her," showing that she had passed these initiations in other lives and was spiritually prepared to fulfill her mission. "Thus," comments Matthew, "the Lord did, in the infancy of his Virgin, work this extraordinary work and evidence by this miracle how great she was like to be hereafter."[18]

Therefore Mary was left with other virgins in the apartments of the temple to be brought up there. And her parents, having offered up their sacrifice according to the custom of the law and perfected their vow, returned home.

For those who know the beauty of the soul of Mary, Matthew's account of her daily communion with the heavenly hierarchy is precious. "The Virgin of the Lord, as she advanced in years, increased also in perfections; and according to the saying of the Psalmist, her father and mother forsook her but the Lord took care of her. For she every day had the conversation of angels and every day received visitors from God which preserved her from all sorts of evil and caused her to abound with all good things; so that when at length she arrived to her fourteenth year, as the wicked could not lay anything to her charge worthy of reproof, so all good persons who were acquainted with her admired her life and conversation."[19]

According to Matthew, when Mary was fourteen years old, the high priest made a public order that all temple virgins "as they were now of a proper maturity should according to the custom of their country endeavour to be married. To which command, though all the other virgins readily yielded obedience, Mary the Virgin of the Lord alone answered that she could not comply with it. Assigning these reasons, that both she and her parents had devoted her to the service of the Lord and besides that she had vowed virginity to the Lord, which vow she was resolved never to break."[20]

The priest, being perplexed, commanded "that at the approaching feast all the principal persons both of Jerusalem and the neighbouring places should meet together that he might have their advice, how he had best proceed in so difficult a case. When they were accordingly met, they unanimously agreed to seek the Lord and ask counsel from him on this matter. And when they were all engaged in prayer, the high priest, according to the usual way, went to consult God.

"And immediately there was a voice from the ark and the mercy seat which all present heard, that it must be inquired or sought out by a prophecy of Isaiah to whom the Virgin should be given and be betrothed; for Isaiah saith, there shall come forth a rod out of the stem of Jesse, and a flower shall spring out of its root, and the Spirit of the Lord shall rest upon him, the Spirit of Wisdom and Understanding, the Spirit of Counsel and Might, the Spirit of Knowledge and Piety, and the Spirit of the fear of the Lord shall fill him.

"Then, according to this prophecy, he appointed that all the men of the house and family of David who were marriageable and not married should bring their several rods to the altar, and out of whatsoever person's rod after it was brought a flower should bud forth and on the top of it the Spirit of the Lord should sit in the appearance of a dove, he should be the man to whom the Virgin should be given and be betrothed."[21]

But, Matthew tells us, Joseph, being advanced in years, "drew back his rod when every one besides presented his. So that when nothing appeared agreeable to the heavenly voice, the high priest judged it proper to consult God again, who answered that he to whom the Virgin was to be betrothed was the only person of those who were brought together who had not brought his rod. Joseph therefore was betrayed. For when he did bring his rod and a dove coming from heaven pitched upon the top of it, every one plainly saw that the Virgin was to be betrothed to him."[22]

Thus Mary was betrothed to Joseph. Matthew's version is that Joseph returned to Bethlehem to make ready for the marriage, and Mary, accompanied by seven virgins, returned to her parents' house in Galilee, whereas James says that Joseph took Mary to his house and then went to mind his trade of building, leaving her alone. James, in the Protevangelion, says that while she was yet betrothed, Mary was one of several virgins chosen to spin the new veil for the temple and that as she was spinning the true purple, "she took a pot and went out to draw water and heard a voice saying unto her, Hail, thou who art full of grace, the Lord is with thee; thou art blessed among women."[23] This, then, is his account of Archangel Gabriel's annunciation of Mary's conception of the Christ by the power of the Holy Ghost:

"And she looked round to the right and to the left to see whence that voice came, and then trembling went into her house; and laying down the waterpot, she took the purple and sat down in her seat to work it. And behold the angel of the Lord stood by her and said, Fear not, Mary, for thou hast found favour in the sight of God; which when she heard, she reasoned with herself what that sort of salutation meant.

"And the angel said unto her, The Lord is with thee, and thou shalt conceive: to which she replied, What! shall I conceive by the living God and bring forth as all other women do? But the angel returned answer, Not so, O Mary, but the Holy Ghost shall come upon thee, and the power of the Most High shall overshadow thee; wherefore that which shall be born of thee shall be holy and shall be called the Son of the Living God, and thou shalt call his name Jesus; for he shall save his people from their sins. And behold thy cousin Elisabeth, she also hath conceived a son in her old age. And this now is the sixth month with her, who was called barren; for nothing is impossible with God. And Mary said, Behold the handmaid of the Lord; let it be unto me according to thy word."[24]

When Mary had completed the spinning of the true purple, she took it to the high priest, who blessed her, saying, "Mary, the Lord God hath magnified thy name, and thou shalt be blessed in all the ages of the world."[25] Like the account in the Gospel of Luke, James's description of Mary's visit to the house of her cousin Elisabeth is punctuated by the leap and the blessing of the fires of John the Baptist. Elisabeth, who was carrying the messenger of the Lord that would go before the face of Jesus, exclaimed upon her arrival: "Whence is this to me, that the Mother of my Lord should come unto me? For lo! as soon as the voice of thy salutation reached my ears, that which is in me leaped and blessed thee."[26]

As Mary became great with child, Joseph was sorely troubled concerning her condition and determined to put her away privily. The angel of the Lord, however, appeared to him, telling him that this was not the work of man but of the Holy Ghost. James tells us that Annas the scribe then visited Joseph and, seeing Mary with child, informed the high priest that Joseph had privately married her.

"Upon this both she and Joseph were brought to their trial, and the priest said unto her, Mary, what hast thou done? Why hast thou debased thy soul and forgot thy God, seeing thou wast brought up in the Holy of holies and didst receive thy food from the hands of angels and heardest their songs? Why hast thou done this? To which with a flood of tears she answered, As the Lord my God liveth, I am innocent in his sight, seeing I know no man. Then the priest said to Joseph, Why hast thou done this? And Joseph answered, As the Lord my God liveth, I have not been concerned with her.

"But the priest said, Lie not, but declare the truth; thou hast privately married her and not discovered it to the children of Israel and humbled thyself under the mighty hand of God that thy seed might be blessed. And Joseph was silent. Then said the priest to Joseph, You must restore to the temple of the Lord the Virgin which you took thence. But he wept bitterly, and the priest added, I will cause you both to drink the water of the Lord, which is for trial, and so your iniquity shall be laid open before you.

"Then the priest took the water and made Joseph drink and sent him to a mountainous place. And he returned perfectly well, and all the people wondered that his guilt was not discovered. So the priest said, Since the Lord hath not made your sins evident, neither do I condemn you. So he sent them away. Then Joseph took Mary and went to his house, rejoicing and praising the God of Israel."[27]

The accepted version of the events surrounding the birth of our Lord are well known. The following sequence, which the early fathers did not include in the New Testament, is thought to be from the Gospel of Thomas:

"In the three hundred and ninth year of the aera of Alexander, Augustus published a decree that all persons should go to be taxed in their own country. Joseph therefore arose, and with Mary his spouse he went to Jerusalem and then came to Bethlehem, that he and his family might be taxed in the city of his fathers. And when they came by the cave, Mary confessed to Joseph that her time of bringing forth was come, and she could not go on to the city and said, Let us go into this cave. At that time the sun was very near going down.

"But Joseph hastened away that he might fetch her a midwife; and when he saw an old Hebrew woman who was of Jerusalem, he said to her, Pray come hither, good woman, and go into that cave, and you will there see a woman just ready to bring forth. It was after sunset when the old woman and Joseph with her reached the cave, and they both went into it. And behold, it was all filled with lights greater than the light of lamps and candles and greater than the light of the sun itself. The infant was then wrapped up in swaddling clothes and sucking the breasts of his mother Saint Mary.

"When they both saw this light, they were surprised; the old woman asked Saint Mary, Art thou the mother of this child? Saint Mary replied she was. On which the old woman said, Thou art very different from all other women. Saint Mary answered, As there is not any child like to my son, so neither is there any woman like to his mother. The old woman answered and said, O my Lady, I am come hither that I may obtain an everlasting reward. Then our Lady, Saint Mary, said to her, Lay thine hands upon the infant; which, when she had done, she became whole. And as she was going forth, she said, From henceforth, all the days of my life, I will attend upon and be a servant of this infant.

"After this, when the shepherds came and had made a fire and they were exceedingly rejoicing, the heavenly host appeared to them, praising and adoring the supreme God. And as the shepherds were engaged in the same employment, the cave at that time seemed like a glorious temple, because both the tongues of angels and men united to adore and magnify God on account of the birth of the Lord Christ. But when the old Hebrew woman saw all these evident miracles, she gave praises to God and said, I thank thee, O God, Thou God of Israel, for that mine eyes have seen the birth of the Savior of the world."[28]

I will bless the Lord at all times: His praise shall continually be in my mouth.

My soul shall make her boast in the Lord: the humble shall hear thereof, and be glad.

O magnify the Lord with me, and let us exalt his name together.

I sought the Lord and he heard me, and delivered me from all my fears. —Psalms

PART ONE

The Wisdom Aspect of the Christ Flame
Fourteen Letters from a Mother to Her Children

And in the sixth month the angel Gabriel was sent from God unto a city of Galilee named Nazareth, to a virgin espoused to a man whose name was Joseph, of the house of David; and the virgin's name was Mary.

And the angel came in unto her and said, Hail, thou that art highly favoured, the Lord is with thee: blessed art thou among women.

And when she saw him, she was troubled at his saying and cast in her mind what manner of salutation this should be.

And the angel said unto her, Fear not, Mary: for thou hast found favour with God. And behold, thou shalt conceive in thy womb, and bring forth a son and shalt call his name JESUS. He shall be great and shall be called the Son of the Highest: and the Lord God shall give unto him the throne of his father David: and he shall reign over the house of Jacob for ever; and of his kingdom there shall be no end.

Then said Mary unto the angel, How shall this be, seeing I know not a man?

And the angel answered and said unto her, The Holy Ghost shall come upon thee, and the power of the Highest shall overshadow thee: therefore also that holy thing which shall be born of thee shall be called the Son of God. And behold, thy cousin Elisabeth, she hath also conceived a son in her old age: and this is the sixth month with her, who was called barren. For with God nothing shall be impossible.

And Mary said, Behold the handmaid of the Lord; be it unto me according to thy word.

And the angel departed from her. —Luke

1

Darkness Shall Be Overcome by Light!

The Self-Righteousness, Selfishness and Spiritual Pride of the Blind Leaders of the Blind Are Confounded by the Bible of Nature

To the Freeborn and Those Who Would Be:

Each day many among mankind awaken from their sleep plagued with uncertainty. Their concerns extend to the Christian church, to their nation, to their children and members of their society. They fear what is coming upon earth. Is the population of the world increasing too rapidly or too slowly? Why is there such tremendous violence upon the planetary body?

Why, in this beautiful world that can be filled with the hope of the Divine Mother and the carefree attitude of the holy innocents which many have experienced in childhood, do sophisticated mankind fail to comprehend the meaning of life's experiences? Let it be made clear that human struggle is the result of humanity's selfishness, of their failure to appropriate the divine abundance and to apprehend the universal purpose. Seeing life, then, in its smallest dimensions, they are not able to grasp the perspective of the overall picture. For they have already circumscribed the potential of their life with their own sense of limitation.

Long before there was a compendium of the Law known as the Christian Bible, combining the ancient writings of the prophets of Israel with the followers of Christ who set forth the New Testament, there existed at the time of Enoch[1] prior to the Flood mere fragments of what could be called a sacred scripture.

Yet the bible of nature, the recording of the Law in engrams of light, was then and has always been present within the very atoms of the earth itself. Just as man today does not build without a blueprint, so cosmos was designed after that universal perfection which God was from the Beginning and is forever.

Don't you see, then, inasmuch as perfection is ever the divine lot, how easy it would have been had mankind chosen to walk within the confines of the Great Law to perpetuate perfection throughout the world? Yet in the dispensation of free will as it is held by embodied mankind today, there is a chastening that comes from man's inherent freedom to create imperfectly and to live in error. Among the errors which mankind have perpetuated are errors of dogma adhered to by countless individuals who are the blind leading the blind that all mankind may fall into the ditch.[2]

Now there has come before the Karmic Lords the question of what shall be done about modern man and his behavior patterns, his violations of cosmic law, the torment he has inflicted upon nature and upon his fellowmen. All of life is offended, and that mortally so, beloved ones. Whereas the Karmic Board and the hosts of heaven have sought to stave off the karmic recompense which should long ago have been loosed upon mankind, they have persistently held back the onslaught of the world's misqualified energies in the fond hope that the terrible inhumanities practiced against God and man by the people of the earth would cease and the trend toward more and more evil be checked.

Men are prone to believe in a personal saviour, one who can deliver them from their sins as well as from those circumstances which cause them pain and suffering. Then there is the tendency toward radicalism, which engenders human hatred against those who either in politics or religion are not as radical as the radicals think they ought to be. There is human self-righteousness and spiritual pride that has become a terrible weight swung upon the thread of mankind's oppressive sense of foreboding and the desire to inflict punishment upon one another. This has caused untold sorrow in spiritual realms as well as hardship upon earth.

Like a sword of Damocles, humanity's damning indictments of one another's faith in God and in Christ hang over their heads as an indictment of their own sinful consciousness, while their challenges of the universality of divine purpose and the beauty of the pure in heart continue to reinforce the brutal walls mankind have erected among themselves.

I, who sought so often and so earnestly in past lives as well as during my embodiment as the Mother of Jesus to be a peacemaker, have much to give to those who would pour oil upon the troubled waters of mankind's consciousness. Contrary to the opinions of some, the early disciples and apostles often squabbled, as do disciples of Christ today. It was no easy task to show them the error of their ways and to place in perspective the little concerns that they so frequently voiced, which were not nearly as important as the state of the altar of being, the chalice of the heart and mankind's attunement with the purposes of God.

Men have often strained at a gnat and swallowed a camel.[3] And how they still need with all their getting, even of things spiritual, to get understanding[4] and compassion. It is not enough for men to be bold in their search for truth. For all require that bountiful humility which, like a great magnet of cosmic love, draws the love of God through the whole net and fiber of creation, infusing it with the glow of cosmic intent and true spiritual compassion.

Why is it that from time to time in my numerous appearances to many among the faithful, as at Fátima and Garabandal, I have often sought to warn? It is because in reality in mankind's free will there is an element of divine grace which can be called into action, a focus of great love and understanding that can remove the hardness of heart with which mankind have so frequently cloaked their activities. Sometimes it appears to us as though man does not really understand the power that God wields. In the universal macrocosmic sense, the all-power of God is the "all power in heaven and in earth"[5] which is given to those who attain Christ-mastery and their joint heirship with God[6] through the reality of the universal Son.

What a pity it is that self-righteousness is such a barrier to divine reality and to the teachings of the Holy Spirit. For the Holy Spirit guides all men into all truth.[7] And truth, beloved mankind, is not just the letter of the Law as it is interpreted by various groups, which may well differ in their comprehension of sacred scripture and still be composed of hearts that truly seek the light. To have love without the illumination of the Christ mind and the power to rightly divide the Word[8] is often not enough to promote the universal righteousness of God-activity within the consciousness of the individual that brings divine justice to all.

That the perfect balance of the Holy Trinity may permeate the consciousness of the true followers of God is our prayer. For truly the will of God that is above ought to be done below.[9] But as long as men allow themselves to be hung on the various pegs of their human concepts—or even those of their divine concepts as they understand them—when those concepts are not rightly divided by the Spirit, so long will they remain in separate camps. In reality there is one cosmic purpose; and that purpose, which is the ultimate merging of the flames of God and man, will one day reveal itself to all by the light of the one Spirit.[10]

I call for your consideration of these matters, even in an elementary way. For if thought will not provide easement to humanity's struggles, then prayer will. Therefore I urge all to pray with me and with the masters of light and love that the Christian world be stripped of the elements of hardness of heart and cruelty toward those it regards as nonbelievers or heretics, of its shouting-forth of charge and countercharge, of its sense of struggle that is like the thrashing of a dying animal.

Truly darkness shall be overcome, but it shall ever be overcome by light. For darkness cannot overcome itself. And when the light that is in man is darkness,[11] that is, when his light is misqualified by darkness, its fruit cannot bring about a Christ-victory either for humanity or for the little monad of self. We await that greater understanding which descends upon the world as a giant curtain of light and enfolds the hearts of those who would follow God as dear children.

Devotedly, I remain,

Mary

Retreat of the Resurrection Spiral
Colorado Springs, Colorado
July 16, 1972

2

A Secret Covenant with God through Total Surrender

*The Masterful Ones Walk as Servant-Sons
Dispelling Subtle Pressures of Condemnation,
Patterns of Destructivity and Ignorance of the Law of Love*

To the Beloved Children of the Sun:

When you greet the morning's first light, which continually appears somewhere upon the planetary body as the great cosmic clock rolls the lovetide of the dawn round the giant ball of the world, will you try to realize that each planetary center, like a human being or an individual, is constantly being bathed in the light of the physical sun. At the same time that the physical light is shed abroad upon the earth, a spiritual radiation and divine presence, a divine omnipresence, floods forth through the physical light of the sun. It is the Sun behind the sun. This is the reality of God that engenders spiritual resurrections which overcome the temporary consciousness of mankind's death and dying and bring about the eternal sense of living.

When spiritually minded men and women contemplate the true significance of the Angelus, they are able to feel the holy peace that comes with sweet prayer engaged in by the soul who is unashamed to extend from the cathedral of the heart the magnificent afflatus of love born of holy communion with God. The waning light of the sun, as it recedes from the place where the petitioner stands, is aware of the fruit of the day, of the beautiful blessings of the light that has shone not only upon the one but upon countless others. Hopefully, receptive souls have used its cosmic energies to bring forth a day of achievement, a day that is not without fruit, a day that is not without love.

Whereas we recognize that there are many kinds of love, the love of which we speak is ever the love of God that is broken in the bread of those who serve mankind and understand that it is not just physical bread alone that they dispense, meeting their physical needs, but also the bread of the Spirit that nourishes their souls. Will you consider, then, the beauty of the whole loaf of the Christ consciousness, whose qualities are focused in each tiny crumb as it falls from the Lord's table, the Eucharist that gives unto all that impartation of spiritual unity whereby all are enfolded in his love.

The senses of mankind ought to be correctly used and never abused. For they are indexes to the consciousness of self whereby the individual experiences the conditions of his environment and his relationship to them—where he is, what he is doing, how he lives and breathes and functions through his four lower bodies. It is just as easy for the trained soul who has applied his heart unto God to use these senses to reach up out of the deep well of the human consciousness into the abundance of the water of life that flows from the Source that is above into the vessel that is below.

At no time should men fear to expand their consciousness under the domain of the Father's love. For his love, when it covers the altar of man's true consciousness, is like the covering cherubim keeping their vigil over the mercy seat.[12] In reality, man can make a secret covenant with God which is far above the prying eyes of the profane. Accomplishing this through total surrender, he finds coming into manifestation on the altar of his heart a sense of the omnipresence of God and of his own unity with that Presence.

When others also feel this selfsame calmness within the abundant sense that is born of dedication to the practice of the laws of God, they are made aware that surging within their own being is the very power that is native to the whole universe. And wherever they go, they recognize that the Lord inhabits space and that he hallows and blesses it. With this awareness of the Presence of God, it is more difficult for mankind to become involved in those subtle pressures of condemnation against which both Saint Germain and El Morya have spoken.

It is in the hope of bringing into the world community, the religious as well as the secular, a greater sense of purpose in God, of dedication to the Christ and of inner striving for unity with the Great Law that I speak. For so long as mankind continue to involve themselves in karmic patterns of destructivity, so long will they reflect destruction in their actions and the peace of my Son be manifest only in part. Wrong action is a barrier to mankind's manifestation of that perfect love which casts out all fear.[13]

Be aware, then, of the hopes that blaze throughout the pores of space awaiting an opening into the doorway of the heart of each man that he may truly honor the Father's laws according to his highest understanding. God often winks at man's ignorance. And the masterful ones who walk as servant sons in the footsteps of the great heartbeat of life will never add to the weight of the world's condemnation but will serve instead to lift mankind out of darkness into light. As Jesus said to the adulterous woman, "Neither do I condemn thee, go and sin no more,"[14] so shall compassion expand its wings of healing joy over the earth through mercy and forgiving love, and the Angelus of peace crown each day with the sense of divine achievement.

I am a peacemaker as well as a mother. And as we meet on the road of life, there shall come through all measures of mutual striving the finalizing activity that will free each son to accept the fullness of the love of God in Christ Jesus.

With increasing blessing, I AM

Mary

Retreat of the Resurrection Spiral
Colorado Springs, Colorado
July 23, 1972

3
Peace, Be Still!

The Compassionate Ones Raise Up the Downtrodden to a Higher Response

To the Beloved Sons and Daughters Who Consciously Recognize Their Divine Origin:

The hopes of God lie in mankind's conscious willing acceptance of universal harmony, which must first be established in each one.

You cannot manifest the harmony of God if you continually allow yourself to be drawn into worldly situations through the play of your emotions. In truth, all of creation was brought forth in its primordial reality by the spark of God's desire made manifest through the agency of the Holy Spirit. This desire of the Creator to amplify the qualities of perfection is closely related to the desire nature of man, which is expressed through his emotional or feeling world. Therefore when you permit your feelings to be ruffled, the surge of emotional energy which passes through your feeling world has a detrimental effect upon the harmony of self and is counter to the love, the peace, the wisdom and the joy of the Holy Spirit.

How simple it is for even a child to disturb the emotional world of any among mankind, save those who have established themselves in the determined, fruitful intent to guard the vehicles of the mind and feelings so that they remain tethered solely to the operations of the Holy Spirit. This is not easy, beloved ones. We fully recognize that the mind, accustomed to ordinary thoughts and feelings, is easily caught up in the revolving of the mundane and the amplification of the mass consciousness. In effect man has become a reactor both to his environment and to the haphazard activities of his companions, and his energies are almost totally engaged in the human situations that arise in his world from day to day. And like the rising and falling of a surging sea, his emotional energies are maneuvered by his reactions from one disturbing condition to the next.

The image of their own Christ Self commanding the emotional waves and saying, "Peace, be still!" is needed by mankind in every walk of life, for there are none in the world that are not subject to trying conditions. When people let their thoughts and feelings become reactive, triggered by the words and deeds of others, the flow of their precious energies becomes subject to whimsy.

But there is one great danger that often arises when individuals on the path first begin to apply the laws of harmony. This I should like to point out to the students of the light. It is the danger of insulating oneself against the doings and attitudes of others whereby one becomes hardhearted, cold and sterile in the attempt to implement the great desire to maintain harmony in his world. Under these circumstances, the individual is not even willing to respond favorably to others, all in the guise of maintaining harmony.

Men should learn to stand within the citadel of being, insulated by the currents of the Holy Ghost but capable of reaching out in mercy's name with the response that is dictated by their own inner God-nature. They should lovingly place themselves upon the ladder of availability, going up or down so that their awareness can coincide momentarily with the ups and downs of others as the elevatorlike consciousness of humanity rises and falls. Thus the compassionate ones, taking no thought for their lives,[15] descend to the level of greatest need to raise up the downtrodden to a higher response. They do not leave them where they find them, at the level of reaction to the lower nature, but provide a way of escape through the door of the Christ Self—I AM the open door which no man can shut.[16]

How does all this fit in with the great struggles going on in religious movements today? Politics and religion, which are intended to show forth the standards of the governing of the world and the governing of the self under divine ordinances, have been misused to promote discord and dissension among the masses, providing a smoke screen for the manipulators. And where is the fruit of the Spirit?[17] It is far from being a manifest reality.

Oh, how quickly mankind turn from a face of smiles to one of frowns and fears as they enter into a defense of their pet theories and personal dogmas or as they discuss the darkening aspects of their lives, all in the name of Christ. Frequently men search the scriptures looking only for a justification of their questionable conduct without understanding that the seat of mercy and understanding dwells also in the soul and that humility is the great expanding magnet of the soul that unerringly draws God's energy into one's world, making each one in effect a child of the light.

It is almost as though men themselves had created the religious tenets to which they adhere, and by and by their loyalty to their own beliefs transcends their loyalty to God. But God is above mankind's religion. He is even above those doctrines which they have come to accept, wherever these differ with the true aspects of love.

I wonder if mankind have ever mused upon what would happen in the world if all men professing to work for God were really doing so. Their loyalties, then, would be to him rather than to their egos, to the bringing-in of the kingdom rather than to the building of a tower of Babel, to the establishment of the joys of God in the lives of others rather than to the indulgence of their appetites and passions. That adherence to cosmic law which only waits as a beast of prey ready to pounce upon some statement of the Law that one of us has made which will support their own desires and desire patterns is not religion pure and undefiled.[18]

Don't you understand, beloved ones, that the harmony of the whole is of far greater importance than the temporary satisfaction of a part, even allowing that the part might be momentarily correct in its application of a tenet of the Law? Oh, the Law—how beautiful it is! And how wonderful it is when mankind can reach out to the Law and see it as the counterpart of love and mercy that will establish the unifying power of the Holy Spirit upon earth! Then much of the chastening of the children of God will become unnecessary, for they will be one with the Law even as we are one with him.[19]

Never at any time were the admonishments of the apostles or of my Son intended to be wrongly divided. Yet how frequently the Word—which is both a sword to divide good from evil and a shield to protect eternal truth from the onslaught of error's divisive ways—is misunderstood in the realm of applications. We know full well that there are many tenets of cosmic law recorded in scripture that ought to be regarded as the living Word of God. But of a truth, theologians who are part of orthodox movements have overlooked many concepts that are the pure teachings of the Spirit because of false premises injected into the printed word in the early centuries of the Christian dispensation and into later interpretations thereof.

I know the great difficulty mankind have in departing from tradition that has become accepted as divine decree. I also know how easily they wrest the laws of God to their own destruction.[20] But it is wrong to forsake one's faith in God in those moments when being true to oneself means going against orthodox tradition. For unless the Spirit of God is permitted to lead man into the laws of truth, even that progressive truth which defies tradition and the warps of the carnal mind, the present generation may well continue to be divided on both fundamental and disputed points of the Law.

Above all, men should understand and apply the law of brotherhood and not be so hasty in their judgments of one another. For in many cases, right when we have sought to establish a very special assistance to one whose prayers evoked that assistance, his own dogmatism and loyalty to traditional concepts have become the enemy of all truth, barring him from receiving our intercession.

So deeply dyed is the consciousness of mankind with many wrong concepts about God and Spirit's intent that they have failed to apprehend the basic laws of the universe so apparent in man and nature. The reason we continue to discuss the problems of religious bigotry is that the spiritual progress of the world will be effectively stayed until the people rise above the level of their dogmatic interpretations of life, their ego-centered logic and their sense thralldom, as some might say, above the world, the flesh and the devil. For it is those who deify evil through the instating of spiritual wickedness in high places[21] who are guilty of perpetuating darkness in the world, even more so than that which is the result of what men have called pure evil. And so the liar is often more deadly than the lie.

We long to see the effect of the divine level of understanding upon mankind, for we know that only through understanding will the nations promote true brotherhood in place of their brittle intellectual concepts and human conquests. So many the world over still move in the realms of mortal thought and feeling wherein they desire to be thought well of, without realizing that this in itself is a reflection of their own inadequacy, their own feelings of inferiority and insufficiency.

With God all things are possible![22] And by him the true divine nature will be established within the hearts of all. Thus there will be a natural blending of the flame that is below in man with the fire that is above in God.

I remain devoted to your divine Sonship.

Your Mother,

Mary

Retreat of the Resurrection Spiral
Colorado Springs, Colorado
July 30, 1972

4

It Is the Sense of Struggle That Makes the Struggle

Man's Twofold Responsibility to Be His Brother's Keeper and to Take Dominion over the Earth

To the Timeless Children of My Heart:

Have you thought upon the grace that can be called timeless, the infinite grace that God has had from the origin of all things which he has extended not only to the end of cycles but also to the end of each sosophoric round, to the end of each *manvantara*,* and to the eternal beginning of each fresh cycle of ever ascending regeneration?

It is not the purpose of God to thwart the progress of the ages but rather to enhance it. The current snarl of mankind's entanglement in those struggles of mind and spirit that cause him to become enmeshed in the mechanics of civilization has already created frustration piled on frustration. And the spirit of man, as well as the mind of man, becomes wearied with the endless sense of struggle that is intended to divide and conquer his very soul.

Your beloved Saint Germain has often said, "It is the sense of struggle that makes the struggle." Can you understand, blessed ones, how easy it is to relinquish your fears and your awareness of humanly contrived bondage—bondage to hatred and the creations of hatred and to the mental and emotional burdens that constantly cry out, "I cannot! I will not!"—seeing that the unity of life and of all that lives can be summoned as an act of grace to intervene at any point in time or space to alter those conditions

---

*Manvantara: Sanskrit for cycle in cosmic history.

within yourself which need to be changed so that the fullness of the Godhead may dwell in you bodily[23] as it did and does in my Son, Christ Jesus.

Your True Self can never be removed from the valedictory manifestations of the ages, from the spirit of achievement that is inherent within the Godhead and the universe. Chaos and confusion are no part of God! For the sifting and sorting process within the natural order, when it is allowed to function according to the natural selection of the Holy Spirit—that is, the natural elevation of the divine qualities in man—without that interference which mankind by wrong thoughts and feelings continue to thrust upon the universe, is pure victory on the move. In accordance with the universal plan, nature herself is a beautiful selector of grace on man's behalf, contriving to adorn his being with the highest and noblest forms of Christ-mastery.

Surely, beloved ones, somewhere along the line of even your human thought and reasoning you must have recognized that imperfection which *appears* to manifest and that perfection which you know within your hearts and souls *is* the very nature of God. Can you not see, then, that due to the presence of imperfection in the appearance world, the letter of the Law is far more subject to human manipulation than the spirit thereof, which remains inviolate in the world of perfection?[24] Yet it is to the letter of the Law that so many adhere rather than to the spirit. But God, in all of his power and wisdom, still looks at the motivation of the heart.[25]

Ah yes, we are fully aware of those changes in the interpretation of both the letter and the spirit that occur betwixt the dark and the daylight of the human consciousness, even as we are aware of those transformations of the human consciousness that occur in the sunlight of God's love and Christ-illumination. While mankind persist in engaging in those dreary activities of the mind that burden the soul in every age, they can look upon the drama of religious nonfulfillment without ever recognizing

It Is the Sense of Struggle That Makes the Struggle 67

that what their blind leaders have passed off as genuine religion has very little to do with God.

Yet the spiritual founders of religious movements, working hand in hand with those who have sustained a momentum of great hope for the salvation of the world and served the needs of the multitudes, cannot be expected to continue to bear the burden of humanity when that humanity allows its misunderstanding of the letter of the Law to interfere with its spiritual outreach.

Just as man is intended to be his brother's keeper,[26] so he is also intended to be the keeper of the domain of his destiny, proclaimed in the fiat "Take dominion over the earth!"[27] His acceptance of this twofold responsibility constantly creates newness of life and re-creates the spirit of justice in all the earth. Now, the spirit of justice is a part of the spirit of divine love, for all things of God agree in one. It is never permissible for anyone at any station in life or point of advancement in spiritual service to indulge in any action which would create further bondage to forms of hatred or result in a lack of the true expression of divine love.

What a pity it is that humanity can allow themselves in the name of righteousness, in the name of truth, to crucify one another over their disagreements on moot points of the Law or to allow their misunderstandings mixed with their understanding thereof to thwart their united effort. When we speak of humanity's need to espouse the virtue of God-control, it is because we know that this quality of Christ-mastery will bind the mankind of earth into one common body of light-servers. Thus we emphasize the flow of Christ-reality, of regeneration in the unity of the purpose of the Fatherhood and Motherhood of God.

I represent the Motherhood of God, as every woman can. And I seek to affirm and reaffirm those precepts of divine safety within the conscious awareness of each evolving monad so that in the hour of trial only light shall prevail. Past ages of failure or success are no guarantee of what shall prevail today. For each day is sufficient unto itself.[28] If man, then, desires to do the will of God and to hold fast to that which is good,[29] he must do so oblivious of all momentums of human destruction which have ever manifested in his world. For these have no power to perpetuate themselves except the power man gives to them.

Mankind speak of the current age as though it were unique. So is each precious moment. But just how unique mankind little dreams of. For at any time, at any moment in the history of the earth, man could have either failed or succeeded. The elements of God-reality have always been there as the great pondering of the mind of God to produce the fruit of his holy will in the consciousness of man. How fragile are moments in time as opportunities for the perfectionment of eternity! Their use, however, depends upon the sensitivity of men's souls and to what measure they can hold firmly to the great realities of God.

Stay with the dream of God, then, and shut out the clamoring wakefulness of the outer mind, whether in self or others, never losing touch with the components of reality in all parts of life; and you will succeed beyond your farthest dreams, for

> The house of divine Sonship
> Holds open still the door.
> The darkness of the mortal mind
> Cannot, shall not, be anymore.
>
> For just beyond the mortal sunset
> Lies the light's immortal dawn,
> Trembling on the face of morning,
> Shining promise from now on.
>
> Day of life's immortal gladness
> Echoes from the dim-lit past,
> Shimmering freshness of the Daystar,
> Crystal diamonds in the grass.

Like a dewdrop ever fairer
You reveal the bright new day;
In the fervor ever nearer
Christ's own face is seen today.

Like a gossamer veil atremble
With the thunder of the sun,
Beauteous doorway of forever
Swings wide open for each one!

Devotedly, I AM

Mary

Retreat of the Resurrection Spiral
Colorado Springs, Colorado
August 6, 1972

5

O Mankind, How Lovely You Are in Your God-Identity

Through the Trial by Fire the Real Self of Man Is Perceived as the Universal Spirit

To All Who Seek Knowledge That the Infinite God Be Glorified:

Some men rejoice in the fact that the fashion of the world passeth away.[30] But remember, blessed hearts of love, that it is your victory won right within the framework of your experiences that skims off the dross of human misbehavior and produces the divine alchemy of purification. This is the trial by fire[31] that separates your darkness from your light.

Man should understand that one day all qualification, both good and evil, must receive its reward. Through the great mercy of God, the karma of a planet and its people has again and again been withheld that new opportunities for experience might continue to come to all. This is that aspect of the Law which allows little children, maturing through the round of experience, to find the emancipation that reveals the grace of God to those whose eyes are open to his benign bestowal and to his desire to create out of the substance of opportunity the best possible gifts to life in all of its manifold parts. It is the Mother aspect of God that can examine human hurts with the eye of understanding and then yield the heart back to God with total surrender.

Now, in examining the fabric of what in this age has been called a Christian civilization, we cannot stop with just the present era but must reach back into the pages of history where we find manifesting the oh so frequent barbarities that have been brought forth upon humanity in the name of my Son, Christ Jesus. It is a great pity that today's smug and conceited Christianity often fails to utilize the honest eyes of the heart and soul to extract a valued lesson from both present and past Church history.

It is the yielding of the heart to the beat of joy in every situation that purifies the understanding of man that it might one day become a repository of strength to those who are willing to surrender unto God all human desires and their need for self-importance. This does not mean, O hearts of light, the extinguishing of man's life or light. Rather it brings about an intensification of its shine, for the intensifying power of the Christ does descend from the Godhead into the chalice of individual lives.

It should always be a joy to contribute thoughts of dignity and worth into the flowing stream of energy which constitutes life. How often men sit on the bank of the river of life and watch it flow, taking from it all that they possibly can yet contributing nothing to its course or movement. Surely justice and mercy must follow man,[32] both contemporary man and man to come. Surely all shall come to understand one day that it is only that which is yielded unto God through love that endures. As Saint Paul said long ago, "Now abideth faith, hope, charity, these three; but the greatest of these is charity."[33]

You who read my words through the *Pearls of Wisdom* should understand that these are not written for the glorification of the human ego but for the exaltation of the soul in the divine flame and light. Thus one day mankind will come to know and to understand how beautiful and complete the light is because he will have added to that light the best gifts of his own self-realization, intensifying them in the filaments of his being so that he too may let his light shine.[34] It is the energy of God that glorifies the soul of each one. And when the electrifying concepts of his grace are made known to the world, the right use of both his masculinity and his femininity will be adhered to and the androgynous being of God seen at last in fuller measure in the stature of the Christ.

Mankind often say that it is a tragedy that greater understanding does not prevent wars, rumors of wars[35] and the darkening attitudes of the race of men. But after all, beloved ones, it is to high places in human thought rather than to high places in divine thought that mankind aspire. Is it any wonder, then, that they yield themselves so easily to self-glorification and self-righteousness? Is it any wonder, then, that they are prone to error almost from the beginning of their mistaken monadic expressions, which are in reality no part of the Divine Monad but are of the synthesized personality they have come to regard as the Real Self?

When the Real Self of man is perceived as the universal Spirit, all-flowing and all-enfolding, the power of love comes to be realized to such a marked degree as to produce the profoundest of changes in the nature of man. And if these changes be produced in the individual, must they not, then, permeate all substance and structuring?

"Let not your heart be troubled," my Son declared. "Ye believe in God, believe also in me."[36] Why, in the name of heaven, if all men were really created by God, should they deem it an unworthy act to hold, in addition to self-esteem, esteem for other parts of life? Certainly we do not say that mankind should respect evil or those things which are hurtful to men. But there is enough virtue in the soul of man which God so lovingly placed there that those who look can surely perceive that virtue in man and, seeing it, amplify it so that all may partake of the sacred Eucharist, the tiny wafer of life by which they are made aware of their unity in Christ.

The world today lives in a time of the great depreciation of values, in a time of the deterioration of a sense of their own worth and hence of the worth of others. Because of this and because mankind do not understand true religion nor the fact that the world has produced saints in the past as well as in the present, they seem to look askance at all who hold fast to good.[37] There is a trend today to expose all action of a truly divine nature as if it were fraudulent, as if it were deceptive. I am sure that more shall be said on this subject, but let mankind perceive how seldom men really do believe in motives of worth in others.

Little do they dream of what is in the heart, for we perceive the virtue of God in the hearts of many. But by the same token, we also observe in the temporary strands of human petulance and greed the tendency on the part of many to condemn others for the same thing that they themselves desire to do but in some cases have not done and in other cases have done. It is dangerous for mankind to point an accusing finger at others when many times they are not aware of their own imperfect patterns from past ages. They do not foresee what they will one day do as a result of the very trends they are now creating.

O mankind, how lovely you are in your God-identity! And so it is with our prayer for the redemption of all that is beautiful and real about you that in this hour of mounting human affliction and distress the hearts of many will turn to my Son as a part of their Real Self, as a part of their God-identity. His mission in life was not for self-glorification but for the eternal glory of God. If men are able to perceive this glory in all, then all will find themselves identifying with such perfection as has never come to earth before. And the divine genius native to man will let fly out the window of life, never to be anymore, those elements of human distress that presently conceal the face of God from a weary and a hungry world.

Christ said so long ago, "Blessed are they which do hunger and thirst after righteousness, for they shall be filled."[38] The moments of that infilling are thrilling beyond belief! The soul gasps in individualized mankind that it might receive a breath of this reality, that it might perceive the infinite hand of God reaching through all experience and beckoning all to move onward into the universal light without fear and with the fullest of confidence.

I remain ever your Mother in the service of the universal Christ,

Mary

Retreat of the Resurrection Spiral
Colorado Springs, Colorado
August 13, 1972

6

My God Shall Supply All Your Need

*The Love of Money and the Possessiveness of Things
Deprives Humanity of Christ and His Kingdom*

To Men of Good Will in All Lands:

The physical framework of the world, consisting of the planetary platform of mountains and plain, of the strata of the rock and the verdure of nature, including the torrid regions of the earth and the snowcapped mountain heights, reflects but a rock-ribbed dignity, a plane for human endeavors, a world stage upon which events array themselves.

Man, possessed with his God-given right of mobility, moves to and fro upon the earth just as his consciousness traverses the realm of manifold experience. But wherever he goes, he utilizes the one consciousness, the one flow of the generosity of God which gives to embodied mankind the gift of access to the mind of God, to the mind of Christ. And it is through the mind of God and the mind of Christ that he is able to achieve at last the perspective that enables him to rule the kingdom of nature as well as the realm of selfhood.

Do you not realize, O blessed mankind, that the fabric and outreach of the mind are a specific endowment of God which is given to mankind in order that he may integrate his consciousness with the Holy Spirit in nature and in man? What folly it is, then, for mankind to play the peacock and strut about as though his endowment were greater than that of another. All should come to the humble realization of the grace of God shining in the face of nature and behind the screens of the human monad with all of its selfishness and deceit. For of old and to the present day, the greatest grief is brought to mankind, as well as an outpouring of the vials[39] of his own karma, strictly because of his unending tolerance of human greed within heart and mind.

Is it not recorded that the *love* of money is the root of all evil?[40] The summation of the propensity to love money can be perceived in world commerce and world thought. It is not necessary that mankind despise that medium of exchange which they have called money but rather that they learn its correct use as my Son taught it two thousand years ago.[41] For through the correct use of money, mankind will understand that money is but a little part of the abundance of God. It is a medium of exchange between nations and peoples, intended never to be manipulated but always to be expanded as a breaking of the loaf[42] of God's substance by the action of the flame of God-maturity among men, that the crumbs that fall from the Master's table[43] should be given to all as a part of the whole loaf of universal abundance.

When individuals allow themselves to be attached to mortal things, when they permit their mind and consciousness to become involved in elements of human greed until all other considerations of life are excluded, they will most certainly lose sight of the abundant life. All fleshly gain should be seen in the light of the statement "Naked came I out of my mother's womb, and naked shall I return thither: the LORD gave, and the LORD hath taken away."[44] For unless man understands that all that can be attached to his being, to his soul, to his individuality is grace, he will not understand the proper use of either money or the energies of life.

The reason the Brotherhood deems it desirable to call these matters to the attention of the students at this time is to avoid their becoming a part of the world struggle for the control of money and the economies of the nations. Money of itself would be of little value if men were anhungered and could find no bread, if they were in need of shelter and could find no home. What is needed, then, by all is a correct understanding of life and its abundance.

Some men may ask why it is that I choose to discourse on the love of money and its effect on monetary releases. Don't you see, beloved ones, how important it is to the evolution of humanity that men understand, not only in words but also in spirit, the need to establish themselves in God and his goodness? The fashions of the times change and men are no sooner born than the process of decay sets in. They no sooner acquire a vast storehouse of worldly wisdom, of nomenclature and much superficial knowledge of all things than they are borne from the world to which they have become attached.

Freedom from the love of money, which is the root of all evil, will free men from those attachments which have created such a quantity of discord and darkness in the world. Furthermore, it will bring to everyone who is able to free himself from this love, from this attachment, from this grossness, the refining and ennoblement of his spirit. The reason it is so wrong for humanity to become attached to the love of money is that the quality of possessiveness of things deprives humanity of the promise of the Christ "Fear not, little flock; for it is your Father's good pleasure to give you the kingdom."[45] Indeed it is God's good pleasure to give to mankind all dominion, all power and all glory once he has demonstrated his willingness to use these gifts as a wise steward of the grace of God.

In gazing at the record of mankind's doings through the ages, ever and anon the love of money has shown its ugly head as the serpentine force which creates in the labyrinth of human life those tortuous movements which enslave mankind the world around. Thus the love of money prevents mankind from entering into the kingdom simply because the very things that God would so gladly give to all are denied to the many because this or that one desires to keep, to retain, to hold in esteem the things of the world above the things of the kingdom of God.

In this series I have felt it necessary to touch the heart of heaven in order that I might also learn what specific quality of understanding or assistance can be imparted unto mankind that will enable him to move with the avant-garde into the advancing era of the kingdom of God.

For me to say that the churches of the world have not over the centuries involved themselves or allowed themselves to be involved in the activities of human greed and injustice would be sheer falsehood. In my Son's name, in my name and in the name of heaven, acts have been committed again and again which are a perversity of the Spirit, which have denied bread to the hungry while erecting altars of gold and silver. Yet in the eyes of heaven, there is some justification for the adorning of the temples of God and the honoring of the hosts of heaven with the abundance of God that the matrix of his supply might be expanded for all upon the altar of the Lord.

Therefore, in dividing the word of righteousness, men must understand that condemnation of any act of man must be tempered not only by justice and mercy but also by the higher criticism of the divine Logos. Men must love God above all things. For in loving God first, they will come to love all things, all men, all the adornments of nature and the graces of life, both seen and unseen, as the manifestation of God. And they will be free of the desire to covet. Hence, wise is the man who does not judge his neighbor but understands the nature of service to his God, to his home, to his church and to his fellowmen.

By spreading abroad the sense of the abundance of God as attainable by every man—"but my God shall supply all your need"[46]—each man is imbued with the fire of sacred trust whereby he sees the world as an abode of usefulness where dwell the Spirit of God and the spirit of usefulness and the harmony of the artisans that can work together and spread the balm of the true kingdom everywhere.

Let perish from your mind, then, the thoughts of darkness, of greed and the condemnation of human greed. For by the illuminating sense that gives to each one the true knowledge of the right attitudes of the spiritual thoughts that are the thoughts of Christ, man can at last ascend in consciousness to the place where true Christhood does manifest.

Devotedly, I AM

Mary

Retreat of the Resurrection Spiral
Colorado Springs, Colorado
August 20, 1972

7

He Was Made Man That We Might Be Made God!

*By the Invincible Light of Cosmic Victory,
Valiant Spirits Weave a New Culture of Understanding
in the Heart's Chalice*

To Men and Women of the Hour:

The shafts of light that penetrate the world darkness and maya must be seized upon hourly by embodied mankind. They cannot afford to continue to ally themselves with cherished institutions which have ceased to serve the purposes for which they were founded. They cannot deny the reality of perspective that is conveyed to the soul when the soul attains that perfection of attunement which reveals the reality of God.

It is not our wish to destroy those human instruments and traditional organizations which have in some measure served the divine plan. Nevertheless, they are already self-destroyed. And those remnants of their followers that remain as confused sheep that cannot find their pasture do not yet realize that through the greater power of the Great White Brotherhood and the greater dedication of the ascended masters of wisdom there have been preserved in the heavens, by divine decree and through divine intervention, the standards of sublime grace that are sufficient for all mankind's needs.

As the old has exhibited its failures again and again, as those who profess to represent the Deity have shown themselves to be lovers of gold more than lovers of God, the divisive attempts of the brothers of the shadow have removed from view the real images of divinity in the true spiritual leaders of the race and supplanted them by those human warps and distortions which indeed reflect the abomination of desolation standing in the holy place where it ought not.[47]

We have said before and we say again that the world is in grave danger. But we cite as evidence of the eternal presence of hope the manifestations of nature—the trees, the rocks and the so-called inert aspects thereof—that endure long after the physical body of man. I say they endure in order to once again become a part of a planetary platform for the hopeful appearance of life regenerate.

The statements made by my Son have been added to and in many cases enhanced by the spiritual experiences of men who in the centuries following his mission have entered into divine association with the heavenly hosts. As the great patriarch Athanasius said, "For he was made man that we might be made God."[48] But the rising turbulence of human emotion generated in wars and rumors of wars[49] and in all manner of strife does not indicate that this process of man's rapprochement with the Deity is being accelerated.

The perceptive, who see not merely the speck of the moment but the grandeur of the accumulations of the spark of God within the heart and soul of mankind, are refreshed with the hope which, regardless of human appearances, is summoning from far-off worlds those valiant spirits that are even now approaching the planetary body to increase mankind's awareness of grace. They are determined, by the invincible light of cosmic victory, to fasten together the loose-knit strands of a new culture and to weave the understanding within the heart's chalice and the mind's altar of mankind's own Christ-awareness.

Blatant have been the chatterings of those mortal magpies that have always sought to carry from nest to nest the burdens of carnal commentaries framed by those who are known to us as the destroyers of the cult of the Mother. But one day their opportunity shall pass. For they will reap the reward of having separated themselves into levels of sensuality that while extinguishing the flame of God within the souls of their victims also blot out the very best possibilities for themselves.

Now is the time for the elect to determine so to be! I cannot say in cosmic honor that many orthodox institutions are serving aught else than the causes of Satan. That they have summoned some appearance of goodness yet have denied the power thereof in no way provides them with a valid excuse in the eyes of the living God.

How deep has been our heart's grief to see in this age the repudiation of Christ-wholeness that would have knit the body of God upon earth into a solid spiritual organism that could well have assured humanity that the hour of the Second Coming was indeed now. Daily the conceptions of Antichrist are thrust upon the world religious scene. And daily the religious leaders, as well as our students, have failed to distinguish between the Christ and the appearances of Antichrist, which proclaims itself to be that which it is not. Those who claim to be the allness of God must understand that the spark is only the allness when the spark is merged with the flame.

They have not understood that whereas the spark can and should increase its size and magnificence, achieving within its own framework of identity a greater measure of the Godhead, it is only in the progressive movement of concerted action in harmony with the universe that the great rotation of the cosmic spheres is served. Hence those who proclaim themselves light but are filled with darkness should look to the Christ-hope of universal dimension whereby they can at last be free from all that is less than perfection within themselves.

Man is indeed a being of mingled light and darkness. His light is the Christ light; his darkness is that to which he has been subjected and that which he has accepted of that which opaques light. Let all understand, then, that the purging of the self, which may excite many tests and trials and may well provide elements of chastisement, is still the most valiant way whereby individuals may come at last to a state of purification and a greater extension of the light of God through the clear pane of their own crystal awareness.

I AM devoted to the expansion of the kingdom of heaven upon earth.

Mary

Retreat of the Resurrection Spiral
Colorado Springs, Colorado
August 27, 1972

8

The Son Shall Also Be Subject unto Him That Put All Things under Him

Through the Gnosis of Life and the Love of the Christ of Every Man, Human Interpretations of Dogma Are Overcome

To the Children of the Sacred Chalice:

As you ride through the busy streets of life, do you stop long enough to consider the reality of your being tied to the chalice of your heart? Your consciousness is a sacred connection. When it is correctly used, it can, like a giant beam of a searchlight, pierce the gloom of human night and nebulousness and then involve itself in unerring contact with the Presence of God or with those divine emissaries to whom he has assigned specific functions in the universe.

Have you thought, beloved ones, of the multitudinous manifestations of life, of how here in the physical world there are so many diverse manifestations as to almost dazzle the eyes of the mind? In a spiritual sense, there are even more manifestations, yet all are manifestations of the One.

It is vital that man should cease to allow himself to be confused by human interpretations of dogma which seek to separate the creations of heaven or earth from the Lord that hath made all things.[50] Men choose so frequently to honor him with their lips and by supposedly directing their consciousness toward God alone. But while they seek to honor him, they exclude all of the functional and beautiful manifestations which he has made and charged with specific uses to the glory of the light in man.

How many there are in the world today who always seek to

reach the Christ on the throne without understanding that the tiniest grain of sand or blade of grass and the smallest individual from the standpoint of human esteem is also, by God's decree, a manifestation of that universal Christ. Won't you try to understand that it is only an activity of darkness that attempts to separate humanity into segments, allowing individuals to think that this lesser manifestation is the all of God, whereas there are higher manifestations which all can find through the attainment of the Christ consciousness. Through the schemes of false esteem, through the improper placement of values, mankind reject God in Matter or they reject God in the temple of the heart's chalice or they reject God in all of the secondary phases of his expression save the Central Sun or what they consider to be the central reality of creation.

This is not pleasing to God. It is direct disobedience to the principles of "Love one another."[51] For it is loving life free that changes in mankind's actions will take place which will bring in the golden age. It is so vital that the great pressures of love, of the very Godhead itself, be transmitted into the chalice of the heart, the focal point of the individual's consciousness, and then sent out to love every manifestation of God that is bound and blinded by human dogmas and human greed to free them all—free at last.

Don't you see that life is not intended to be an orgy that demoralizes, degrades and destroys the central theme of love's purpose, which has ever in view the harmony of the sacred spheres and that work which Jesus referred to so long ago when he said, "My Father worketh hitherto, and I work"?[52] One day as all advance in their spiritual consciousness through the chalice of their own heart, they will come to the similitude of God, to the place where they will understand the work of God, the labors of his love, the labors of his creativity, the labors in which all are intended to share.

From the first dawn of creation, it was God's hope that man, made in his own image,[53] would learn how to be one with him[54] and elect so to be. Thus the Father foreknew that many blessed souls would enjoy the spirit of wholeness through imbibing the spiritual gnosis of life. By this process they would be able to bring their consciousness into complete harmony with the consciousness of God through the ministration of the Holy Spirit and through the complete acceptance of the reality of God.

It is recorded in the scriptures that "every knee should bow at the name of Jesus"[55] and that "the Son [should] also himself be subject unto him that put all things under him, that God may be all in all."[56] Let all understand, then, the nature of the office of Mediator, the office held by the Christ of every man, not as one of worldly position and pomposity but as one of humility before God and authority before man.

My Son, whose identity became totally merged with the Christ, long ago rejected the temporal crown upon the celebration of Palm Sunday. He desired only the crown of service in the kingdom of God and to bring many sons into captivity to the will of God. Don't you see, then, that it is not the worship of his person that he craves, but the identification of every son and daughter with the inner Christ-radiance which God placed within the chaliced being of man?

Through utter devotion, man will one day be able to understand that true worship is the worship of God as Spirit,[57] both in its universal aspect and in its specific individualization in hearts abiding in the dimensions of Matter. Thus the diadem of lives lived in and for him may indeed provide the encircling crown of the World Mother, which she may hold in her hands and offer unto God. For Spirit is one. And though, as has been said, there be gods many and lords many, "there is but one God, the Father, of whom are all things, and we in him."[58]

To him be "blessing, and honour, and glory, and power."[59] Let the temples of individual lives, the temples of the world and the varying religions of the world learn to understand this cardinal truth that they may cease in their warrings and begin to express universal compassion.

Devotedly, I AM

Mary

Retreat of the Resurrection Spiral
Colorado Springs, Colorado
September 3, 1972

9

As Men Sow, So Shall They Reap

*The Magnificence of God and of His Spirit
and the Christ Transmutes All Harshness
in Human Life and Human Suffering*

To All Who Love God—to All Who Profess to Love God:

I now make a plea for the avoidance of harshness in human life. How much suffering there is in the world order because of human selfishness and a lack of understanding between people! And O mankind of earth, how much suffering occurs each day in the various countries of the world simply because of carelessness and human cruelty.

If individuals only knew the Law! For it is impossible to do harm to anyone without receiving the last jot and tittle of recompense,[60] whether in this world or in the world to come. It is folly to think that men will escape the result of their own acts. In accordance with the consistency of cosmic law, it is ever true that as men sow, so shall they reap.[61] The fact that the mercy of heaven has extended pardon to men again and again is no sign that in matters of human relations where mankind fail to express a reasonable kindness to one another they are not forging a yoke of drudgery around their own necks.

But, then, I think of how true it is that this is not the will of God. I think also of his great mercies, which endure forever,[62] because those who are the recipients of the greatest mercy are those who receive eternal life. Mankind gaze at the spectacle of their years as though they were entitled to eternity in their present state. Certainly it ought to be apparent to the discerning thinker that God could not limit his creation or the measure of its progress to the confusing aspects of life that are in the world today. It is never the intent of God to neglect his creation and its marvelous opportunity to progress.

Let every heart pause to reflect upon the goodness of God, to realize his care and consideration, not only in this year but in all past times, and to behold the hand of his grace extending itself into the whole domain of the future for all. Worlds aborning and worlds adying are simply the fulfillment of infinite Law, which governs the cycles of life in all parts of cosmos. In a like manner, the process of metamorphosis and the entire spectrum of change in human life are intended to follow the measured cadences of God's care.

It is in receiving comfort from the Holy Spirit that mankind are imbued with the sense of complete peace and rest. Yet how marvelous is the balance that enables them to see once and for all that peace is not a cessation of activities but a blessed expansion of God at rest in service, as being is intended to be God in action. For both manifestations are necessary polarities of his grace.

If men and women would only recognize the creative motions of the universe as their own, as a part of their spiritual heritage, they would see quite plainly that the present regime of struggle against confusion and against false management of the lives of others by diverse forms of tyranny is only a darkening cloud that, like burned-out cinders, clogs the atmosphere of man's consciousness. The infamous history of human tyrants and ungodly people involves far too great a percentage of human life when one considers the multitudes who have mimicked the wickedness of both their lords and their peers.

Only the few have understood the true meaning of life not as a continuing struggle but as a pulling-together for a higher glory than that of the human ego. These have held out the hand of faith to the purposes of Deity.

Men who witness the magnificence of God and of his Spirit

could, in the name of pure reason, scarcely believe him incapable of dominating all mankind. The fact that he does not shows that he has placed a contract of life in the hands of embodied mankind. It is up to them as they pursue the highest goal in the universe, oneness with God, to find those regenerative faculties of light and hope for themselves, that their hearts might thereby bow low in reverent gratitude to God for the gift of himself. While flesh and blood cannot inherit the kingdom of God,[63] the triumph of the soul arrayed in its divine vestments is one of mastery over all man's darkness by the expansion and acknowledgment of his light.

Have you thought how closely Christ identifies with this magnificent outpouring that I refer to as light? Christ is light, and the Christ within you, each one, is light. I make an impassioned plea to humanity, before it is too late and the karmic vials are poured out upon the earth, to seek to alleviate harshness, to repudiate it in all of its forms by the action of their thoughts powerfully centered in God. For man's inhumanity to man and his failure to meet the human need with divine love, whenever and wherever it appears, are often the result of hardness of heart,[64] which must be challenged by fervent supplication and the careful doing of the will of God.

Only by the grace of God can the world order be moved forward into the domain of divine kindness and all people find at last the great possibilities of the kingdom envisioned so long ago by my Son, Jesus Christ, by others before him[65] and by the All-Father from the first page of the cycle unto the present.

That the anointing of God be sought, that his Spirit be encouraged to do its mighty work among men to alter the structure of weakness and bind up the wounds of humanity is my prayer.

Devotedly,

Mary

Retreat of the Resurrection Spiral
Colorado Springs, Colorado
September 10, 1972

10

Let Us Not Be Weary in Well Doing

*Being Self-True, Rising into
the Essential Greatness of the Soul,
Man Overcomes*

To the Cherished Ones:

The fashion of the times changes, but the kingdom of God changes not. Think! This which is within you, this beautiful focus you call soul, made in the image of God,[66] is intended to endow your consciousness with its fragrances, its passion for delight, its outreach into reality.

What shall I say, then, of the synthetic overlay fed by the constant drippings of human dreariness? Long ago Paul said, "Let us not be weary in well doing."[67] There is a human tendency, which the scientists understand as inherent within metal, for the very atoms of substance to rebel against the constant outpicturing of sameness. Hence as a result of their rebellion, there sets in what is known as metal fatigue, the weariness of the particles of substance of their continual manifestation within the matrix of a specific object or activity.

When men understand life better, they will see that unless the joyous dancing electrons of which substance is composed were able to express spontaneously the beauties and perfection of the ongoingness of God, they could not possibly bear the burden through the millenniums of those undesirable forms and endowments of the human consciousness which are such an abomination to the progress of life.

O hearts of light, the shadows of the world are not of God!

The fact that they are permitted at all is a manifestation of law and forward movement. It is ever God's hope that men will do better, that men will accept the great legacy of life which he has so generously given to all, and that they will restrain themselves from dipping into those caldrons of seething human emotion which regurgitate upon the screen of life those awful manifestations of pain and hardship which are no part of the reality of God.

When we urge men to recognize the perfection of God, there are times when, for purposes of contrast, we unveil those unfortunate astral sequences and scenarios of half existence which offer a shadowland of enticement to the human monad. We pray that men will swiftly learn to discern the differences between the glamour of the astral existence and the brilliance of real living that frees man to rise into the arms of God with the balm of sweet surrender that lends serenity to the soul moving onward.

If you stop and think about it, no one can hold riches or fame or family name generation after generation with any degree of certitude. One day the lesser aspect of man must joyously relinquish the little stair steps which he has climbed to enter into the magnetic pull of his God Presence. Rising, then, into his essential greatness, the soul claims at last all that God envisioned for it. Heaven conspires to give every advantage to the individual monad and remembers his iniquities no more,[68] casting them aside as though they had never existed.

How true it is that men are prone to honor that which is traditional and to look askance upon even the highest reality when it does not appear through traditional channels. Would it not be wise, then, if embodied mankind began to consider the accuracy of their reason and the integrity of their own souls and to attune with the blessed focus of the eternal coal of fire upon the altar of being?

By being self-true, men are able to see what is real instead of relying upon the words of men. Can't you see, beloved ones, that we are simply trying to give you a greater measure of perspective?

Let Us Not Be Weary in Well Doing

Be careful that you do not use this perspective to reject what is real, but do learn to discern, and that well. The fact that many men accept a certain idea as being correct does not mean that it is, nor does it mean that it is not. Hence out of the crucible of experience, trial and error, continual faith and a determination to know God will man come at last to the place where he will know himself *as* God.

To be a god of your own universe does not defeat the plan of the eternal Father. His greatest desire is to see that perfection which he has placed in all life realized by man. As his offspring, all men are expected to follow the stream of the Law as it pertains to the perfect life. It is not as though men cannot; it is so frequently that they will not. And for what purpose do men despise the higher law of their being when by adhering to it they can, once the negative momentums of life are overcome, walk with less effort into the dominion of their spiritual treasure, the bounty of the Christ consciousness that overcomes the world, and into that perfect life which is God?

Oh, I know how the enemy has sown the tares[69] that despise even the hearing of his name or the affirmation of his being. They can hardly stand the concept of his existence. Well, don't you think, beloved ones, that it is a little foolish for them to muster all this opposition against a God whose existence they deny?

One day humanity will perceive en masse the goal of life after they emerge from the crucible of their self-created trials to that position where they will summon that great measure of understanding which will make of all men the universal Christ in consciousness. What some do not understand is that the days of man's travail can be shortened, that it is the will of God to shorten those days wherever possible.[70] The elect are usually those who elect to pursue the higher path. This means that they have chosen even as they were chosen, and their generated response precedes them upon the path that leads to regeneration.

The universal Mother would gather men and women from

the four corners of the earth into the court of the Temple of Understanding, which is a spiritual temple built out of the giant hopes of God. No lilliputian world is this but a world of experience in beauty, in the divine arts, in the divine sciences, and in the recognition of man's opportunity to create and to enjoy his creation. The pities of life must go down under the triumphs. But so long as men ally themselves with darkness and with their failure to exert upon life the pressures of their own understanding, they will continue to manifest in the mirror of consciousness those warps and waves of imperfection in which they dwell.

We would see men who have been lifted out of the socket of mortal density accept the fullness of their God-endowment and decide here and now that the quality of life upon earth shall be as it is in heaven. Don't you know, beloved mankind, how many powers of a spiritual nature are yours for the asking? Don't you know that the more they are correctly used, the greater the talent endowment becomes? "Choose you this day whom ye will serve,"[71] for his is the light of beginning.

> Like the pale and pastel morning,
> The dawn of life appears to all
> Expressing warning.
> The shadow of the years,
> In its essence bright and shining,
> Contains the strands eternally
> That are the substance
> Of the morning
> Grasping all eternity.

Devoted to the fire mist of creative essence within your heart,
I AM

   Mary

Retreat of the Resurrection Spiral
Colorado Springs, Colorado
September 17, 1972

11

For the Letter Killeth but the Spirit Giveth Life

*The One Source of Power, Wisdom and Love
Is Victorious over the Vibrations of Defeat and Defeatism*

To the Children of the Living God:

To understand from the divine level is totally different than to understand from the level of the human consciousness. The first vision is of all perfection. The second varies greatly in its comprehensions of life. Yet surely all can understand, if they will, that life's purposes were woven into the universal fabric of creative opportunity and that in the beginning every soul was given the same opportunity, the same radiant goal.

It is often difficult to convince men and women of the temporal power they wield. They do not understand why they cannot seem to make contact with God. All hindrances, inasmuch as they do not emanate from the Godhead or from the divine plan, must of necessity come from another source. As there is only one source of power, wisdom and love in the universe—only one Godhead and one radiant emanation of that Godhead extending itself throughout the whole domain of time and space—hindrances must originate outside of Being itself, beyond the hallowed circle of reality.

If you stop and think about it, it is a change in the frequency of your thoughts and feelings, in the attunement of mind and heart, that cuts out the great God-controls which would otherwise make you so effective in mastering your world and taking command of your life. Instead of giving you the victory of your Divine

Presence, this step-down in vibration causes you to become attuned with the lower vibrations of defeat and defeatism that are already in the world. These releases do not come from nowhere; therefore they have to come from somewhere. Where is it that they come from if not from the misqualification of light and consciousness by someone? And when individuals engage in the misqualification of energy, they automatically place themselves at that moment within the bounds of unreality.

Is it possible that men and women can be so simple that they fail to understand that misunderstandings are often compounded as one person catches the ball of someone's misunderstanding and then passes it to another, having added his own misunderstanding to it? As inaccuracies pile up layer upon layer in the minds of people, they retain an electrical impulse that can be transmitted to other minds of a similar frequency. Those who remain constant with their mind fixed on God and the purposes of love are unmoved by the subtle influences that abound in the mass consciousness. But those who adjust the frequency of their thoughts to negative manifestations rather than to the perfection of their God Presence easily become the victims of all types of human thought and feeling.

It is with a view to showing mankind the way to deliverance that I speak. Unless people are able to escape those thoughts and feelings that are not to their liking, they will be affected to a greater or lesser degree by the thoughts and feelings of others. How easy it is through the generation of excitement to attract mankind's attention and then lead him where you want him to go. It is not that we recommend that individuals always hold to thoughts of suspicion. It is simply that a certain amount of soul vigilance is required in order for men to achieve the goal of spiritual discernment lest they be swept out of the way by a flood of human opinions.

The greatest tragedies of life have arisen from those dogmas that through the years have aborted mankind's true sense of reality—ideas, for example, that create feelings of distrust, doubt and fear. In the matter of reembodiment, how frequently those in orthodox circles, whose fathers and forefathers before them have leaned upon what they term Christian traditions, feel that any instruction on the subject is a dividing of the way. They but pinpoint the fact that their devotion to my Son and to his great example is secondary to their devotion to a false teaching based upon the doctrines of those who have proved themselves to be lovers of man rather than lovers of God.

This is a great misfortune, for when individuals have believed a certain thing for many years, their feelings gradually intensify concerning the absoluteness of their belief. This often prevents a clear seeing of the structures of life.

Some base their rejection of a teaching upon a single tenet or an idea taken out of context without understanding the need to "try the spirits"[72] and to "in patience possess their souls."[73] When I consider the numbers of wars that have been fought and the conflicts that have been engaged in by mortal men in defense of political or religious ideals, I pray that more men and women will develop that strength of character which will afford them a greater degree of tolerance for one another's views and their right to hold them and thus bring about a state of peace on earth with goodwill to all.[74]

The concept of reembodiment is one of the ancient truths which were handed down by men of God long before the Christian era. The way of life of the majority of the world's population was at one time completely oriented around this idea. They understood the continuity of existence—that God had not planned for souls to come into the world with one chance for salvation and then to be either accepted or rejected at the hour of judgment.

Don't you see how in keeping with the mercy of God the

divine plan is, as renewed opportunity for self-mastery is given to the soul lifetime after lifetime? For each embodiment is like a day in itself. It is an epoch during which the individual is expected to master certain aspects of life, to understand how he can gain spiritual stature and at the same time convey peace and harmony to his fellowmen.

Because of world conflicts and the generation of a sense of conflict within the human consciousness, I urge upon all the understanding that the mind of man, in reality, need not be so vulnerable that those who have pursued God for years will allow themselves to be cast down and destroyed by a sudden wind of doctrine or some new religious philosophy. For men can submit their hearts to God without necessarily submitting their minds to dogma. Dogma is like unto dead letter. It does not contain in and of itself the spiritual potential, which man himself must invoke, of bringing comfort and understanding to humanity. The Holy Spirit does. The Presence of God does. Therefore let men learn to be in contact with the living essence of the spirit of truth rather than with the manifestation of the letter that killeth.[75]

What a pity it is that through the years so many conflicts have raged concerning so many things. If men would only realize that a fair consideration, an objective analysis, of what some have termed the hidden side of life is not wrong. There are those who feel that if a man even contemplates an idea that is foreign to his established beliefs or accepted tradition, he is consorting with evil. Oh, how many more evil things there are in the world than that! There is far greater potential for evil in mankind's associations with one another—the way in which they live, their behavior toward and regard for their fellowman. A man's actions remain the supreme test of his philosophy. And these are far more important than his meat or his drink, what he concedes in his mind or what he does not.

> For all is well
> If all will tell
> The soul perfection within them
> To express, to unfold,
> To release, to behold
> A new heaven and a new earth,[76]
> A new mind and a new heart,
> Cleansed by the ongoing of the Spirit
> That leads and guides men
> Into all truth.[77]

Nevertheless, it is very necessary in the disciplining of the mind and the tethering of the heart's devotion to the Law for men to adhere to some form of ritual and certain tenets of faith. It is almost impossible to think that man in this day and age would have no religious teaching whatever. But his consideration of the gentle activities of cosmic law, as they unfold within his understanding, should help him more through the open door that leads to reality than through the closed door that signifies a closed understanding and a search that ended before it was begun.

Will you think about that razor's edge, that fine line which enables you to contemplate the nature of truth, to understand the precepts of the Law, and ask God to lead you into the paths of righteousness for his name's sake?[78]

How mighty indeed would be our thrust for light's purpose if men would bring themselves into harmony with the universe and with one another! When they see each meeting as a confrontation between opposing philosophies, a testing of egos, when they transfer thoughts of fear and failure to one another, they lose the balance of the Middle Way and quite frequently do not recover their loss in the space of a lifetime. Would it not be better, rather than sparring with the world, if men sought to please God and to know him—not to know him merely through the eyes of mentors and friends but to know him for themselves, that they may be justified by the Holy Spirit that is even now leading the race into all truth?

For the glory of peace in the religious world, I remain

Your Mother,

Mary

Retreat of the Resurrection Spiral
Colorado Springs, Colorado
September 24, 1972

12

Father, into Thy Hands I Commend My Spirit

*Pruning the Tree of Life Opens the Door
to Divine Intercession and the Thread of Contact*

To All Who Would Understand:

How strange it is that men are so often caught up in the glamour of economic station or social position. They do not seem to understand the greatness that God has placed within the heart of the divine seed, which he has also placed within them. They do not seem to understand the great brand of cosmic equality that does not favor one son of God over another, that places the same potential within the grasp of all.

The image of God is the highest rung upon the ladder. It is the rung of perfection. Whereas individuals may differ in their comprehensions of life and in the speed with which they grasp divine principles or even human principles, men should understand, as in the fable of the hare and the tortoise,[79] that what is important is that they arrive at the place where the knowledge of God has meaning to them and where their faith is anchored in that magnificent achievement of divine perfection which will one day manifest as fruit upon their tree of life.

Individuals are prone to either undersell or oversell themselves. They think that balance is not within their grasp simply because of aberrations in the human consciousness that swing to the left or to the right of the Christ mind. In reality, even a middle-of-the-road position is not the desired goal when it is sought from the level of the human ego. For the perfection of God is more than a human standard: it is a tangible reality that comprises the whole spectrum of man's divinity. This reality can never be subject to human opinion as it moves from the right to the center or to the left of any position. For God's outreach is involved solely with the allness of himself, which includes the total manifestation of Christed man.

There are many problems facing the world today that should be the direct concern of all of humanity. God himself has given a great deal of thought to mankind's problems, and he has placed within man's grasp the ability to cope with current conditions even though it does not seem that he has.

The best position for any man to take, then, is one of trust whereby he recognizes the holy concern of the Comforter[80] that does not necessarily involve itself with human problems and human solutions but rather inculcates within the consciousness of embodied humanity an inner sense of God's reality that adapts itself freely to meet the needs of any situation. Thus if man will let him, God, who is in his heaven, will ultimately produce through man's own consciousness right action in the world of material form.

How difficult it seems for people to maintain their patience, their fortitude and their perspective long enough to keep their hands off the ark of God.[81] But if they would have the perfect solution to every problem, they must be willing to wait for the salvation of our God and the moving of his Spirit upon the troubled waters. Surprisingly, there is a tendency for men to feel that they are better able to deal with problems in the physical realm than God. It is almost as if they thought that the perfection of God does not possess the ability to invade the world of man's imperfection!

Man's trust in God creates a bond between Father and son that produces perfection wherever it is realized and affirmed. Men are seldom willing to admit that the fault of their failure lies

Father, into Thy Hands I Commend My Spirit

within their own domain. But when they tamper with that which ought to be left to the powers of heaven, they set up various interference patterns, astral grids and forcefields, which block the ray of the perfect solution from cycling into manifestation from higher levels of consciousness to lower levels of being.

You have heard the saying that man proposes but God disposes,[82] and this is correct according to the principles of cosmic law. But when the individual submits himself into the keeping of God as Jesus did when he said, "Father, into thy hands I commend my spirit,"[83] God gives his angels the authority to immediately move in and take dominion over those conditions in the individual's world that do not conform to the true nature of his being. Because that which is beneath the allness of God has willingly forfeited its position of the temporal disposition of its own affairs in an attitude of complete trust that the allness of God possesses both the means and the end to produce perfection, it becomes the immediate benefactor of the divine intercession.

The line between the rights of man and the right of God is very fine. When man acts with the authority of God, he can say, *"Dieu et mon droit."*[84] But only when he becomes the Christ incarnate has he the right to say, *"L'etat, c'est moi!"*[85] We who walk upon the spiritual pathway as surely as you do upon the physical retain within our causal body and etheric consciousness the memory of earthly experiences from our past lives and from the continuity of life which was ours between embodiments. Through examining the memory of the unascended state from our present perspective, we have a better understanding of life on earth than we did when we were in physical embodiment.

I know it is difficult on your side of the veil to realize the certitude and naturalness of the divine unfoldment which originates in the inner planes. As you now "see through a glass darkly," when one day you enter this realm, you will see "face to face"[86] with the clearness of divine reality. Until you do, I suggest that you relinquish, ever so gladly, those elements of life which pertain to the outer realm of experience and which seem right unto men and yet lead to death and destruction.[87]

This is an activity of pruning the tree of life that you and you alone can perform through self-surrender and self-effacement. This may seem hard at first, but when you call God into action in each human problem, his response can result in a perfect outpicturing of the divine ideals for you. This attitude of letting God in and letting the human out is the best means of achieving greater peace of mind and greater involvement in your affairs by the Godhead and those powers whom he has assigned to be your guardians and protectors.

We who are on the other side of the veil want you to understand the uses of, as well as the meaning of, perfection. We want you to understand how you can cope with each of life's problems and receive the comfort of the Holy Spirit that will make you a very real part of the intent of the Godhead for the earth as well as for yourselves. It does not matter if mankind do not perceive God's care and consideration for them released through you and countless others who are so dedicated. In a very real way, you who possess this understanding are keeping the flame of your divinity and maintaining a greater closeness to your Divine Self in your daily life. And for the millions who know not the workings of cosmic law, you are also holding a focus of the flame.

In the days of old, Sanat Kumara and his retinue kept the flame at Shamballa on behalf of embodied mankind who had lost the thread of contact with their divinity. Little did humanity at large realize by what a slender thread the destiny of the planet was held—the thread of one Master's consciousness attuned with God. Yet surely this was a giant thread of throbbing compassion! For the infinite love of God which these avatars retained in their hearts was a love that extended itself to all mankind.

Today with many more to carry the flame, the many who have followed in the way of his great sacrifice, with many more whose examples are arousing divine sentiments in the hearts of the many, kindling faith and giving assurance of the divine purpose unto the family of nations, embodied mankind are in a position to have greater trust—trust in the God flame expanding from within, trust in the God Spirit expanding from without—even as the hierarchy is in a position to have greater trust in mankind because some among them are steadfastly keeping the flame.

Albeit many among mankind neither know nor understand cosmic law as it has been given unto the devotees to know and understand, they have been given an inner assurance within their souls that is strengthened and intensified by each effort of the devotees to keep the flame. Therefore trust is God working within you and within your hearts. Trust is the chalice of the Divine Mother and the Divine Father. Trust is the beneficent activity of the Christ Selves of all mankind.

Trust is a universal blessing to the planet, producing the bonanza of the Holy Spirit's manifestation of comfort to all. The Spirit teaches them that the Lords of Karma and those who govern the affairs of the world from both a human and a divine level are able to summon the elect from the four corners of the earth and to bestow upon them compassion and a correct knowledge of the use of energy which will day by day advance the human race into all right knowledge.

How unfortunate it is that men and women will hold organizations or individuals responsible for their own failures. Often, just at the hour of victory, they are ready to separate themselves from an activity which God himself has ordained as one great doorway to his heart. If they would only understand that it is God whom they are actually serving in every part of life, if they would only understand that it is his grace by which they serve other parts of life, they would not need to feel the pressure upon their being which causes them to become restless of heart and to long for other times and other climes.

Right in the midst of a service that requires the greatest constancy, they suddenly become unwilling to submit their being and consciousness to that great cosmic law which requires every man, woman and child upon the planet to balance every erg of energy they have misused. Paul[88] stated it thusly: "Whatsoever a man soweth, that shall he also reap."[89] And Jesus said: "Verily I say unto you, Till heaven and earth pass, one jot or one tittle shall in no wise pass from the law, till all be fulfilled."[90]

What a pity it is that men do not understand the depth of the spiritual wisdom that is within them, that they feel the need to dogmatize and then to peddle their dogmatizations without understanding the magnetization of cosmic love that attracts people to the true wisdom of the heart. The magnetization of cosmic love in itself gives new courage to the mind, strengthens the bond of spiritual reality and reveals at last those hidden mysteries which the soul has ever understood.

Men do not always understand how these mysteries are conveyed from the Spirit of God to the soul of man. This is because they intrude a barrier of human thought and feeling patterns which positions itself between the divine revelation and the human monadic expression. Thus they defeat cosmic purpose with the limitations they have superimposed upon the variables of their own evolving consciousness. But when the barrier is finally removed, the matrix of perfection, which is God-ordained, removes the last vestiges of opacity in the minds of men and reestablishes that clear realization of the realities of life which the mind of Christ, as one with the mind of God, is always able to do.

Beloved hearts,

> Be slow to condemn, be swift to love,
> Be firm in your endeavors and look above!

The way of hope he does make plain—
The rule of Christ fore'er to reign.
For 'tis his hand removes all pain
And lifts men to the heart of love
Where life reveals the God of love
And casts down idols, sense of blame,
As man becomes a living flame.

Devoted to the expansion of your light, I AM

Mother Mary

Retreat of the Resurrection Spiral
Colorado Springs, Colorado
October 1, 1972

13

I and My Father Are One

*The Tearing-Down of the Old City of Jerusalem,
Prophetic of the Leveling of Man's False Concepts of Himself,
Must Precede the Building of the New Jerusalem*

To the Beloved Children of Precipitation upon Earth of God's Will:

How generous is the heart of God! Yet how many have failed to concede this fact because they see him only through their own eyes and through the limited aperture of their own mind. Hence they see only the limitations of those eyes and of a mind that holds a focus of limitation and never relinquishes it—no, not even for a moment. O embodied mankind, won't you allow within the domain of your thought and feelings a penetration of the mercy flame of God, of the flame of his universal compassion for each child, each child of his heart?

I know how easy it is for individuals sitting within the frame of a body of limitation, a body of concepts, a body of opinions, to look upon other individuals and to make a judgment without in any way attuning with their souls or attempting to understand the weight of human problems that beset them. From this position of limitation, of seeming separation from God and man, though mindful of the weight of their own human problems, people fail to practice the ritual of mercy toward other parts of life. If they would only permit barriers between hearts to be set aflame by the Holy Spirit, how quickly would human problems melt away in a great gust of divine love!

For after all, is not God's love also a very important expression of his will? And is not his will, by reason of its very nature, the highest intent for the universe as a whole as well as for every individual? No matter how long I pondered in my embodiment as the Mother of Jesus, I could never conceive of anything more precious than heaven's will. It was with this thought in mind that I mused hour after hour upon the rightness of the divine intent, upon the supremacy of universal purpose, and the means to exercise that intent and that purpose within the framework of my own life.

The trivial tasks of the day seemed at times far apart from me. At first I sat as one dazed, for the necessary duties seemed but to consume the precious substance of which the day was made, as though material things resembled a hole of darkness, a yawning chasm which would devour the hours. Light and perfection was the allness of that which was real; hence, to those around me I seemed frequently to dwell in a state of contemplation of the other side of life, the divine side.

I must admit that at first this preoccupation also seemed impractical to me. But gradually, through the ritual of contemplation, the obscurities were dissolved and I was able to see those elements of divine grace which are not always real to the average person but rather dimly perceived, if at all. Much later I came to realize that I could dwell both in the consciousness of God and in the consciousness of man, which must of necessity be involved in the practical aspects of living in the world and in the community.

One of the more difficult matters confronting the seeker after spiritual grace is the resolving of those problems of an emotional nature which arise between people as the result of their misunderstandings. Quite frankly, much human difficulty is involved with human jealousy and with patterns of resentment of the achievements of others. We have found it of great help for those who desire to overcome this type of situation to recognize achievement as God's.

For when men perceive all human achievement as the mark of wonder upon the page of the ages, when they begin to understand that their achievement can be greatly enhanced through calls to God for assistance, when they understand that true greatness is the greatness of God made manifest in man, they will not resent the achievement of others nearly as much. They will look behind the screen of the human monad and behold the hand of divine grace helping to mold a better world, a world of understanding in preparation for the coming of the kingdom.

The tearing-down of the old city of Jerusalem was not only an act of prophecy but also a leveling of man's false concepts of himself, of those limiting concepts which in the old man had a tendency to go unrecognized because each man sought to exalt himself. Once the destruction of the human ego with its false set of values takes place, the New Jerusalem,[91] symbolizing the spiritual recognition of all achievement as God's, comes into view in individual man. When man's energy is not expended in a manifestation of carnal-mindedness, when he is able to retain the perspective of the working-together of mankind for the achievement of universal values to the end that all may share in those values, he is able to sunder his connection with those nefarious acts of karma in his own life that have held him back for so long.

Even in the world order, the purposeless dissipation of energies that occurs as one segment of life does battle with another invariably uses up the resources that ought to be directed to the overcoming of all human problems. What a beautiful world can be built as the amplification of those Christic values which are the light of the Foursquare City[92] kindle the imagination of the many! History has clearly shown that mankind have been inspired by the few, whereas the many, like lost sheep, wander thither and yon subject to every wind of man's discord that has been spread abroad over the whole earth as a network of destruction.

Now as we look for a time of greater harmony, of greater dialogue, of greater assessment of man's position in the world of form—as we look not from the standpoint of man alone but from a realization of the loftiness of God's compassion and his grace—we are certain that great changes can be wrought upon earth and that these changes will be as Above, so below.

For man himself, in the domain of his expanding consciousness, is the City of God. The human monad is intended to reflect the ultimate grace of God, of the Divine Monad. For born out of the oneness of God is the oneness of man's union with God—"I and my Father are one."[93] How beautifully did my Son express this concept! How complete is the work of the City Foursquare, the New Jerusalem, which is lowered into every man's consciousness as he becomes one with the foundations of perfection. These heaven is ready to convey to each monadic expression as that expression determines to have and to hold its eternal oneness in the never failing light of God.

I AM and I remain a servant of the Cosmic Mother of all,

Mary

Retreat of the Resurrection Spiral
Colorado Springs, Colorado
October 8, 1972

14

The Correct Understanding of Universal Purpose

The Recognition of the Inexorable Law of Cosmos Governs the Return of Energy Misqualified, Faith in Ultimate Goodness and Patience

To Those Attending the Rebirth of the Christ in Human Hearts:

How true it is that if men had the correct understanding of universal purpose, they could never commit those acts or align themselves with those activities which slaughter righteousness and the unfoldment of universal love. The bane of ignorance cloaks their hearts' rays, and in consort with the carnal mind they have again and again opaqued the light of divine wisdom and love.

The little gems I bring are for those whose every thought reaches out to the implementation of an improved world situation, to an evolvement of self, and to cooperation with the hand of God moving even midst ordinary human affairs.

It has been rightly said that nothing happens by chance, and so the word *chance*, in its current usage, has become another name for the outworking of karma and the fulfillment of the law of universal desire. That individuals can and do influence the manifestation of cosmic law in human affairs is a foregone conclusion. Justice is nowhere more blind than in the courts of men. If the free will of man were not the key factor in the bringing-in of the kingdom, the triumph of universal love would have been accomplished in ages long past. But who can deny that Virtue has done her perfect work in all ages, most especially in the lives of those who have held to the faith in the goodness of God and in their own ability to serve him in the humblest task allotted to them?

Certain features of cosmic law go unrecognized by humanity. One that is often overlooked is the divine answer to humanity's calls that is always forthcoming from God. Yet he has said, "Before they call, I will answer."[94] Because his ignorance or his ignoring of the Law is no excuse, the man of faith cannot rightly persist in allowing elements of doubt in the Creator's word to color his mind and emotions without paying the penalty of being cut off from the answers to his calls. For doubt is the wall that man erects between himself and his God, and it is a self-imposed penalty that only he can remove through corrective measures.

It is never the desire of the personal God to place the weight of responsibility for wrong action upon a recalcitrant generation. Rather it is the inexorable law of cosmos, which governs the return of energy misqualified by erroneous thought and feeling to those who send it forth, that determines the burden man shall bear for past mistakes.

I wish to convey the immense yet simple knowledge that every gift of God given to man in answer to prayer must either be kept, used or dissipated. It is always hoped by those among the heavenly host through whose hands the gift is bestowed that if it is kept and then used, it will be for the constructive good of the individual or of another part of life.

Unfortunately, those who dissipate the divine gifts of mercy and grace, either through misqualification of the God-ordained intent or by spending the light upon paltry human desires, will one day find that they are without the answers to their prayers. For one day the karmic hammer will surely fall and they will have dissipated God's energies for the last time. And that which has been faithfully given them from on high—in recognition of the divine spark within and as opportunity to renew their vows through the many avenues of service to life—will be withheld. As James said, "Ye ask, and receive not, because ye ask amiss, that ye may consume it upon your lusts."[95]

What a pity it is that individuals regard us as dead! Because we live and move and have our being in God,[96] we are cognizant each moment of every human thought and feeling. Therefore, we are vitally aware of the universal need of humanity to hold fast to the life triumphant and immortal, the life that pulsates as the threefold flame within and holds the solution to every problem. Those who believe that "God is dead," simply because their own concepts of him are lifeless, find no difficulty in applying the same concepts to the ascended hosts of light, thereby relegating us to the realm of the dead. Those who deny our existence would do well to reexamine their concepts of God, whose life necessarily includes our own.

Conversely, those who understand and recognize the immortality of the cosmic gifts God gives from his heart to those whose every thought is directed toward him have no difficulty in accepting either his reality or the living presence of his servant sons and daughters, both in heaven and on earth. Their blessed faith starts a circuit of light that moves from hearts kindled with gratitude to the heart of God, carrying more of his energy on the return current. These are full of joy as they see cosmic mutations taking place within themselves—a metamorphosis of the soul brought about through the ritual of divine love.

Those who seek us will realize almost from the beginning of their search, and then again when the moment of truly knowing us comes, that our hearts are full of love for embodied humanity and that our only desire is to create, through proper education, a spiritual uplift in the human consciousness that will enable mankind to avoid both the shedding of tears for human failures and their remorse for divine ones. The fact that individuals have turned the pathway of selflessness into the pathway of selfishness is due not alone to their lack of knowledge but to their great lack of conclusive faith in the ultimate goodness of God.

Born out of his heart's desire for the salvation of the current age, the continual motions of divine love move throughout the universe, engendering new hope for the ages. Thus the wonder of his love is measured out of the very heart-steps of God himself. And there is a focus, a place prepared within each one's heart, where he shall abide forever if man wills it so.

All that man is and does is by the grace of God. Therefore, in the outworkings of divine grace in man, those spiritual works of which his faith is but a symbol do appear. This substance of things hoped for, this evidence of things not seen,[97] can also be kept by man as a divine gift. Those who desire to increase their faith may call for an intensification of the measure of grace given unto them and see the miracle of immortal life as it unfolds before them the magnificent faith of cosmos in its own fiery destiny.

Expectancy is a much needed virtue, blessed hearts of love, and this cannot be the expectancy of personal fulfillment through another but the expectant hope that waiteth on the LORD day and night.[98] And when the triumph of an individual's faith brings him at last out of the smoke of doubt and self-delusion into the fire of cosmic purpose, how very wonderful is the counsel of God to each one concerning his life that is so precious.

Each life, like a locket around the neck of the living God, is the fulfillment of a wish he made as he fashioned the soul, a wish for its creative expression and for the best gifts to adorn the Christ aborning in each one of his children. Won't you, then, O humanity, for all time let go of the awful struggle in which you have engaged your energies? For in your present state of limited self-awareness, instead of fulfilling the divine plan you fulfill only the karmic recompense of the law of return. And by reason of your own evil thoughts about one another—often based on mere surmise—you remain bound to the karmic wheel that keeps turning, ultimately bringing to your doorstep the malice which, if unchecked today, can destroy the very fabric of your souls tomorrow.

Will you, then, out of a heart akin to God's own heart, learn to be patient with individuals at various levels of development? Do not expect too much of those who, far down the ladder of life, leap, childlike, toward what may seem to you only a bauble or a trinket. One day they will come to understand infinite values as you do, and then the joy bells will ring out as the angels of heaven rejoice in the overcoming of undesirable conditions by an individual or a segment of humanity.

Oh, what a pity it is that men do not understand the need to express patience toward other parts of life! When they are on the receiving end of this and other gifts of God, they hold out expectant hands. How necessary it is that men learn not only to receive the mercy of God but also to extend it graciously to others.

Let us, then, build a tower of light and hope in the world that shall shift man's interests and intents from the mundane to the heavenly and, drawing him from the murky darkness of failures and follies, polarize his consciousness to the goal of rebirth in Christ. Thus he moves toward the gentle Christ-attainment that thunders forth the peal of universal purpose made available to all because it has been realized by one.

With these thoughts from my heart, I remain devotedly
Your spiritual Mother,

Mary

Retreat of the Resurrection Spiral
Colorado Springs, Colorado
October 24, 1971

PART TWO

The Love Aspect of the Christ Flame
Eight Mysteries of the Rosary by the
Mother for Her Children

And Mary arose in those days, and went into the hill country with haste into a city of Juda;

And entered into the house of Zacharias, and saluted Elisabeth.

And it came to pass that when Elisabeth heard the salutation of Mary, the babe leaped in her womb; and Elisabeth was filled with the Holy Ghost:

And she spake out with a loud voice, and said, Blessed art thou among women and blessed is the fruit of thy womb.

And whence is this to me, that the mother of my Lord should come to me? For lo, as soon as the voice of thy salutation sounded in mine ears, the babe leaped in my womb for joy.

And blessed is she that believed; for there shall be a performance of those things which were told her from the Lord. —Luke

Christian Prayer Forms and the Evolution of the Rosary

Jesus taught his disciples how to pray the Lord's Prayer saying, "When thou prayest, enter into thy closet, and when thou hast shut thy door, pray to thy Father which is in secret; and thy Father which seeth in secret shall reward thee openly."[1] By this his followers knew that to pray effectively they must enter the Holy of holies, the white-fire core of being that is focused in the flame of life blazing upon the altar of the heart.

This threefold flame of love, wisdom and power anchored in the body temple is the seat of the Christ consciousness in every man, woman and child. To enter into this cloister of oneness and to seal one's consciousness in the ineffable light of the Trinity is to secure one's energies in sacred service to God and man. The Father Presence, called the I AM Presence, dwelling in the secret place of the Most High that is the fiery core of the causal body, responds to every prayer uttered in the secret chambers of the heart. The reward for prayerful application is always forthcoming as the release of the energies of Being into tangible manifestation through the blessed Mediator, the Holy Christ Self.

The repetition of prayers, meditations and mantras accomplished by the power of the spoken Word need not be vain if they are offered sincerely and scientifically. On the contrary, by the action of the light, the verbalization of affirmations made in the name of the beloved I AM Presence and the Christ Self is the fulfillment of cosmic law. This law has been made known to man through Old and New Testament prophets.

For example, Isaiah wrote that concerning the work of his hands (the manifestation of his Spirit in the planes of earth), the Holy One of Israel said, "Command ye me."[2] In other words, God instructed his sons and daughters to command him to come down from heaven and work his works upon earth. The logic of this injunction, *"Command ye me,"* can be understood only in the light of certain principles and precepts of God's laws, which we herewith set forth. It is our hope that out of this writing mankind will gain a greater appreciation not only for the rosary, but also for all forms of prayer.

When God created man and woman and gave them free will to be co-creators with him in the plane of Matter, saying, "Take dominion over the earth,"[3] he turned over to them an entire world pulsating with light and life and energy in order that male and female, whom he had made in his image and likeness, might exercise their free will by learning the conscious control of cosmic forces through initiative and ingenuity, through discovery and invention. Thus the twain were sent forth with a challenge and a fiat from the Lord: *"Go Be!"* To experiment with the forces of creation and to conquer time and space—whether by an innate genius or by the trial-and-error method—sons and daughters of God spiraled into form.

Planetary homes provided by the Elohim served as platforms for the evolution of the soul and the mastery of the four lower bodies. Each planet was a sphere of influence—a forcefield for experiment, yes, but an unlimited one, no. By solar edict, boundaries were established around each separate world and each separate system of worlds. These finite platforms suspended in infinity were designed and built for each new lifewave consisting of millions of souls created by the Father-Mother God with a common origin and a common destiny.

Because their uses of creative energy were yet in the experimental stage, because their correct application of free will was not yet tried and true, pairs of souls like Adam and Eve were allowed freedom of self-expression within the confines prescribed as the bounds of their habitation. These bounds, actually bonds of love, could not and would not be broken until man and woman should prove themselves worthy to penetrate infinity with perfection by consciously choosing God's will to reinforce the absolute goodness of their manifest creation.

Having turned over to man the administration of his world, having given him the right to rule in the footstool kingdom,[4] the Lord withdrew in order that his sons and daughters might show forth their determination and their desire to use their freedom to glorify God in man and to use God's energies for the carving-out of their divine destiny in the plane of Matter. If man wanted God to be a part of his life, of his taking dominion over the earth, then he would have to ask him. By his own law, set forth out of the necessity to let man and woman prove themselves, God, unless invited, not only would not but could not intervene in the lives of his sons and daughters.

As soon as man would surrender to God the free will which God had given him, saying, "Not my will but thine be done,"[5] then God could and would intercede on man's behalf, assisting him each step of the way. Total surrender on the part of man—of his will, his life, his energies and his purpose—allows God to manifest that total oneness of which Jesus spoke when he said, "I and my Father are one"—that is to say, "I and my Father are one in will, in life, in energy flow and in cosmic purpose." In the light of this knowledge, we are able to understand more clearly why the Lord would instruct his sons and daughters to command him into action in the world of Matter form. Without that command, neither he nor the heavenly hosts are free to act in mankind's domain.

God *will* not—he *cannot*, according to his own law—act in our daily lives or in our world unless we by right prayer and right action consciously, willingly invoke him into our midst. Therefore the Lord himself has said: "*Because* he hath set his love upon me, therefore will I deliver him. I will set him on high, *because* he hath known my name (*because* man has known and affirmed the name of God as the I AM that I AM). He shall call upon me, and I will answer him: I will be with him in trouble; I will deliver him and honour him. With long life will I satisfy him and shew him my salvation."[6] This is a covenant between God and man which the Lord can keep only when man loves God through daily devotions, when he affirms God's name as the fiat of Being, and when he calls upon God directly for assistance.

The statement "The call compels the answer" is well known to the initiate on the Path. When the Lord says, "Command ye me," he is letting us know that the call of man will compel the answer from God. Without the call, there can be no answer. Therefore we understand that there is a necessity for man to invoke God's energies with the authority of the Christ—to actually command life to manifest the perfection of "Thy kingdom come" and "Thy will being done on earth as it is in heaven."[7] Of this ritual of commanding the law of the Lord, it is also written in the Book of Job: "Thou shalt decree a thing, and it shall be established unto thee: and the light shall shine upon thy ways."[8]

The authority to pray and decree which the Lord gives to his sons and daughters was clearly outlined by Jesus when he said, "If two of you shall agree on earth as touching any thing that they shall ask, it shall be done for them of my Father which is in heaven."[9] Jesus also taught his disciples to pray to the Father in his name, saying, "Whatsoever ye shall ask the Father in my name, he will give it you."[10] Thus the early Christians prayed to the Father without ceasing in the name of Jesus the Christ or simply in the name of the Christ.

Jesus himself was wont to pray fervently to his Father. He prayed in the mountains, in the wilderness, on the sea and as he interceded for the sick and the sinful. Sometimes he prayed by supplication, as in the Garden of Gethsemane when he said, "Father, if thou be willing, remove this cup from me; nevertheless, not my will but thine be done." At times his prayer was a fiat: "Arise, take up thy bed, and walk!...Thy faith hath made thee whole!...Thy sins be forgiven thee!" On other occasions he prayed by a direct and fervent appeal, crying "with a loud voice," as in the case of the raising of one who had been dead four days: "Lazarus, come forth!" He also commanded the elements with his "Peace, be still!" And he did not fail to rebuke the adversary directly with the words "Get thee behind me, Satan!"[11]

In his final hours, Jesus lifted up his eyes to heaven and spoke to the Father directly, articulating the need for every son and daughter of God to pray fervently for the souls of an evolving humanity, saying: "I pray for them...which thou hast given me, for they are thine. And all mine are thine, and thine are mine; and I am glorified in them....Neither pray I for these alone, but for them also which shall believe on me through their word, that they all may be one, as thou, Father, art in me and I in thee, that they also may be one in us: that the world may believe that thou hast sent me."[12]

Jesus' impassioned plea to Peter, "Feed my sheep,"[13] spoken three times, showed the longing that has remained in his heart these two thousand years that his followers should meet the needs of all mankind through intercessory prayer and through ministering love. Was this not a prayer to the very Christ flame of Peter upon which he built his Church,[14] that the Church headed by the Vicar of Christ should serve him by serving the light in all of its members who comprise the body of God upon earth?

The most eloquent benediction of the Father through the Son, a blessing of all facets of the Christ consciousness as these are expressed in mankind, was given in Jesus' Sermon on the Mount. This, too, is a form of prayer that we would class as an affirmation of truth which unlocks the blessings of each one's causal body: "Blessed are the meek: for they shall inherit the earth....Blessed are the pure in heart: for they shall see God. Blessed are the peacemakers: for they shall be called the children of God. Blessed are they which are persecuted for righteousness' sake: for theirs is the kingdom of heaven."[15]

Jesus' teaching was enriched by the mantras he received from his teacher, Lord Maitreya, during the period in which he journeyed to the Himalayas between the ages of twelve and thirty. These and other mantras released in the retreats of the Himalayan masters became the "I AM" meditations of his inner circle of devotees, and to the present hour they are recited by Christian mystics the world around: "I am the resurrection and the life.... I am the light of the world....I am come that they might have life and that they might have it more abundantly....I am the way, the truth, and the life....I am in the Father, and the Father in me."[16]

Thus in the two-thousand-year history of Christian prayer, Jesus set the example of communion with the Father through prayer and intercession, not only as a life of love in action but also as the conversation of the beloved Son with the beloved Father. All these forms have their place in Christian ritual. In the tradition of the Master himself have Christians prayed to the Father in his name, and through the years many legitimate prayer forms have evolved even as man's conscious awareness of the Christ has evolved.

Down through the centuries since the birth of Enos, the son of Seth, who was the son of Adam,[17] men have called upon the name of the LORD. And as Paul says, their sound has gone into all the earth and their words unto the ends of the world.[18] The use of stones or beads carried on a chain or in the pocket has long been a means of keeping count of prayers in both the Eastern and Western traditions of chanting praises to the Lord in supplication and in song. The promise of salvation through calling upon the name of the Lord[19] has led devotees of the Holy Spirit to affirm not only the sacred name of Mary and Jesus but also the "I AM that I AM" (in the West) and the sacred Aum (in the East).

The pattern for the rosary can be traced to ninth-century Ireland, when monks chanted the 150 Psalms of David daily. The illiterate peasants, wishing to join in the devotion, were allowed to substitute the Lord's Prayer (the Our Fathers) for each psalm. While in the East the invocations were to Brahma, Vishnu and Shiva and to Durga as the interpolator of the heavenly triumvirate, in Europe many devotees of Mary recited the angelic salutation of Gabriel, "Hail, Mary, full of grace, the Lord is with thee."[20] To this was added Elisabeth's salutation to Mary, "Blessed art thou among women, and blessed is the fruit of thy womb."[21] Thus those who sought out the Virgin as the Mother of the Christ and the Mediatrix of the Father began offering their prayers to her as a bouquet of roses. In time these prayers became an important Christian ritual known as the rosary (from Latin *rosārium*, rose garden).

On the occasion of Mother Mary's appearance to Saint Mechtilde, the Blessed Mother explained the salutation:

"My daughter, I want you to know that no one can please me more than by saying the salutation which the most adorable Trinity sent to me and by which he raised me to the dignity of Mother of God. By the word Ave (which is the name Eve, Eva), I learned that in his infinite power God had preserved me from all sin and its attendant misery which the first woman had been subject to. The name *Mary*, which means 'lady of light', shows that God has filled me with wisdom and light, like a shining star, to light up heaven and earth. The words *full of grace* remind me that the Holy Spirit has showered so many graces upon me that I am able to give these graces in abundance to those who ask for them through me as Mediatrix.

"When people say *the Lord is with thee*, they renew the indescribable joy that was mine when the eternal Word became incarnate in my womb. When you say to me, *blessed art thou among women*, I praise Almighty God's divine mercy which lifted me to this exalted plane of happiness. And at the words *blessed is the fruit of thy womb, Jesus,* the whole of heaven rejoices with me to see my Son Jesus Christ adored and glorified for having saved mankind."

The third part of the Hail Mary was inspired by the Council at Ephesus in A.D. 470. The prayer "Holy Mary, Mother of God, pray for us sinners, now and at the hour of our death" settled the Nestorian heresy, which arose from the mouth of Anastasius, "Let no one call Mary the mother of God, for Mary was a human being; and that God should be born of a human being is impossible."[22] With this additional affirmation, the Council at Ephesus affirmed the Motherhood of God for all of Christendom.

Mother Mary explained her calling as the Mother of God to the Keepers of the Flame: "I AM a cosmic mother, and as much your mother as I am the mother of beloved Jesus. Some who are adherents of the Christian faith call me the Mother of God. To those of the protesting branch of orthodox Christianity, this seems a sacrilege. For men may well ask, 'Who is worthy to be the Mother of God?' But this concept, when understood to mean the mother of the embodiment of the Divine Spirit, reveals the glorious truth that every mother who understands that which was spoken—'and the Word was made flesh and dwelt among us'[23]—may be the Mother of God."[24]

To mother means to give birth to, to give rise to, to care for and to protect. Therefore, to be the Mother of God is to give birth to, to give rise to, to care for and to protect his flame on earth. To mother the flame of Spirit in the plane of Matter is the calling of the feminine ray in both man and woman. That male and female whom God created in his image and likeness cannot find fulfillment on earth without mothering or nurturing the flame of life in themselves or in these little ones. How empty and alone are we poor mortals and how void of meaning is mortal existence when we fail to embrace this our highest calling—to be fruitful and multiply the flame of the Most High in this world that is our proving ground for the eternal wonder to come.

Mary is the fair maid of our hearts' love. She shows us how to not only love and adore the Father but also how to bring forth his light and to anchor it in the plane of Matter by giving birth to the Divine Manchild. She shows us that by the exaltation of the feminine ray, every woman can become the Woman clothed with the Sun[25] of righteousness, and that by fastidiousness in her application of the Law, every woman can wear the crown of twelve stars as the sign of the attainment of the twelve godly virtues. She shows us how Eve may return to the state of grace in the garden paradise, placing the moon, symbolizing the mirage of maya, beneath her feet.

Mary has indeed set the pattern for the liberation of woman in this and every age. If we would be truly liberated, we must follow her all the way—and that way is the consecration of body, soul and mind—to the nurturing of Alpha's seed throughout the cosmos that is the body of Omega.

Behold not one but many mothers of God! Let the dragon challenge us all, for we stand as one united in the authority of the Christ with the shield of Michael the archangel to fulfill our cosmic destiny! This is the cry of New Age women everywhere. To be the Mother of God is our reason for being, and we shall by his grace proclaim the victory of the light in all ages to come. Thank you, Mary, for showing us the way!

Thus Mother Mary has spoken: "The Christ must be born in every man and woman. The Christ seed must be nurtured and expanded as the threefold flame of love, wisdom and power holding dominion over every ideological concept of man, over every teleological matter prescribed by cosmic law and ruling supreme as the master function of life. Then I (the God flame in me) automatically become (because the God flame in me is so consecrated) the Cosmic Mother of each son and daughter of heaven. Then you automatically become that to which you have consecrated the energies of your I AM Presence. That which I AM you can be also, if you will it so by the power and authority of the I AM."[26]

The Hail Marys later given by the European Christians strengthened the devotion to the Mother, encouraging the further expansion of the rosary in the thirteenth century. New forms of the rosary appeared. One hundred fifty Praises of Jesus, devotions which related the Psalms to Jesus' life, were composed. And shortly after this form of the rosary was in use, 150 Praises of Mary appeared. When only 50 of the Praises to Mary were given, it was called a rosarium.

Throughout this period there were four distinct forms of the rosary in use: (1) 150 Our Fathers, (2) 150 Hail Marys, (3) 150 Praises of Jesus, and (4) 150 or 50 Praises of Mary. The first synthesis of these four forms occurred in the fourteenth century when Henry de Kalker, a Carthusian monk, synthesized the Our Fathers and 150 Hail Marys, grouping the Hail Marys into tens with one Our Father between each decade.

Further synthesis occurred in 1409, when Dominic the Prussian assigned a thought from the lives of Mary and Jesus to each of the Hail Mary beads. The Hail Marys were again grouped into decades with an Our Father between each decade. In 1470 Alan of Rupe spread this particular rosary throughout Europe, popularizing the use of this form to such a degree that it provided the foundation for the present-day scriptural rosary.

Picture rosaries became popular around 1500, when woodcuts were inexpensively reproduced for the first time. Because of the complexity of printing 150 pictures for the Hail Mary beads, a new rosary with 15 pictures (1 for each Our Father bead) was introduced. During the Renaissance, the 150 thoughts for each Hail Mary bead were used less and less, until only the 15 thoughts for the Our Fathers remained, surviving as the 15 mysteries used in the Catholic Church today. Supplementary prayers or meditations were usually read before each decade to augment the brief mysteries. A return to the medieval form of the rosary began in the twentieth century with the appearance of several series of Hail Mary meditations in Germany, Switzerland and Canada.

On a fall morning in 1972, Mother Mary appeared to the Mother of the Flame during her morning meditation in the prayer tower of the Retreat of the Resurrection Spiral, saying: "I want to give you a ritual of the rosary for Keepers of the Flame. It is to be a scriptural rosary for those who adhere to the true teachings of Christ as taught by the ascended masters and for the bringing-in of the golden age. It is to be used as a universal adoration of the Mother flame by people of all faiths. For, you see, the salutation 'Hail Mary' simply means 'Hail, Mother ray' and is an affirmation of praise to the Mother flame in every part of life. Each time it is spoken, it evokes the action of the Mother's light in the hearts of all mankind.

"Thus the rosary is a sacred ritual whereby all of God's children can find their way back to their immaculate conception in the heart of the Cosmic Virgin. The New Age rosary is the instrument for mankind's deliverance from the sense of sin and from the erroneous doctrine of original sin. For every soul is immaculately conceived by Almighty God, and God the Father is the origin of all of the cycles of man's being. That which is conceived in sin is not of God and has neither the power nor the permanence of reality. All that is real is of God; all that is unreal will pass away as mankind become one with the Mother flame. The daily giving of the rosary is a certain means to this oneness."

As was mentioned in the foreword, Mother Mary released a rosary for each of the seven rays of the Christic light to be used each morning of the week and a rosary for the eighth ray to be used on Sunday evening. A rosary for each of the five secret rays of the Holy Spirit was given for communion with the Paraclete on the five evenings of the week. These mysteries outline the testings which the soul must face, the demonstrations of the Law which it must make, and the temptations which it must overcome ere the devotee of the Mother and the Son be wholly integrated within the consciousness of the Christ. Mary promised to release a fourteenth rosary that she said would be very different from the others when enough people had built a momentum of devotion in giving the thirteen rosaries. Without question, all of these rosaries prepare the disciple for the initiations on the Path which are narrated in the mysteries.

The evolution of the ever transcending form of the rosary manifested in Mary's release of the proper recitation of the Hail Mary. The third part of the Hail Mary, which was not biblical but was added by the Council at Ephesus, "Holy Mary, Mother of God, pray for us, sinners, now and at the hour of our death," succeeded in affirming the Motherhood of God. However, it also assigned to man the role of sinner and emphasized death as the end of the life of the sinner. Mary said that Keepers of the Flame ought not to affirm their sinful nature but rather their rightful inheritance as sons and daughters of God. Nor should they dwell upon the hour of death but rather upon the hour of victory.

The Mother of Jesus therefore asked the Mother of the Flame to teach the Keepers of the Flame to pray for her intercession "now and at the hour of our victory over sin, disease and death," thereby drawing their attention to the hour of victory over all conditions of time and space which her blessed Son proved in his life and in the hour of his victorious ascension. She affirmed the "hour of our victory" to be the eleventh hour when the greatest vigilance is required to countermand the backlash of the tail of the dragon depicted by Saint John the Revelator as being wroth with the woman and going forth to make war with the remnant of her seed.[27] She promised to assist Keepers of the Flame, disciples of Christ and devotees of the Mother flame in winning their victory and the victory for all mankind if they would thus pray to her:

Hail, Mary, full of grace. The Lord is with thee. Blessed art thou among women and blessed is the fruit of thy womb, Jesus.

Holy Mary, Mother of God, pray for us, sons and daughters of God, now and at the hour of our victory over sin, disease and death.

The content of the Scriptural Rosary for the New Age which the Blessed Mother then proceeded to dictate reflects the flow of the Father-Mother God—of God as Father and God as Mother, revealed to John in the words "I am Alpha and Omega, the beginning and the ending."[28] The first adoration of the rosary marks the four aspects of God's being as Father, Mother, Son and Holy Spirit. As we make the sign of the cross, we are reinforcing the consciousness of these aspects in body and soul, mind and heart. The Latin cross (usually suspended from the rosary) is the emblem of the converging lines of Spirit (Alpha) and Matter (Omega), signifying the place where Christ is born and where the energies of the Logos are released to a planet.

Touching the forehead as the north arm of the cross, we say, "In the name of the Father." Touching the heart as the south arm of the cross, we say, "and of the Mother." Touching the left shoulder as the east arm of the cross, we say, "and of the Son." Touching the right shoulder as the west arm of the cross, we say, "and of the Holy Spirit, Amen." By including the name of the Mother in our salutation of the Trinity, we invoke the consciousness of the Cosmic Virgin, who makes each aspect of the sacred Trinity meaningful to our evolving consciousness. Indeed Mary is the daughter of God, the Mother of Christ and the bride of the Holy Spirit. Fulfilling the intimate role of the feminine counterpart of each aspect of the masculine principle of God, she is best able to portray to us the nature of Father, Son and Holy Spirit.

The second adoration of the rosary, the Keeper's Daily Prayer, is a universal creed which may be pronounced by men of all religions. As the Apostles' Creed provided the theme for the Christian dispensation, this prayer is a declaration of faith that can be made in the New Age by sons and daughters of God wherever they may be—whether in this world or beyond the Milky Way—for it centers the consciousness in the flame of God and does not bind the soul to man-made doctrine or timeworn dogma.

Jesus' I AM Lord's Prayer—the very one he taught to the inner circle of his disciples two thousand years ago—was released to the whole world at the dawn of the golden age in an Easter dictation given by the Galilean master through the messenger Mark L. Prophet on April 14, 1963. This prayer reveals the name of God as "I AM," the same revelation that was given to Moses when God spoke to him out of the bush that burned but was not consumed, declaring himself to be the I AM that I AM.[29]

With this key to his identity pattern, God unlocked for the multitudes yet evolving in time and space the knowledge of their potential divinity. This flaming Presence—the Presence of the I AM—was seen by both Moses and Jesus as man's sublime opportunity to become a Christed Being. By using the name of God, I AM, as an affirmation of that Being in each line of the Lord's Prayer, the disciple in his third adoration of the rosary, after hallowing the name of God, I AM, is actually affirming:

> God in me is *(the action of)* thy kingdom come
> God in me is *(the action of)* thy will being done
> God in me is *(the action of Being)* on earth even
>   as God in me is *(the action of Being)* in heaven
> God in me is *(the action of)* giving this day daily
>   bread to all
> God in me is *(the action of)* forgiving all life this
>   day even as
> God in me is also *(the action of)* all life forgiving me
> God in me is *(the action of)* leading all men away
>   from temptation

God in me is *(the action of)* delivering all men from
  every evil condition
God in me is *(the action of)* the kingdom
God in me is *(the action of)* the power, and
God in me is *(the action of)* the glory of God in
  eternal, immortal manifestation
All this God *is* in me

To thus affirm the action of the Creator within the creation is not blasphemy. On the contrary, it is the fulfillment of the judgment of the Lord recorded in the Book of Psalms "God standeth in the congregation of the mighty; he judgeth among the gods [he pronounces his judgments through the ascended masters]: How long will ye judge unjustly and accept the [testimony of the] persons [sons] of the wicked?...I have said, *Ye are gods;* and all of you are children of the Most High."[30] This declaration of the Lord was intended to be a refutation of the lies of the Liar and of the accusations leveled against the children of the Most High by the accuser of the brethren,[31] namely that all mankind are sinners conceived in sin and therefore do not have the potential of God-good to rise to the fullness of the stature of Christ.

Inasmuch as a fundamental misunderstanding of the teachings of Jesus predominates in Christian theology, we again set forth the Law in these pages in order that those who would enter into the fullness of the spirit of giving the rosary might have the bulwark of the Law to reinforce their faith and their hope in the Second Coming of the Christ as they keep the flame of charity with the Divine Mother. For she also prays without ceasing on behalf of the sons and daughters of God whom, in the flame of oneness, she has made her own.

When Jesus declared his divine Sonship and his oneness with God, saying, "*I and my Father are one,*"[32] he also declared not only for himself but for all sons and daughters of God the great law that allows the Creator to *act* through his creation and therefore to be one with it. For the *action* of oneness—the act of being one—is the only oneness that God and man can share. Bearing witness to this active oneness, Jesus testified, "My Father worketh hitherto, and I work."[33] In this true oneness of God and man, whether man affirms "I and my Father are one" or "I AM that I AM," he is acknowledging the individed wholeness of God in and as the manifestation—man.

After Jesus made this profound statement of the Law—that God and man are one being and not separate entities—it is recorded that the Jews took up stones to stone him: "Jesus answered them, Many good works have I shewed you from my Father; for which of those works do ye stone me? The Jews answered him, saying, For a good work we stone thee not, but for blasphemy and because that thou, being a man, makest thyself God. Jesus answered them, Is it not written in your law, I said, Ye are gods? If he called them gods unto whom the word of God came, and the scripture cannot be broken, say ye of him whom the Father hath sanctified and sent into the world, Thou blasphemest, because I said, I am the Son of God? If I do not the works of my Father, believe me not. But if I do, though ye believe not me, believe the works, that ye may know and believe that *the Father is in me and I in him.*"[34]

As Jesus was ordained of God to give to "as many as received him power to become sons of God, even to them that believe on his name,"[35] so we must recognize that to receive the Christ and to believe upon the name of God, I AM—the I AM that I AM—is to begin to use that very potential of our divinity which Moses beheld firsthand, which the Lord himself declared and which Jesus the Son proved by doing the works of his Father. The Jews' interpretation was essentially correct: To declare oneself to be the son of God by a statement of oneness is to make oneself in effect equal with God. This equality they could not accept in Jesus because they could not accept it in themselves. They could not see the Christ light as the extension of God's very Being in themselves; therefore, they could not see it as the extension of God's being in Jesus.

We are willing to accept with the apostle John that "we are now the sons of God"[36] and that we have been made worthy to be called sons of God by believing in the Christ light which God placed not only in Jesus but also in all of his sons and daughters. For this is the light, John says, that lighteth *every* man that cometh into the world. We are willing to accept the fact that we have been made sons of God by believing in the name I AM. Therefore, if it be true, as Jesus said, that the son of God is in the Father and the Father is in him, we must also believe the statement of the Almighty that we are gods. This we understand to mean that we have the *potential* of manifesting God, of being the *action* of God in the plane of Matter, by the very fact of our indissoluble oneness with him.

In order to correctly use the name of God, I AM, as an affirmation of Being and as an affirmation of the action of Being, we must first be convinced of our oneness with God through a correct interpretation of his laws. By the grace of God, the statement of these laws has not been entirely removed from sacred scripture. Those who are willing to examine the Bible in the light of historical truth as well as in the light of the ascended masters' teachings will begin to realize that the doctrine of original sin and the belief that man is sinful by nature do not originate in either the laws of God or in the teachings of Jesus.

Once relieved of the burden of sin and the sense of sin, mankind can truly affirm their oneness with God, which can be accomplished only through Christ the Mediator—the only begotten Son of God. As there is but one God, one Lord, so there is but one Christ. As God individualized himself in the Presence of the I AM for each one, so he has also individualized the Christ for each one in the Christ Self and in the Christ flame that blazes upon the altar of the heart sustaining life as the opportunity for oneness.

To continue with our analysis of the adorations of the rosary, we note that the three Hail Marys which comprise the fourth adoration set the pattern for the entire rosary in the tripartite flame of faith, hope and charity, of God's will, his wisdom and his love. By and in this trinity of oneness—of Father, Son and Holy Spirit—the action of the adorations which follow is multiplied by the power of the three-times-three for the salvation of mankind.

The "Call to the Fire Breath," as the fifth adoration of the rosary, is the call to the Holy Spirit who breathed into man's nostrils the breath of life and man became a living soul.[37] Again we affirm by using the spiritual energies released through the name of God, I AM, that *God in me is the action of* the fire breath from the heart of Alpha and Omega, whose twin flames represent the Father-Mother God in the very center of the cosmos. *God in me is the action of* the immaculate concept—the pure pattern, the divine blueprint—of his original wholeness, his original purity, his original love whence I came forth into manifestation. This call is a sacred ritual commemorating the origin of man in God and the gift of life that is bestowed by the Holy Spirit.

The "Transfiguring Affirmations," which are given as the sixth adoration of the rosary, were also dictated by Jesus the Christ through the messenger Mark L. Prophet just as the master taught them to his inner circle of disciples. As in the Lord's Prayer, they affirm that, by the power of the I AM that I AM,

>God in man is *(the action of)* the open door
>   which no man can shut
>God in man is *(the action of)* the light which
>   lighteth every man that cometh into the world
>God in man is *(the action of)* the way
>God in man is *(the action of)* the truth
>God in man is *(the action of)* the life

Chart of the Rosary

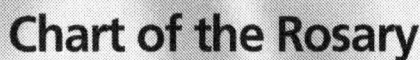

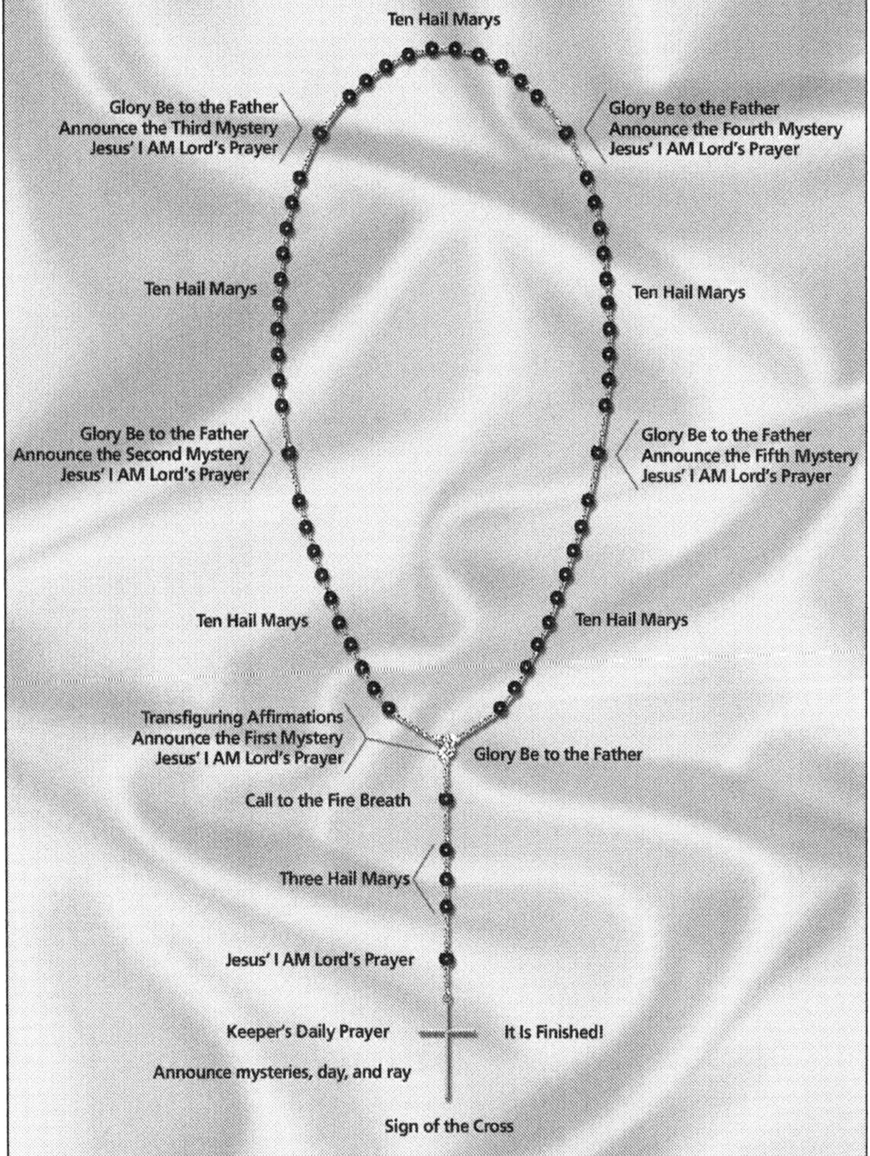

Ten Hail Marys

Glory Be to the Father
Announce the Third Mystery
Jesus' I AM Lord's Prayer

Glory Be to the Father
Announce the Fourth Mystery
Jesus' I AM Lord's Prayer

Ten Hail Marys

Ten Hail Marys

Glory Be to the Father
Announce the Second Mystery
Jesus' I AM Lord's Prayer

Glory Be to the Father
Announce the Fifth Mystery
Jesus' I AM Lord's Prayer

Ten Hail Marys

Ten Hail Marys

Transfiguring Affirmations
Announce the First Mystery
Jesus' I AM Lord's Prayer

Glory Be to the Father

Call to the Fire Breath

Three Hail Marys

Jesus' I AM Lord's Prayer

Keeper's Daily Prayer

It Is Finished!

Announce mysteries, day, and ray

Sign of the Cross

Proceed from left to right in a clockwise direction, beginning with the *Sign of the Cross* and ending with *It Is Finished!*

God in man is *(the action of)* the resurrection
God in man is *(the action of)* the ascension in the light.
God in man is *(the action of)* the fulfillment of all
my needs and requirements of the hour
God in man is *(the action of)* abundant supply poured
out upon all life
God in man is *(the action of)* perfect sight and hearing
God in man is *(the action of)* the manifest perfection
of Being
God in man is *(the action of)* the illimitable light
of God made manifest everywhere
God in man is *(the action of)* the light of the
Holy of holies
God in man is *(the action of)* a Son of God
God in man is *(the action of)* the light in the
holy mountain of God

In each of the five decades that form the body of the rosary, the Jesus' I AM Lord's Prayer, the ten Hail Marys and the Glory to the Father anchor one of the secret rays of Christ in the heart of the devotee for his self-mastery and his entering into the Holy of holies known as the white-fire core of being. These twelve parts of each of the five decades are a tribute to the oneness of the Father-Mother God.

The Lord's Prayer, seventh in the order of adorations, establishes the flow of energies from our heart's altar back to the very source of life whence we came. The ten Hail Marys, eighth in the order of adorations, are the gift of our devotion to the Starry Mother. She has borne us in her cosmic womb and held for us the immaculate concept of our divinity within her diamond heart. By the action of the ritual of the ten, the Mother helps us overcome all self-love and crowns us with a vision of the kingdom of heaven as we crown her with a garland of our love. The Glory to the Father, ninth in the order of adorations, is our giving-forth of joy-

Christian Prayer Forms and the Evolution of the Rosary

ful praise to Almighty God for the victory of the Woman clothed with the Sun, who in turn bestows upon us the rule of the Divine Manchild.

The rosary concludes with the affirmation of Jesus the Christ made in his hour of ultimate surrender and ultimate triumph—"It is finished!" This tenth adoration of the rosary, our offering to the Son of Mary given in the name of the living Christ, seals the prayers we selflessly give to Mary as well as the energies she gives to us on the returning current of her love. These are the last words which Jesus spoke on the cross—heard not by man but by God as the final devotion of his Son, "in whom," he declared, "I am well pleased."[38]

In her appearance to the children at Fátima on July 13, 1917, Mother Mary requested that the Vicar of Christ consecrate Russia to her immaculate heart to prevent the great destruction that would otherwise occur there: "I come to ask the consecration of Russia to my Immaculate Heart and the Communion of reparation on the first Saturdays. If they listen to my requests, Russia will be converted and there will be peace. If not, she will scatter her errors through the world, provoking wars and persecutions of the Church. The good will be martyrized, the Holy Father will have much to suffer, various nations will be annihilated."[39]

Since the Vicar of Christ is the representative of Christ both as Jesus and as the Christ Self of each individual, the Christ in us gives us the authority to implore the I AM Presence to consecrate Russia and all of the energies of her people to the immaculate heart of Mary. Following the Scriptural Rosary for the New Age, we ask the Blessed Mother to multiply this consecration not only for the people of Russia but also for her children in China, America and the whole world.

The ascended master El Morya (better known as Saint Thomas More), who founded The Summit Lighthouse activity in 1958, heartily endorsed the rosary released by Mother Mary when he said through Mark: "I have observed also the manifestation of your intention in the spiritual rosary which has been brought forth now through the hand of the universal Mother. Do you understand that everything that firms in you those elements of devotion tends to bind up the wounds of the world? For you are not serving for yourselves alone but for the fulfillment of the Brotherhood's eternal purpose."[40]

When Mother Mary completed the dictating of the rosary, she said: "This is the one key. If the student body will take it up, the giving of this rosary daily will enable the flame of the Mother to be anchored in the world and to prevent a great deal of destruction of human life during the days that are ahead."

In return for our devotion and for the garland of roses woven out of our ten affirmations of the rosary, Mary made the promise "When you come to a certain place in your momentum of attainment in the giving of the rosary, I will come to you and I will place about your neck a rosary of roses composed of fiery stars—each bead a star of light. And you will know when I come in that very hour, for you will feel the garland of light around your neck. And it will be as a reward for faithful service to my Immaculate Heart and to the rose which symbolizes the unfolding of the Mother flame in the consciousness of mankind."[41]

The heavenly hosts await the energies we release in the giving of the rosary that they may in turn release their energy in concerted action on behalf of all of the children of God on earth. Mary exhorts us to give the rosary as heaven joins us in devotion to the beloved Mother and together we pray for the salvation of all mankind:

"Some among you must hold the love of the Mother to hold the balance. And thus I asked that the rosaries be released to you that you might tie in to the momentum of the voices of the saints—saints in heaven....You know, they gather also for the giving of the rosary and blend their voices with your own."[42]

Thus the New Age rosary consists of ten steps to our victory in the test of the ten, which is the test of selflessness, sacrifice and surrender. Fortunate are we who have the opportunity to follow in the footsteps of Jesus and Mary to our own ultimate surrender, our own ultimate triumph.

As we give the rosary, we become partakers of the thirteen mysteries. And through this holy communion, we are made a part of the body (the substance) and of the blood (the spiritual essence) of Christ. He in turn makes us one in him and in the Father as he prayed "that they may be one, even as we are one."[43] Moreover, we share in the mystical union that is between Christ and his Church, the holy Jerusalem coming down from God out of heaven prepared as a bride adorned for her husband.[44] Through the daily giving of the rosary, we enter into a sacred awareness of life and a sacred union with every part of life, until we in truth become the rosary, a rose of light in the garland of the Mother; and we rejoice to be a star in her crown of rejoicing.

Not only are we found as the starry rose, but we move across the entire chain of stars. Confined to none, ensouling all, we are truly one in this fiery chain of Being that is an endless succession of hierarchy-devotee, hierarchy-devotee, hierarchy-devotee—each conscious awareness of Father, Mother, Son and Holy Spirit a focal point for worlds infolding worlds and of God becoming more of himself in man and of man transcending himself in God.

Give unto the LORD, O ye mighty, give unto the LORD glory and strength.

Give unto the LORD the glory due unto his name; worship the LORD in the beauty of holiness.

The voice of the LORD is upon the waters: the God of glory thundereth: the LORD is upon many waters.

The voice of the LORD is powerful; the voice of the LORD is full of majesty….

The voice of the LORD divideth the flames of fire.

—Psalms

Adorations of the Rosary

The Sign of the Cross
In the name of the Father
and of the Mother
and of the Son
and of the Holy Spirit,
Amen.

The Keeper's Daily Prayer
A flame is active—
A flame is vital—
A flame is eternal.

I AM a God flame of radiant love
From the very heart of God
In the Great Central Sun,
Descending from the master of life!
I AM charged now
With beloved Helios and Vesta's
Supreme God consciousness
And solar awareness.

Pilgrim upon earth,
I AM walking daily the way
Of the ascended masters' victory
That leads to my eternal freedom
By the power of the sacred fire
This day and always,
Continually made manifest
In my thoughts, feelings, and
   immediate awareness,

Transcending and transmuting
All the elements of earth
Within my four lower bodies
And freeing me by the power of the sacred fire
From those misqualified foci of energy
   within my being.

I AM set free right now from all that binds
By and through the currents of the divine flame
Of the sacred fire itself
Whose ascending action makes me
God in manifestation,
God in action,
God by direction and
God in consciousness!

I AM an active flame!
I AM a vital flame!
I AM an eternal flame!
I AM an expanding fire spark
From the Great Central Sun
Drawing to me now every ray
Of divine energy which I need
And which can never be requalified by the
   human
And flooding me with the light
And God-illumination of a thousand suns
To take dominion and rule supreme forever
Everywhere I AM!

Where I AM, there God is also.
Unseparated forever I remain,
Increasing my light
By the smile of his radiance,
The fullness of his love,

The omniscience of his wisdom,
And the power of his life eternal,
Which automatically raises me
On ascension's wings of victory
That shall return me to the heart of God
From whence in truth
I AM come to do God's will
And manifest abundant life to all!

The I AM Lord's Prayer
by Jesus the Christ

Our Father who art in heaven,
Hallowed be thy name, I AM.
I AM thy kingdom come
I AM thy will being done
I AM on earth even as I AM in heaven
I AM giving this day daily bread to all
I AM forgiving all life this day even as
I AM also all life forgiving me
I AM leading all men away from temptation
I AM delivering all men from every evil condition
I AM the kingdom
I AM the power and
I AM the glory of God in eternal, immortal manifestation—
All this I AM.

Hail Mary

Hail, Mary, full of grace. The Lord is with thee. Blessed art thou among women and blessed is the fruit of thy womb, Jesus.

Holy Mary, Mother of God, pray for us, sons and daughters of God, now and at the hour of our victory over sin, disease, and death.

Call to the Fire Breath

I AM, I AM, I AM the fire breath of God
From the heart of beloved Alpha and Omega!
This day I AM the immaculate concept
In expression everywhere I move!
Now I AM full of joy,
For now I AM the full expression
Of divine love!

My beloved I AM Presence,
Seal me now
Within the very heart
Of the expanding fire breath of God:
Let its purity, wholeness, and love
Manifest everywhere I AM today and forever!

I accept this done right now with full power!
I AM this done right now with full power!
I AM, I AM, I AM
God-life expressing perfection
All ways at all times!
This which I call forth for myself
I call forth for every man, woman, and child
   on this planet!

Transfiguring Affirmations of Jesus the Christ

I AM that I AM
I AM the open door which no man can shut
I AM the light which lighteth every man that
   cometh into the world
I AM the way
I AM the truth

I AM the life
I AM the resurrection
I AM the ascension in the light
I AM the fulfillment of all my needs and
   requirements of the hour
I AM abundant supply poured out upon all life
I AM perfect sight and hearing
I AM the manifest perfection of Being
I AM the illimitable light of God made manifest
   everywhere
I AM the light of the Holy of holies
I AM a son of God
I AM the light in the holy mountain of God

> Glory Be to the Father
>
> Glory be to the Father
> And to the Son
> And to the Holy Spirit!
> As it was in the beginning,
> Is now and ever shall be,
> Life without end—
> I AM, I AM, I AM!

> It Is Finished!
> by Jesus the Christ

It is finished!
Done with this episode in strife,
I AM made one with immortal Life.
Calmly I AM resurrecting my spiritual energies
From the great treasure house of immortal knowing.

The days I knew with thee, O Father,
Before the world was—the days of triumph,
When all of the thoughts of thy Being

Soared over the ageless hills of cosmic memory,
Come again as I meditate upon thee.
Each day as I call forth thy memories
From the scroll of immortal love,
I AM thrilled anew.
Patterns wondrous to behold enthrall me
With the wisdom of thy creative scheme.
So fearfully and wonderfully am I made
That none can mar thy design,
None can despoil the beauty of thy holiness,
None can discourage the beating of my heart
In almost wild anticipation
Of thy fullness made manifest within me.

O great and glorious Father,
How shall a tiny bird created in hierarchical bliss
Elude thy compassionate attention?
I AM of greater value than many birds
And therefore do I know that thy loving thoughts
Reach out to me each day
To console me in seeming aloneness,
To raise my courage,
Elevate my concepts,
Exalt my character,
Flood my being with virtue and power,
Sustain thy cup of life flowing over within me,
And abide within me forever
In the nearness of thy heavenly Presence.

I cannot fail,
Because I AM thyself in action everywhere.
I ride with thee
Upon the mantle of the clouds.
I walk with thee

Upon the waves and crests of water's abundance.
I move with thee
In the undulations of thy currents
Passing over the thousands of hills
   composing earth's crust.
I AM alive with thee
In each bush, flower, and blade of grass.
All nature sings in thee and me,
For we are one.

I AM alive in the hearts of the downtrodden,
Raising them up.
I AM the Law exacting the truth of Being
In the hearts of the proud,
Debasing the human creation therein
And spurring the search for thy reality.
I AM all things of bliss
To all people of peace.
I AM the full facility of divine grace,
The spirit of holiness
Releasing all hearts from bondage into unity.

It is finished!
Thy perfect creation is within me.
Immortally lovely,
It cannot be denied the blessedness of Being.
Like unto thyself, it abides in the house of reality.
Nevermore to go out into profanity,
It knows only the wonders of purity and victory.
Yet there stirs within this immortal fire
A consummate pattern of mercy and compassion
Seeking to save forever that which is lost
Through wandering away
From the beauty of reality and truth.

I AM the living Christ in action evermore!

It is finished!
Death and human concepts have no power
   in my world!
I AM sealed by God-design
With the fullness of that Christ-love
That overcomes, transcends, and frees the world
By the power of the three-times-three
Until all the world is God-victorious—
Ascended in the light and free!

It is finished!
Completeness is the allness of God.
Day unto day an increase of strength, devotion,
Life, beauty, and holiness occurs within me,
Released from the fairest flower of my being,
The Christ-consecrated rose of Sharon
Unfolding its petals within my heart.
My heart is the heart of God!
My heart is the heart of the world!
My heart is the heart of Christ in healing action!
Lo, I AM with you alway, even unto the end,
When with the voice of immortal love
I too shall say *"It is finished!"*

Mary's Ritual of the Rosary for Sons and Daughters of Dominion

To give the Rosary, follow these fourteen steps, using the Adorations of the Rosary given on the preceding pages as they are called for in the ritual.

1

Holding the cross in your right hand, make the *sign of the cross* to honor the Holy Trinity within man as you give the *Sign of the Cross:*

> In the name of the Father
> *Touch forehead with right hand*
> and of the Mother
> *Touch heart with right hand*
> and of the Son
> *Touch left shoulder*
> and of the Holy Spirit,
> *Touch right shoulder*
> Amen.
> *Put hands together*

2

Announce the mysteries, the day, and the ray; for example, "The Joyful Mysteries: Tuesday - The First Ray."

3

Still holding the cross, recite the *Keeper's Daily Prayer* to proclaim your identity here and now as a flame of God.

4

On the first large bead, recite Jesus' *I AM Lord's Prayer* to commemorate the oneness of God in universal manifestation.

5

On each of the next three beads, recite one *Hail Mary* for the establishment upon earth of the dominion of faith, hope and charity.

6

On the next bead give the *Call to the Fire Breath* to commemorate the lighting of the threefold flame within the secret chamber of the heart* of man by the Holy Spirit.

7

At the triangle or medal give the *Transfiguring Affirmations of Jesus* released from the Immaculate Heart of Mary to resurrect her sons and daughters with the fires of wholeness (holiness).

8

Announce the First Mystery; for example, "First Joyful Mystery: The Annunciation."

9

Still holding the triangle, recite *Jesus' I AM Lord's Prayer* to commemorate the oneness of God in individual manifestation.

---

*The threefold flame is anchored in the secret chamber of the heart chakra, also known as the secondary heart chakra. This chamber is surrounded by such a forcefield of light and protection that it is called a 'cosmic interval'. It is separated from matter, located in the etheric octave.

10

On each of the next ten beads, recite the scriptures listed under the First Mystery to create a cup of praise, and offer a *Hail Mary* to invoke the light that fills the cup with the essence of the Divine Mother.

11

Conclude the first mystery with an offering of praise to the Holy Trinity in man by singing or reciting the *Glory Be to the Father* on the next bead.

12

Still holding this bead, announce the second mystery; for example, "Second Joyful Mystery: The Visitation."

13

On the same bead give *Jesus' I AM Lord's Prayer* to commemorate the oneness of God in individual manifestation. Complete the next four decades in the same manner as the first.

14

Conclude your ritual by reciting Jesus' Prayer of the Cross, *It is Finished!* to acknowledge your daily victory over sin, disease, and death through the glorious fulfillment of the Son of God.

Give ear to my words, O Lord, *consider my meditation. Hearken unto the voice of my cry, my King, and my God: for unto thee will I pray.*

My voice shalt thou hear in the morning, O Lord; *in the morning will I direct my prayer unto thee, and will look up.* —Psalms

MARY'S SCRIPTURAL ROSARY FOR THE NEW AGE

I know that, whatsoever God doeth, it shall be for ever: nothing can be put to it, nor any thing taken from it: and God doeth it, that men should fear before him.

That which hath been is now; and that which is to be hath already been; and God requireth that which is past.

—Ecclesiastes

I

Sign of the Cross

The Teaching Mysteries
Sunday Morning - The Second Ray

Keeper's Daily Prayer
Jesus' I AM Lord's Prayer
Three Hail Marys
Call to the Fire Breath
Transfiguring Affirmations of Jesus

First Teaching Mystery
The Beatitudes

Jesus' I AM Lord's Prayer

1   And seeing the multitudes, he went up into a mountain: and when he was set, his disciples came unto him: and he opened his mouth and taught them, saying,

Hail Mary

2   Blessed are the poor in spirit: for theirs is the kingdom of heaven.

Hail Mary

3   Blessed are they that mourn: for they shall be comforted.

Hail Mary

4   Blessed are the meek: for they shall inherit the earth.

Hail Mary

5   Blessed are they which do hunger and thirst after righteousness: for they shall be filled.

Note: Exact references to scripture verses used in the mysteries are included in the section of notes in the back of the book.

Hail Mary

6   Blessed are the merciful: for they shall obtain mercy.

Hail Mary

7   Blessed are the pure in heart: for they shall see God.

Hail Mary

8   Blessed are the peacemakers: for they shall be called the children of God.

Hail Mary

9   Blessed are they which are persecuted for righteousness' sake: for theirs is the kingdom of heaven.

Hail Mary

10   Blessed are ye when men shall revile you and persecute you and shall say all manner of evil against you falsely for my sake. Rejoice and be exceeding glad: for great is your reward in heaven: for so persecuted they the prophets which were before you.

Hail Mary

Glory Be to the Father

Second Teaching Mystery
The Marriage Feast and the Wedding Garment

Jesus' I AM Lord's Prayer

1   The kingdom of heaven is like unto a certain king which made a marriage for his son and sent forth his servants to call them that were bidden to the wedding: and they would not come.

Hail Mary

2   Again he sent forth other servants, saying, Tell them which are bidden, Behold, I have prepared my dinner: my oxen and my fatlings are killed, and all things are ready: come unto the marriage.

Hail Mary

The Teaching Mysteries

3   But they made light of it and went their ways, one to his farm, another to his merchandise:

Hail Mary

4   And the remnant took his servants and entreated them spitefully and slew them.

Hail Mary

5   But when the king heard thereof, he was wroth: and he sent forth his armies and destroyed those murderers and burned up their city.

Hail Mary

6   Then saith he to his servants, The wedding is ready, but they which were bidden were not worthy. Go ye therefore into the highways, and as many as ye shall find, bid to the marriage.

Hail Mary

7   So those servants went out into the highways and gathered together all as many as they found, both bad and good: and the wedding was furnished with guests.

Hail Mary

8   And when the king came in to see the guests, he saw there a man which had not on a wedding garment: and he saith unto him, Friend, how camest thou in hither not having a wedding garment? And he was speechless.

Hail Mary

9   Then said the king to the servants, Bind him hand and foot and take him away and cast him into outer darkness; there shall be weeping and gnashing of teeth.

Hail Mary

10   For many are called, but few are chosen.

Hail Mary

Glory Be to the Father

Third Teaching Mystery
The Unmerciful Servant

Jesus' I AM Lord's Prayer

1   Therefore is the kingdom of heaven likened unto a certain king which would take account of his servants. And when he had begun to reckon, one was brought unto him which owed him ten thousand talents.

Hail Mary

2   But forasmuch as he had not to pay, his lord commanded him to be sold, and his wife and children and all that he had, and payment to be made.

Hail Mary

3   The servant therefore fell down and worshipped him, saying, Lord, have patience with me, and I will pay thee all.

Hail Mary

4   Then the lord of that servant was moved with compassion and loosed him and forgave him the debt.

Hail Mary

5   But the same servant went out and found one of his fellowservants which owed him an hundred pence: and he laid hands on him and took him by the throat, saying, Pay me that thou owest.

Hail Mary

6   And his fellowservant fell down at this feet and besought him, saying, Have patience with me and I will pay thee all.

Hail Mary

7   And he would not, but went and cast him into prison till he should pay the debt.

Hail Mary

8   So when his fellowservants saw what was done, they were very sorry and came and told unto their lord all that was done.

Hail Mary

9   Then his lord, after that he had called him, said unto him, O thou wicked servant, I forgave thee all that debt because thou desiredst me. Shouldest not thou also have had compassion on thy fellowservant, even as I had pity on thee?

Hail Mary

10   And his lord was wroth and delivered him to the tormentors till he should pay all that was due unto him. So likewise shall my heavenly Father do also unto you if ye from your hearts forgive not every one his brother their trespasses.

Hail Mary

Glory Be to the Father

Fourth Teaching Mystery
The Ten Virgins

Jesus' I AM Lord's Prayer

1   Then shall the kingdom of heaven be likened unto ten virgins which took their lamps and went forth to meet the bridegroom. And five of them were wise, and five were foolish.

Hail Mary

2   They that were foolish took their lamps and took no oil with them.

Hail Mary

3   But the wise took oil in their vessels with their lamps.

Hail Mary

4   While the bridegroom tarried, they all slumbered and slept.

Hail Mary

5   And at midnight there was a cry made, Behold, the bridegroom cometh: go ye out to meet him.

Hail Mary

6   Then all those virgins arose and trimmed their lamps. And the foolish said unto the wise, Give us of your oil; for our lamps are gone out.

Hail Mary

7   But the wise answered, saying, Not so, lest there be not enough for us and you: but go ye rather to them that sell, and buy for yourselves.

Hail Mary

8   And while they went to buy, the bridegroom came; and they that were ready went in with him to the marriage: and the door was shut.

Hail Mary

9   Afterward came also the other virgins, saying, Lord, Lord, open to us. But he answered and said, Verily I say unto you, I know you not.

Hail Mary

10   Watch therefore, for ye know neither the day nor the hour wherein the Son of man cometh.

Hail Mary

Glory Be to the Father

Fifth Teaching Mystery
The Tares among the Wheat

Jesus' I AM Lord's Prayer

1   Then Jesus sent the multitude away and went into the house: and his disciples came unto him, saying, Declare unto us the parable of the tares of the field.

Hail Mary

2   He that soweth the good seed is the Son of man; the field is the world; the good seed are the children of the kingdom; but the tares are the children of the wicked one.

Hail Mary

3   The enemy that sowed them is the devil; the harvest is the end of the world; and the reapers are the angels.

Hail Mary

4   As therefore the tares are gathered and burned in the fire, so shall it be in the end of this world.

Hail Mary

5   The Son of man shall send forth his angels, and they shall gather out of his kingdom all things that offend and them which do iniquity,

Hail Mary

6   And shall cast them into a furnace of fire: there shall be wailing and gnashing of teeth.

Hail Mary

7   Then shall the righteous shine forth as the sun in the kingdom of their Father. Who hath ears to hear, let him hear.

Hail Mary

8   Verily I say unto you, Whatsoever ye shall bind on earth shall be bound in heaven: and whatsoever ye shall loose on earth shall be loosed in heaven.

Hail Mary

9   Again I say unto you that if two of you shall agree on earth as touching any thing that they shall ask, it shall be done for them of my Father which is in heaven.

Hail Mary

10   For where two or three are gathered together in my name, there am I in the midst of them.

Hail Mary

Glory Be to the Father

It Is Finished!

II

Sign of the Cross

The Masterful Mysteries
Sunday Evening - The Eighth Ray

Keeper's Daily Prayer
Jesus' I AM Lord's Prayer
Three Hail Marys
Call to the Fire Breath
Transfiguring Affirmations of Jesus

First Masterful Mystery
The Temptation in the Wilderness

Jesus' I AM Lord's Prayer

1   Then was Jesus led up of the Spirit into the wilderness to be tempted of the devil.

Hail Mary

2   And when he had fasted forty days and forty nights, he was afterward an hungred. And when the tempter came to him, he said, If thou be the Son of God, command that these stones be made bread.

Hail Mary

3   But he answered and said, It is written, Man shall not live by bread alone, but by every word that proceedeth out of the mouth of God.

Hail Mary

4   Then the devil taketh him up into the holy city and setteth him on a pinnacle of the temple

Hail Mary

5   And saith unto him, If thou be the Son of God, cast thyself down: for it is written, He shall give his angels charge concerning thee: and in their hands they shall bear thee up lest at any time thou dash thy foot against a stone.

Hail Mary

6   Jesus said unto him, It is written again, Thou shalt not tempt the Lord thy God.

Hail Mary

7   Again the devil taketh him up into an exceeding high mountain and sheweth him all the kingdoms of the world and the glory of them;

Hail Mary

8   And saith unto him, All these things will I give thee if thou wilt fall down and worship me.

Hail Mary

9   Then saith Jesus unto him, Get thee hence, Satan: for it is written, Thou shalt worship the Lord thy God, and him only shalt thou serve.

Hail Mary

10   Then the devil leaveth him and, behold, angels came and ministered unto him.

Hail Mary

Glory Be to the Father

Second Masterful Mystery
Raising of Jairus' Daughter and the
Woman Who Touched Christ's Garment

Jesus' I AM Lord's Prayer

1   And behold, there came a man named Jairus, and he was a ruler of the synagogue: and he fell down at Jesus' feet and besought him that he would come into his house.

Hail Mary

2   For he had one only daughter, about twelve years of age, and she lay a dying. But as he went the people thronged him.

Hail Mary

3   And a woman having an issue of blood twelve years, which had spent all her living upon physicians, neither could be healed of any, came behind him and touched the border of his garment: and immediately her issue of blood stanched.

Hail Mary

4   And Jesus said, Who touched me? When all denied, Peter and they that were with him said, Master, the multitude throng thee and press thee, and sayest thou, Who touched me? And Jesus said, Somebody hath touched me: for I perceive that virtue is gone out of me.

Hail Mary

5   And when the woman saw that she was not hid, she came trembling, and falling down before him, she declared unto him before all the people for what cause she had touched him and how she was healed immediately.

Hail Mary

6   And he said unto her, Daughter, be of good comfort: thy faith hath made thee whole; go in peace.

Hail Mary

7   While he yet spake, there cometh one from the ruler of the synagogue's house, saying to him, Thy daughter is dead; trouble not the Master. But when Jesus heard it, he answered him, saying, Fear not: believe only, and she shall be made whole.

Hail Mary

8   And when he came into the house, all wept and bewailed her: but he said, Weep not; she is not dead, but sleepeth. And they laughed him to scorn, knowing that she was dead.

Hail Mary

9   And he put them all out and took the damsel by the hand and said unto her, Talitha cumi; which is, being interpreted, Damsel, I say unto thee, arise!

Hail Mary

10   And her spirit came again, and straightway the damsel arose and walked. And they were astonished with a great astonishment.

Hail Mary

Glory Be to the Father

Third Masterful Mystery
Jesus Walking on the Water

Jesus' I AM Lord's Prayer

1   And straightway Jesus constrained his disciples to get into a ship and to go before him unto the other side. And when he had sent the multitudes away, he went up into a mountain apart to pray: and when the evening was come, he was there alone.

Hail Mary

2   But the ship was now in the midst of the sea, tossed with waves: for the wind was contrary. And in the fourth watch of the

night Jesus went unto them, walking on the sea.

Hail Mary

3   And when the disciples saw him walking on the sea, they were troubled, saying, It is a spirit; and they cried out for fear.

Hail Mary

4   But straightway Jesus spake unto them, saying, Be of good cheer; it is I; be not afraid.

Hail Mary

5   And Peter answered him and said, Lord, if it be thou, bid me come unto thee on the water.

Hail Mary

6   And he said, Come. And when Peter was come down out of the ship, he walked on the water to go to Jesus.

Hail Mary

7   But when he saw the wind boisterous, he was afraid; and beginning to sink, he cried, saying, Lord, save me.

Hail Mary

8   And immediately Jesus stretched forth his hand and caught him and said unto him, O thou of little faith, wherefore didst thou doubt?

Hail Mary

9   And when they were come into the ship, the wind ceased.

Hail Mary

10   Then they that were in the ship came and worshipped him, saying, Of a truth thou art the Son of God.

Hail Mary

Glory Be to the Father

Fourth Masterful Mystery
The Transfiguration

Jesus' I AM Lord's Prayer

1   And it came to pass about an eight days after these sayings, he took Peter and John and James and went up into a mountain to pray.

Hail Mary

2   And as he prayed, he was transfigured before them: and his face did shine as the sun; the fashion of his countenance was altered, and his raiment was white and glistering.

Hail Mary

3   And behold, there talked with him two men, which were Moses and Elias:

Hail Mary

4   Who appeared in glory and spake of his decease which he should accomplish at Jerusalem.

Hail Mary

5   But Peter and they that were with him were heavy with sleep: and when they were awake, they saw his glory and the two men that stood with him.

Hail Mary

6   Then answered Peter and said unto Jesus, Lord, it is good for us to be here: if thou wilt, let us make here three tabernacles: one for thee and one for Moses and one for Elias.

Hail Mary

7   While he yet spake, behold, a bright cloud overshadowed them: and behold a voice out of the cloud, which said, This is my beloved Son, in whom I am well pleased; hear ye him.

Hail Mary

8   And when the disciples heard it, they fell on their face and were sore afraid.

The Masterful Mysteries

Hail Mary

9   And Jesus came and touched them and said, Arise, and be not afraid.

Hail Mary

10   And when they had lifted up their eyes, they saw no man, save Jesus only.

Hail Mary

Glory Be to the Father

Fifth Masterful Mystery
The Raising of Lazarus

Jesus' I AM Lord's Prayer

1   Now a certain man was sick, named Lazarus, of Bethany, the town of Mary and her sister Martha. Therefore his sisters sent unto him, saying, Lord, behold, he whom thou lovest is sick.

Hail Mary

2   When Jesus heard that, he said, This sickness is not unto death, but for the glory of God, that the Son of God might be glorified thereby.

Hail Mary

3   When he had heard therefore that he was sick, he abode two days still in the same place where he was. Then after that saith he to his disciples, Let us go into Judaea again.

Hail Mary

4   Then Martha, as soon as she heard that Jesus was coming, went and met him: but Mary sat still in the house.

Hail Mary

5   Then said Martha unto Jesus, Lord, if thou hadst been here, my brother had not died. But I know that even now, whatsoever

thou wilt ask of God, God will give it thee.

Hail Mary

6   Jesus saith unto her, Thy brother shall rise again. Martha saith unto him, I know that he shall rise again in the resurrection at the last day.

Hail Mary

7   Jesus said unto her, I AM the resurrection and the Life: he that believeth in me, though he were dead, yet shall he live: and whosoever liveth and believeth in me shall never die. Believest thou this?

Hail Mary

8   She saith unto him, Yea, Lord: I believe that thou art the Christ, the Son of God, which should come into the world.

Hail Mary

9   Then they took away the stone from the place where the dead was laid. And Jesus lifted up his eyes and said, Father, I thank thee that thou hast heard me.

And I knew that thou hearest me always: but because of the people which stand by I said it, that they may believe that thou hast sent me.

Hail Mary

10   And when he thus had spoken, he cried with a loud voice, Lazarus, come forth! And he that was dead came forth, bound hand and foot with graveclothes: and his face was bound about with a napkin. Jesus saith unto them, Loose him, and let him go.

Hail Mary

Glory Be to the Father

It Is Finished!

III

Sign of the Cross

The Love Mysteries
Monday - The Third Ray

Keeper's Daily Prayer
Jesus' I AM Lord's Prayer
Three Hail Marys
Call to the Fire Breath
Transfiguring Affirmations of Jesus

First Love Mystery
The Love of John the Baptist and Jesus

Jesus' I AM Lord's Prayer

1   He must increase, but I must decrease.

There was a man sent from God whose name was John. The same came for a witness, to bear witness of the Light, that all men through him might believe.

Hail Mary

2   He was not that Light, but was sent to bear witness of that Light. That was the true Light which lighteth every man that cometh into the world.

Hail Mary

3   In those days came John the Baptist preaching in the wilderness of Judaea and saying, Repent ye: for the kingdom of heaven is at hand. For this is he that was spoken of by the prophet Esaias, saying, The voice of one crying in the wilderness, Prepare ye the way of the Lord, make straight his paths.

Hail Mary

4   John answered, saying unto them all, I indeed baptize you with water; but one mightier than I cometh, the latchet of whose shoes I am not worthy to unloose: he shall baptize you with the Holy Ghost and with fire:

Hail Mary

5   Whose fan is in his hand, and he will thoroughly purge his floor and will gather the wheat into his garner; but the chaff he will burn with fire unquenchable.

Hail Mary

6   Then cometh Jesus from Galilee to Jordan unto John to be baptized of him. But John forbad him, saying, I have need to be baptized of thee, and comest thou to me?

Hail Mary

7   And Jesus answering said unto him, Suffer it to be so now: for thus it becometh us to fulfill all righteousness.

Then he suffered him.

Hail Mary

8   And Jesus, when he was baptized, went up straightway out of the water: and lo, the heavens were opened unto him, and he saw the Spirit of God descending like a dove and lighting upon him:

Hail Mary

9   And lo a voice from heaven, saying, This is my beloved Son, in whom I AM well pleased.

Hail Mary

10   Jesus said unto them, Verily I say unto you, Among them that are born of women there hath not risen a greater than John the Baptist: notwithstanding he that is least in the kingdom of heaven is greater than he.

Hail Mary

Glory Be to the Father

Second Love Mystery
The Love of the Disciples for the Master

Jesus' I AM Lord's Prayer

1   If ye love me, keep my commandments.

Hail Mary

2   And I will pray the Father, and he shall give you another Comforter, that he may abide with you for ever, even the Spirit of truth, whom the world cannot receive because it seeth him not neither knoweth him: but ye know him, for he dwelleth with you and shall be in you.

Hail Mary

3   I will not leave you comfortless: I will come to you.

Hail Mary

4   Yet a little while and the world seeth me no more; but ye see me. Because I live, ye shall live also. At that day ye shall know that I am in my Father, and ye in me, and I in you. He that hath my commandments and keepeth them, he it is that loveth me: and he that loveth me shall be loved of my Father, and I will love him and will manifest myself to him.

Hail Mary

5   Lord, how is it that thou wilt manifest thyself unto us and not unto the world? Jesus answered, If a man love me, he will keep my words: and my Father will love him, and we will come unto him and make our abode with him.

Hail Mary

6   He that loveth me not keepeth not my sayings: and the word which ye hear is not mine, but the Father's which sent me. These things have I spoken unto you, being yet present with you.

Hail Mary

7   But the Comforter, which is the Holy Ghost, whom the Father will send in my name, he shall teach you all things and

bring all things to your remembrance, whatsoever I have said unto you.

Hail Mary

8   Peace I leave with you, my peace I give unto you: not as the world giveth give I unto you. Let not your heart be troubled, neither let it be afraid.

Hail Mary

9   Ye have heard how I said unto you, I go away and come again unto you. If ye loved me, ye would rejoice because I said, I go unto the Father: for my Father is greater than I.

Hail Mary

10   And now I have told you before it come to pass that when it is come to pass ye might believe. Hereafter I will not talk much with you: for the prince of this world cometh and hath nothing in me. But that the world may know that I love the Father; and as the Father gave me commandment, even so I do.

Hail Mary

Glory Be to the Father

Third Love Mystery
The Love of Christ and His Members

Jesus' I AM Lord's Prayer

1   I AM the true vine, and my Father is the husbandman. Every branch in me that beareth not fruit he taketh away: and every branch that beareth fruit, he purgeth it, that it may bring forth more fruit.

Hail Mary

2   Now ye are clean through the word which I have spoken unto you. Abide in me, and I in you. As the branch cannot bear

fruit of itself, except it abide in the vine, no more can ye, except ye abide in me.

Hail Mary

3   I AM the vine, and ye are the branches: he that abideth in me, and I in him, the same bringeth forth much fruit: for without me ye can do nothing.

Hail Mary

4   If a man abide not in me, he is cast forth as a branch and is withered; and men gather them and cast them into the fire, and they are burned. If ye abide in me and my words abide in you, ye shall ask what ye will and it shall be done unto you.

Hail Mary

5   Herein is my Father glorified, that ye bear much fruit; so shall ye be my disciples. As the Father hath loved me, so have I loved you: continue ye in my love.

Hail Mary

6   If ye keep my commandments, ye shall abide in my love, even as I have kept my Father's commandments and abide in his love. These things have I spoken unto you that my joy might remain in you and that your joy might be full.

Hail Mary

7   This is my commandment: that ye love one another, as I have loved you. Greater love hath no man than this, that a man lay down his life for his friends.

Hail Mary

8   Ye are my friends if ye do whatsoever I command you. Henceforth I call you not servants; for the servant knoweth not what his lord doeth: but I have called you friends; for all things that I have heard of my Father I have made known unto you.

Hail Mary

9   Ye have not chosen me, but I have chosen you and ordained you that ye should go and bring forth fruit and that your fruit

should remain: that whatsoever ye shall ask of the Father in my name, He may give it you.

Hail Mary

10   These things I command you, that ye love one another.

Hail Mary

Glory Be to the Father

Fourth Love Mystery
The Love of the Master for His Disciples

Jesus' I AM Lord's Prayer

1   Simon Peter saith unto them, I go a fishing. They say unto him, We also go with thee. They went forth and entered into a ship immediately; and that night they caught nothing.

Hail Mary

2   But when the morning was now come, Jesus stood on the shore: but the disciples knew not that it was Jesus.

Hail Mary

3   Then Jesus saith unto them, Children, have ye any meat? They answered him, No.

Hail Mary

4   And he said unto them, Cast the net on the right side of the ship, and ye shall find. They cast therefore, and now they were not able to draw it for the multitude of fishes.

Hail Mary

5   As soon then as they were come to land, they saw a fire of coals there and fish laid thereon, and bread. Jesus saith unto them, Bring of the fish which ye have now caught.

Hail Mary

The Love Mysteries

6   Simon Peter went up and drew the net to land full of great fishes, an hundred and fifty and three: and for all there were so many, yet was not the net broken.

Hail Mary

7   Jesus saith unto them, Come and dine. And none of the disciples durst ask him, Who art thou? knowing that it was the Lord.

Hail Mary

8   So when they had dined, Jesus saith to Simon Peter, Simon, son of Jonas, lovest thou me more than these? He saith unto him, Yea, Lord; thou knowest that I love thee. He saith unto him, Feed my lambs.

Hail Mary

9   He saith to him again the second time, Simon, son of Jonas, lovest thou me? He saith unto him, Yea, Lord; thou knowest that I love thee. He saith unto him, Feed my sheep.

Hail Mary

10   He saith unto him the third time, Simon, son of Jonas, lovest thou me? Peter was grieved because he said unto him the third time, Lovest thou me? And he said unto him, Lord, thou knowest all things; thou knowest that I love thee. Jesus saith unto him, Feed my sheep.

Hail Mary

Glory Be to the Father

Fifth Love Mystery
The Love of the Father

Jesus' I AM Lord's Prayer

1   Behold what manner of love the Father hath bestowed upon us that we should be called the sons of God: therefore the world knoweth us not, because it knew him not.

Hail Mary

2   Beloved, now are we the sons of God, and it doth not yet appear what we shall be: but we know that when he shall appear, we shall be like him; for we shall see him as he is.

Hail Mary

3   And every man that hath this hope in him purifieth himself, even as he is pure.

Hail Mary

4   Whosoever committeth sin transgresseth also the law; for sin is the transgression of the law.

Hail Mary

5   And ye know that he was manifested to take away our sins; and in him is no sin.

Hail Mary

6   Whosoever abideth in him sinneth not: whosoever sinneth hath not seen him, neither known him.

Hail Mary

7   Little children, let no man deceive you: he that doeth righteousness is righteous, even as he is righteous.

Hail Mary

8   He that committeth sin is of the devil; for the devil sinneth from the beginning. For this purpose the Son of God was manifested, that he might destroy the works of the devil.

Hail Mary

9   Whosoever is born of God doth not commit sin; for his seed remaineth in him: and he cannot sin, because he is born of God.

Hail Mary

10   In this the children of God are manifest, and the children of the devil: whosoever doeth not righteousness is not of God, neither he that loveth not his brother. For this is the message that ye heard from the beginning, that we should love one another.

Hail Mary

Glory Be to the Father

It Is Finished!

IV

Sign of the Cross
The Joyful Mysteries
Tuesday - The First Ray

Keeper's Daily Prayer
Jesus' I AM Lord's Prayer
Three Hail Marys
Call to the Fire Breath
Transfiguring Affirmations of Jesus

First Joyful Mystery
The Annunciation

Jesus' I AM Lord's Prayer

1   And in the sixth month the angel Gabriel was sent from God unto a city of Galilee named Nazareth, to a virgin espoused to a man whose name was Joseph, of the house of David; and the virgin's name was Mary.

Hail Mary

2   And the angel came in unto her and said, Hail, thou that art highly favoured, the Lord is with thee: blessed art thou among women.

Hail Mary

3   And when she saw him, she was troubled at his saying and cast in her mind what manner of salutation this should be.

Hail Mary

4   And the angel said unto her, Fear not, Mary: for thou hast found favour with God. And behold, thou shalt conceive in thy womb and bring forth a son and shalt call his name JESUS.

Hail Mary

The Joyful Mysteries

5   He shall be great and shall be called the Son of the Highest: and the Lord God shall give unto him the throne of his father David: and he shall reign over the house of Jacob for ever; and of his kingdom there shall be no end.

Hail Mary

6   Then said Mary unto the angel, How shall this be, seeing I know not a man?

Hail Mary

7   And the angel answered and said unto her, The Holy Ghost shall come upon thee, and the power of the Highest shall overshadow thee: therefore also that holy thing which shall be born of thee shall be called the Son of God.

Hail Mary

8   And behold, thy cousin Elisabeth, she hath also conceived a son in her old age: and this is the sixth month with her, who was called barren.

Hail Mary

9   For with God nothing shall be impossible.

Hail Mary

10   And Mary said, Behold the handmaid of the Lord; be it unto me according to thy word. And the angel departed from her.

Hail Mary

Glory Be to the Father

Second Joyful Mystery
The Visitation

Jesus' I AM Lord's Prayer

1   And Mary arose in those days and went into the hill country with haste, into a city of Juda, and entered into the house of Zacharias and saluted Elisabeth.

Hail Mary

2   And it came to pass that when Elisabeth heard the salutation of Mary, the babe leaped in her womb; and Elisabeth was filled with the Holy Ghost; and she spake out with a loud voice and said, Blessed art thou among women, and blessed is the fruit of thy womb.

Hail Mary

3   And whence is this to me, that the mother of my Lord should come to me? For lo, as soon as the voice of thy salutation sounded in mine ears, the babe leaped in my womb for joy. And blessed is she that believed: for there shall be a performance of those things which were told her from the Lord.

Hail Mary

4   And Mary said, My soul doth magnify the Lord, and my spirit hath rejoiced in God my Saviour. For he hath regarded the low estate of his handmaiden: for behold, from henceforth all generations shall call me blessed.

Hail Mary

5   For he that is mighty hath done to me great things; and holy is his name. And his mercy is on them that fear him from generation to generation.

Hail Mary

6   He hath shewed strength with his arm; he hath scattered the proud in the imagination of their hearts. He hath put down the mighty from their seats and exalted them of low degree.

Hail Mary

7   He hath filled the hungry with good things; and the rich he hath sent empty away. He hath holpen his servant Israel in remembrance of his mercy; as he spake to our fathers, to Abraham, and to his seed for ever.

Hail Mary

8   Now Elisabeth's full time came that she should be delivered;

The Joyful Mysteries

and she brought forth a son, a man child sent from God, whose name was John.

Hail Mary

9   And his father Zacharias was filled with the Holy Ghost and prophesied, saying, And thou, child, shalt be called the prophet of the Highest: for thou shalt go before the face of the Lord to prepare his ways; to give knowledge of salvation unto his people by the remission of their sins,

Hail Mary

10   Through the tender mercy of our God; whereby the dayspring from on high hath visited us, to give light to them that sit in darkness and in the shadow of death, to guide our feet into the way of peace.

Hail Mary

Glory Be to the Father

Third Joyful Mystery
The Nativity

Jesus' I AM Lord's Prayer

1   In the beginning was the Word, and the Word was with God, and the Word was God. The same was in the beginning with God. All things were made by him; and without him was not any thing made that was made.

Hail Mary

2   In him was life; and the life was the light of men. And the light shineth in darkness; and the darkness comprehended it not.

Hail Mary

3   And Joseph also went up from Galilee, out of the city of

Nazareth, into Judaea, unto the city of David, which is called Bethlehem, to be taxed with Mary his espoused wife, being great with child.

Hail Mary

4   And so it was that while they were there, the days were accomplished that she should be delivered. And she brought forth her firstborn son and wrapped him in swaddling clothes and laid him in a manger, because there was no room for them in the inn.

Hail Mary

5   And there were in the same country shepherds abiding in the field, keeping watch over their flock by night. And lo, the angel of the Lord came upon them, and the glory of the Lord shone round about them: and they were sore afraid.

Hail Mary

6   And the angel said unto them, Fear not: for behold, I bring you good tidings of great joy, which shall be to all people. For unto you is born this day in the city of David a Saviour, which is Christ the Lord. And this shall be a sign unto you; ye shall find the babe wrapped in swaddling clothes, lying in a manger.

Hail Mary

7   And suddenly there was with the angel a multitude of the heavenly host praising God and saying, Glory to God in the highest, and on earth peace, good will toward men.

Hail Mary

8   And the shepherds returned, glorifying and praising God for all the things that they had heard and seen, as it was told unto them. But Mary kept all these things and pondered them in her heart.

Hail Mary

9   Now when Jesus was born in Bethlehem of Judaea in the days of Herod the king, behold, there came wise men from the east to Jerusalem, saying, Where is he that is born King of the

The Joyful Mysteries

Jews? for we have seen his star in the east and are come to worship him. And when they were come into the house, they saw the young child with Mary his mother and fell down and worshipped him: and when they had opened their treasures, they presented unto him gifts: gold and frankincense and myrrh.

Hail Mary

10   And the Word was made flesh and dwelt among us. And we beheld his glory, the glory as of the only begotten of the Father, full of grace and truth.

Hail Mary

Glory Be to the Father

Fourth Joyful Mystery
The Presentation

Jesus' I AM Lord's Prayer

1   And when the days of her purification according to the law of Moses were accomplished, they brought him to Jerusalem to present him to the Lord.

Hail Mary

2   And behold, there was a man in Jerusalem whose name was Simeon; and the same man was just and devout, waiting for the consolation of Israel: and the Holy Ghost was upon him.

Hail Mary

3   And it was revealed unto him by the Holy Ghost that he should not see death before he had seen the Lord's Christ.

Hail Mary

4   And he came by the Spirit into the temple: and when the parents brought in the child Jesus to do for him after the custom of the law, then took he him up in his arms and blessed God and

said, Lord, now lettest thou thy servant depart in peace according to thy word:

Hail Mary

5   For mine eyes have seen thy salvation, which thou hast prepared before the face of all people;

Hail Mary

6   A light to lighten the Gentiles and the glory of thy people Israel.

Hail Mary

7   And Joseph and his mother marvelled at those things which were spoken of him. And Simeon blessed them and said unto Mary his mother, Behold, this child is set for the fall and rising again of many in Israel and for a sign which shall be spoken against

Hail Mary

8   (Yea, a sword shall pierce through thy own soul also), that the thoughts of many hearts may be revealed.

Hail Mary

9   And there was one Anna, a prophetess, which departed not from the temple, but served God with fastings and prayers night and day. And she coming in that instant gave thanks likewise unto the Lord and spake of him to all them that looked for redemption in Jerusalem.

Hail Mary

10   And when they had performed all things according to the law of the Lord, they returned into Galilee, to their own city Nazareth. And the child grew and waxed strong in spirit, filled with wisdom: and the grace of God was upon him.

Hail Mary

Glory Be to the Father

Fifth Joyful Mystery
The Finding of Jesus in the Temple

Jesus' I AM Lord's Prayer

1   Now his parents went to Jerusalem every year at the Feast of the Passover. And when he was twelve years old, they went up to Jerusalem after the custom of the feast.

Hail Mary

2   And when they had fulfilled the days, as they returned, the child Jesus tarried behind in Jerusalem; and Joseph and his mother knew not of it.

Hail Mary

3   But they, supposing him to have been in the company, went a day's journey; and they sought him among their kinsfolk and acquaintance.

Hail Mary

4   And when they found him not, they turned back again to Jerusalem, seeking him.

Hail Mary

5   And it came to pass that after three days they found him in the temple, sitting in the midst of the doctors, both hearing them and asking them questions.

Hail Mary

6   And all that heard him were astonished at his understanding and answers.

Hail Mary

7   And when they saw him, they were amazed: and his mother said unto him, Son, why hast thou thus dealt with us? behold, thy father and I have sought thee sorrowing.

Hail Mary

8   And he said unto them, How is it that ye sought me? wist ye not that I must be about my Father's business?

Hail Mary

9   And he went down with them and came to Nazareth and was subject unto them: but his mother kept all these sayings in her heart.

Hail Mary

10   And Jesus increased in wisdom and stature and in favour with God and man.

Hail Mary

Glory Be to the Father

It Is Finished!

V

Sign of the Cross
The Healing Mysteries
Wednesday - The Fifth Ray

Keeper's Daily Prayer
Jesus' I AM Lord's Prayer
Three Hail Marys
Call to the Fire Breath
Transfiguring Affirmations of Jesus

First Healing Mystery
Christ the Light of the World

Jesus' I AM Lord's Prayer

1   I am the light of the world: he that followeth me shall not walk in darkness, but shall have the light of life.

Hail Mary

2   The Pharisees therefore said unto him, Thou bearest record of thyself; thy record is not true.

Hail Mary

3   Jesus answered and said unto them, Though I bear record of myself, yet my record is true: for I know whence I came and whither I go; but ye cannot tell whence I come and whither I go.

Hail Mary

4   Ye judge after the flesh; I judge no man. And yet if I judge, my judgment is true: for I am not alone, but I and the Father that sent me.

Hail Mary

5   It is also written in your law that the testimony of two men is true. I am one that bear witness of myself, and the Father that sent me beareth witness of me.

Hail Mary

6   Then said they unto him, Where is thy Father? Jesus answered, Ye neither know me nor my Father: if ye had known me, ye should have known my Father also.

Hail Mary

7   When ye have lifted up the Son of man, then shall ye know that I am he and that I do nothing of myself; but as my Father hath taught me I speak these things.

Hail Mary

8   And he that sent me is with me: the Father hath not left me alone; for I do always those things that please him.

Hail Mary

9   Then said Jesus to those Jews which believed on him, If ye continue in my word, then are ye my disciples indeed;

Hail Mary

10   And ye shall know the truth, and the truth shall make you free.

Hail Mary

Glory Be to the Father

Second Healing Mystery
At the Pool of Bethesda

Jesus' I AM Lord's Prayer

1   Now there is at Jerusalem by the sheep market a pool, which is called in the Hebrew tongue Bethesda, having five porches.

Hail Mary

The Healing Mysteries

2   In these lay a great multitude of impotent folk, of blind, halt, withered, waiting for the moving of the water.

Hail Mary

3   For an angel went down at a certain season into the pool and troubled the water: whosoever then first after the troubling of the water stepped in was made whole of whatsoever disease he had.

Hail Mary

4   And a certain man was there which had an infirmity thirty and eight years.

Hail Mary

5   When Jesus saw him lie and knew that he had been now a long time in that case, he saith unto him, Wilt thou be made whole?

Hail Mary

6   The impotent man answered him, Sir, I have no man, when the water is troubled, to put me into the pool: but while I am coming, another steppeth down before me.

Hail Mary

7   Jesus saith unto him, Rise, take up thy bed, and walk.

Hail Mary

8   And immediately the man was made whole, and took up his bed and walked.

Hail Mary

9   Verily, verily, I say unto you, The Son can do nothing of himself but what he seeth the Father do: for what things soever he doeth, these also doeth the Son likewise.

Hail Mary

10   Verily, verily, I say unto you, He that heareth my word and believeth on him that sent me hath everlasting life and shall not come into condemnation, but is passed from death unto life.

Verily, verily, I say unto you, The hour is coming, and now is, when the dead shall hear the voice of the Son of God: and they that hear shall live.

Hail Mary

Glory Be to the Father

Third Healing Mystery
One Born Blind

Jesus' I AM Lord's Prayer

1   And as Jesus passed by, he saw a man which was blind from his birth.

Hail Mary

2   And his disciples asked him, saying, Master, who did sin, this man or his parents, that he was born blind?

Hail Mary

3   Jesus answered, Neither hath this man sinned nor his parents: but that the works of God should be made manifest in him.

Hail Mary

4   I must work the works of him that sent me while it is day: the night cometh, when no man can work.

Hail Mary

5   As long as I am in the world, I am the light of the world.

Hail Mary

6   When he had thus spoken, he spat on the ground and made clay of the spittle, and he anointed the eyes of the blind man with the clay,

Hail Mary

The Healing Mysteries

7   And said unto him, Go, wash in the pool of Siloam. He went his way therefore, and washed, and came seeing.

Hail Mary

8   And Jesus said, For judgment I am come into this world, that they which see not might see and that they which see might be made blind.

Hail Mary

9   And some of the Pharisees which were with him heard these words and said unto him, Are we blind also?

Hail Mary

10   Jesus said unto them, If ye were blind, ye should have no sin: but now ye say, We see; therefore your sin remaineth.

Hail Mary

Glory Be to the Father

Fourth Healing Mystery
The Ten Lepers

Jesus' I AM Lord's Prayer

1   And it came to pass as he went to Jerusalem that he passed through the midst of Samaria and Galilee.

Hail Mary

2   And as he entered into a certain village, there met him ten men that were lepers, which stood afar off:

Hail Mary

3   And they lifted up their voices and said, Jesus, Master, have mercy on us.

Hail Mary

4   And when he saw them, he said unto them, Go shew yourselves unto the priests. And it came to pass that as they went, they were cleansed.

Hail Mary

5   And one of them, when he saw that he was healed, turned back and with a loud voice glorified God,

Hail Mary

6   And fell down on his face at his feet, giving him thanks: and he was a Samaritan.

Hail Mary

7   And Jesus answering said, Were there not ten cleansed? but where are the nine?

Hail Mary

8   There are not found that returned to give glory to God save this stranger.

Hail Mary

9   And he said unto him, Arise, go thy way: thy faith hath made thee whole.

Hail Mary

10   And when he was demanded of the Pharisees when the kingdom of God should come, he answered them and said, The kingdom of God cometh not with observation: neither shall they say, Lo here! or Lo there! For behold, the kingdom of God is within you.

Hail Mary

Glory Be to the Father

Fifth Healing Mystery
The Two Witnesses

Jesus' I AM Lord's Prayer

1   And I will give power unto my two witnesses, and they shall prophesy a thousand two hundred and threescore days, clothed in sackcloth. These are the two olive trees and the two candlesticks standing before the God of the earth.

Hail Mary

2   And if any man will hurt them, fire proceedeth out of their mouth and devoureth their enemies: and if any man will hurt them, he must in this manner be killed.

Hail Mary

3   These have power to shut heaven, that it rain not in the days of their prophecy, and have power over waters to turn them to blood and to smite the earth with all plagues as often as they will.

Hail Mary

4   And when they shall have finished their testimony, the beast that ascendeth out of the bottomless pit shall make war against them and shall overcome them and kill them.

Hail Mary

5   And their dead bodies shall lie in the street of the great city, which spiritually is called Sodom and Egypt, where also our Lord was crucified.

Hail Mary

6   And they of the people and kindreds and tongues and nations shall see their dead bodies three days and an half and shall not suffer their dead bodies to be put in graves.

Hail Mary

7   And they that dwell upon the earth shall rejoice over them and make merry and shall send gifts one to another, because these two prophets tormented them that dwelt on the earth.

Hail Mary

8   And after three days and an half the spirit of life from God entered into them, and they stood upon their feet; and great fear fell upon them which saw them.

Hail Mary

9   And they heard a great voice from heaven saying unto them, Come up hither. And they ascended up to heaven in a cloud, and their enemies beheld them.

Hail Mary

10   And the same hour was there a great earthquake, and the tenth part of the city fell, and in the earthquake were slain of men seven thousand: and the remnant were affrighted and gave glory to the God of heaven.

Hail Mary

Glory Be to the Father

It Is Finished!

VI

Sign of the Cross

The Initiatic Mysteries
Thursday - The Sixth Ray

Keeper's Daily Prayer
Jesus' I AM Lord's Prayer
Three Hail Marys
Call to the Fire Breath
Transfiguring Affirmations of Jesus

First Initiatic Mystery
The Last Supper

Jesus' I AM Lord's Prayer

1   And as they were eating, Jesus took bread and blessed it and brake it and gave it to the disciples and said, Take, eat; this is my body, which is broken for you: this do in remembrance of me.

Hail Mary

2   And he took the cup and gave thanks and gave it to them, saying, Drink ye all of it; for this is my blood of the new testament, which is shed for many for the remission of sins.

Hail Mary

3   But I say unto you, I will not drink henceforth of this fruit of the vine until that day when I drink it new with you in my Father's kingdom.

Hail Mary

4   He riseth from supper and laid aside his garments, and took a towel and girded himself. After that he poureth water into a bason and began to wash the disciples' feet and to wipe them with the towel wherewith he was girded.

Hail Mary

5   Then cometh he to Simon Peter: and Peter saith unto him, Lord, dost thou wash my feet? Jesus answered and said unto him, What I do thou knowest not now, but thou shalt know hereafter.

Hail Mary

6   Peter saith unto him, Thou shalt never wash my feet. Jesus answered him, If I wash thee not, thou hast no part with me. Simon Peter saith unto him, Lord, not my feet only, but also my hands and my head.

Hail Mary

7   Jesus saith unto him, He that is washed needeth not save to wash his feet, but is clean every whit; and ye are clean, but not all.

Hail Mary

8   If I then, your Lord and Master, have washed your feet, ye also ought to wash one another's feet. For I have given you an example, that ye should do as I have done to you.

Hail Mary

9   Verily, verily, I say unto you, He that believeth on me, the works that I do shall he do also; and greater works than these shall he do, because I go unto my Father.

Hail Mary

10   And whatsoever ye shall ask in my name, that will I do, that the Father may be glorified in the Son. If ye shall ask any thing in my name, I will do it.

Hail Mary

Glory Be to the Father

Second Initiatic Mystery
The Vigil in the Garden

Jesus' I AM Lord's Prayer

1   These words spake Jesus and lifted up his eyes to heaven and said, Father, the hour is come; glorify thy Son, that thy Son also may glorify thee: I have glorified thee on the earth: I have finished the work which thou gavest me to do.

Hail Mary

2   And he came out and went, as he was wont, to the Mount of Olives; and his disciples also followed him. And when he was at the place, he said unto them, Pray that ye enter not into temptation.

Hail Mary

3   And he was withdrawn from them about a stone's cast, and kneeled down and prayed, saying, Father, if thou be willing, remove this cup from me: nevertheless not my will, but thine be done.

Hail Mary

4   And there appeared an angel unto him from heaven, strengthening him. And being in an agony he prayed more earnestly: and his sweat was as it were great drops of blood falling down to the ground.

Hail Mary

5   And he cometh unto the disciples and findeth them asleep and saith unto Peter, What, could ye not watch with me one hour? Watch and pray, that ye enter not into temptation: the spirit indeed is willing, but the flesh is weak.

Hail Mary

6   Then cometh he to his disciples and saith unto them, Behold, the hour is at hand, and the Son of man is betrayed into the hands of sinners. Rise, let us be going: behold, he is at hand that doth betray me.

Hail Mary

7   Jesus therefore, knowing all things that should come upon him, went forth and said unto them, Whom seek ye? They answered him, Jesus of Nazareth. Jesus saith unto them, I am he. And Judas also, which betrayed him, stood with them. As soon then as had said unto them, I am he, they went backward and fell to the ground.

Hail Mary

8   And one of them smote the servant of the high priest and cut off his right ear. And Jesus said, Suffer ye thus far. And he touched his ear and healed him.

Hail Mary

9   The cup which my Father hath given me, shall I not drink it? Thinkest thou that I cannot now pray to my Father, and he shall presently give me more than twelve legions of angels? But how then shall the scriptures be fulfilled that thus it must be?

Hail Mary

10   Then Jesus said unto the chief priests and captains of the temple and the elders which were come to him, Be ye come out, as against a thief, with swords and staves? When I was daily with you in the temple, ye stretched forth no hands against me: but this is your hour and the power of darkness.

Hail Mary

Glory Be to the Father

Third Initiatic Mystery
The Trial

Jesus' I AM Lord's Prayer

1   When the morning was come, all the chief priests and elders of the people took counsel against Jesus to put him to death:

And when they had bound him, they led him away and delivered him to Pontius Pilate the governor.

Hail Mary

2   Then Pilate entered into the judgment hall and called Jesus and said unto him, Art thou the King of the Jews?

Hail Mary

3   Jesus answered, My kingdom is not of this world. Pilate therefore said unto him, Art thou a king then?

Hail Mary

4   Jesus answered, Thou sayest that I am a king. To this end was I born and for this cause came I into the world, that I should bear witness unto the truth.

Hail Mary

5   Every one that is of the truth heareth my voice. Pilate saith unto him, What is truth?

Hail Mary

6   When Pilate saw that he could prevail nothing, but that rather a tumult was made, he took water and washed his hands before the multitude, saying, I am innocent of the blood of this just person: see ye to it.

Hail Mary

7   Then answered all the people and said, His blood be on us and on our children.

Hail Mary

8   Then released he Barabbas unto them: and when he had scourged Jesus, he delivered him to be crucified.

Hail Mary

9   And the soldiers platted a crown of thorns and put it on his head, and they put on him a purple robe and said, Hail, King of the Jews! and they smote him with their hands.

Hail Mary

10   Pilate therefore went forth again and saith unto them, Behold, I bring him forth to you that ye may know that I find no fault in him. Then came Jesus forth, wearing the crown of thorns and the purple robe. And Pilate saith unto them, Behold the man!

Hail Mary

Glory Be to the Father

Fourth Initiatic Mystery
The Carrying of the Cross

Jesus' I AM Lord's Prayer

1   And he said to them all, If any man will come after me, let him deny himself and take up his cross daily and follow me. For whosoever will save his life shall lose it; but whosoever will lose his life for my sake, the same shall save it.

Hail Mary

2   Come unto me, all ye that labour and are heavy laden, and I will give you rest. Take my yoke upon you and learn of me; for I am meek and lowly in heart: and ye shall find rest unto your souls. For my yoke is easy, and my burden is light.

Hail Mary

3   And he bearing his cross went forth into a place called the place of a skull, which is called in the Hebrew Golgotha: and Pilate wrote a title and put it on the cross. And the writing was JESUS OF NAZARETH THE KING OF THE JEWS.

Hail Mary

4   And as they led him away, they laid hold upon one Simon, a Cyrenian, coming out of the country; and on him they laid the cross, that he might bear it after Jesus.

Hail Mary

5   And there followed him a great company of people and of women, which also bewailed and lamented him. But Jesus turning unto them said, Daughters of Jerusalem, weep not for me, but weep for yourselves and for your children.

Hail Mary

6   For if they do these things in a green tree, what shall be done in the dry?

Hail Mary

7   Remember the word that I said unto you, The servant is not greater than his lord. If they have persecuted me, they will also persecute you; yea, the time cometh that whosoever killeth you will think that he doeth God service.

Hail Mary

8   And ye now therefore have sorrow: but I will see you again and your heart shall rejoice, and your joy no man taketh from you.

Hail Mary

9   Whatsoever ye shall ask the Father in my name, He will give it you. Hitherto have ye asked nothing in my name: ask, and ye shall receive, that your joy may be full.

Hail Mary

10   These things I have spoken unto you, that in me ye might have peace. In the world ye shall have tribulation: but be of good cheer; I have overcome the world.

Hail Mary

Glory Be to the Father

Fifth Initiatic Mystery
The Crucifixion

Jesus' I AM Lord's Prayer

1   Verily, verily, I say unto you, Except a corn of wheat fall into the ground and die, it abideth alone: but if it die, it bringeth forth much fruit.

Hail Mary

2   He that loveth his life shall lose it; and he that hateth his life in this world shall keep it unto life eternal.

Hail Mary

3   And when they were come to the place which is called Calvary, there they crucified him and the malefactors, one on the right hand and the other on the left. Then said Jesus, Father, forgive them; for they know not what they do.

Hail Mary

4   And one of the malefactors said unto Jesus, Lord, remember me when thou comest into thy kingdom. And Jesus said unto him, Verily I say unto thee, To day shalt thou be with me in paradise.

Hail Mary

5 When Jesus therefore saw his mother and the disciple standing by whom he loved, he saith unto his mother, Woman, behold thy son! Then saith he to the disciple, Behold thy mother! And from that hour that disciple took her unto his own home.

Hail Mary

6 And when the sixth hour was come, there was darkness over the whole land until the ninth hour. And at the ninth hour Jesus cried with a loud voice, saying, Eloi, Eloi, lama sabachthani? which is, being interpreted, My God, my God, why hast thou forsaken me?

Hail Mary

7 And when Jesus had cried with a loud voice, he said, Father, into thy hands I commend my spirit: and having said thus, he gave up the ghost.

Hail Mary

8 And the veil of the temple was rent in twain from the top to the bottom.

Hail Mary

9 And when the centurion which stood over against him saw that he so cried out and gave up the ghost, he said, Truly this man was the Son of God.

Hail Mary

10 Now is the judgment of this world: now shall the prince of this world be cast out. And I, if I be lifted up from the earth, will draw all men unto me.

Hail Mary

Glory Be to the Father

It Is Finished!

VII

Sign of the Cross

The Glorious Mysteries
Friday - The Fourth Ray

Keeper's Daily Prayer
Jesus' I AM Lord's Prayer
Three Hail Marys
Call to the Fire Breath
Transfiguring Affirmations of Jesus

First Glorious Mystery
The Resurrection

Jesus' I AM Lord's Prayer

1   In the end of the sabbath, as it began to dawn toward the first day of the week, came Mary Magdalene and the other Mary to see the sepulchre.

Hail Mary

2   And behold, there was a great earthquake: for the angel of the Lord descended from heaven and came and rolled back the stone from the door and sat upon it.

Hail Mary

3   His countenance was like lightning, and his raiment white as snow: and for fear of him the keepers did shake and became as dead men.

Hail Mary

4   And the angel answered and said unto the women, Fear not ye: for I know that ye seek Jesus, which was crucified. He is not here: for he is risen, as he said. Come, see the place where the Lord lay.

Hail Mary

5   And go quickly, and tell his disciples that he is risen from the dead; and behold, he goeth before you into Galilee; there shall ye see him: lo, I have told you. And they departed quickly from the sepulchre with fear and great joy and did run to bring his disciples word.

Hail Mary

6   And as they went to tell his disciples, behold, Jesus met them, saying, All hail. And they came and held him by the feet and worshipped him. Then said Jesus unto them, Be not afraid: go tell my brethren that they go into Galilee, and there shall they see me.

Hail Mary

7   Then the same day at evening, being the first day of the week, when the doors were shut where the disciples were assembled for fear of the Jews, came Jesus and stood in the midst and saith unto them, Peace be unto you.

Hail Mary

8   And when he had so said, he shewed unto them his hands and his side. Then were the disciples glad when they saw the Lord. Then said Jesus to them again, Peace be unto you: as my Father hath sent me, even so send I you.

Hail Mary

9   And when he had said this, he breathed on them and saith unto them, Receive ye the Holy Ghost.

Hail Mary

10   Whose soever sins ye remit, they are remitted unto them; and whose soever sins ye retain, they are retained.

Hail Mary

Glory Be to the Father

Second Glorious Mystery
The Ascension

Jesus' I AM Lord's Prayer

1   Thus it is written, and thus it behoved Christ to suffer and to rise from the dead the third day and that repentance and remission of sins should be preached in His name among all nations, beginning at Jerusalem.

Hail Mary

2   And ye are witnesses of these things. And behold, I send the promise of my Father upon you: but tarry ye in the city of Jerusalem until ye be endued with power from on high.

Hail Mary

3   All power is given unto me in heaven and in earth.

Hail Mary

4   Go ye therefore and teach all nations, baptizing them in the name of the Father and of the Son and of the Holy Ghost: teaching them to observe all things whatsoever I have commanded you:

Hail Mary

5   And lo, I AM with you alway, even unto the end of the age.

Hail Mary

6   But ye shall receive power after that the Holy Ghost is come upon you: and ye shall be witnesses unto me both in Jerusalem and in all Judaea and in Samaria and unto the uttermost part of the earth.

Hail Mary

7   And when he had spoken these things, while they beheld, he was taken up; and a cloud received him out of their sight.

Hail Mary

8   And while they looked stedfastly toward heaven as he went up, behold, two men stood by them in white apparel;

The Glorious Mysteries

Hail Mary

9   Which also said, Ye men of Galilee, why stand ye gazing up into heaven? this same Jesus, which is taken up from you into heaven, shall so come in like manner as ye have seen him go into heaven.

Hail Mary

10   And they went forth and preached every where, the Lord working with them and confirming the word with signs following.

Hail Mary

Glory Be to the Father

Third Glorious Mystery
The Descent of the Holy Spirit

Jesus' I AM Lord's Prayer

1   And when the day of Pentecost was fully come, they were all with one accord in one place.

Hail Mary

2   And suddenly there came a sound from heaven as of a rushing mighty wind, and it filled all the house where they were sitting.

Hail Mary

3   And there appeared unto them cloven tongues like as of fire, and it sat upon each of them.

Hail Mary

4   And they were all filled with the Holy Ghost and began to speak with other tongues as the Spirit gave them utterance.

Hail Mary

5   Now when this was noised abroad, the multitude came together and were confounded, because that every man heard them speak in his own language. And they were all amazed and marvelled, saying one to another, Behold, are not all these which speak Galileans?

Hail Mary

6   But Peter, standing up with the eleven, lifted up his voice and said unto them, Ye men of Judaea and all ye that dwell at Jerusalem, be this known unto you. This is that which was spoken by the prophet Joel:

Hail Mary

7   And it shall come to pass in the last days, saith God, I will pour out of my Spirit upon all flesh: and your sons and your daughters shall prophesy, and your young men shall see visions, and your old men shall dream dreams:

Hail Mary

8   And on my servants and on my handmaidens I will pour out in those days of my Spirit; and they shall prophesy: and it shall come to pass that whosoever shall call on the name of the Lord shall be saved.

Hail Mary

9   Then Peter said unto them, Repent and be baptized every one of you in the name of Jesus Christ for the remission of sins, and ye shall receive the gift of the Holy Ghost. For the promise is unto you and to your children and to all that are afar off, even as many as the Lord our God shall call.

Hail Mary

10   Then they that gladly received his word were baptized: and the same day there were added unto them about three thousand souls.

Hail Mary

Glory Be to the Father

Fourth Glorious Mystery
The Glory of the Woman and the Man Child

Jesus' I AM Lord's Prayer

1   And there appeared a great wonder in heaven; a woman clothed with the sun, and the moon under her feet, and upon her head a crown of twelve stars.

Hail Mary

2   And she being with child cried, travailing in birth, and pained to be delivered.

Hail Mary

3   And there appeared another wonder in heaven; and behold a great red dragon having seven heads and ten horns and seven crowns upon his heads.

Hail Mary

4   And his tail drew the third part of the stars of heaven and did cast them to the earth: and the dragon stood before the woman which was ready to be delivered, for to devour her child as soon as it was born.

Hail Mary

5   And she brought forth a man child, who was to rule all nations with a rod of iron: and her child was caught up unto God and to his throne.

Hail Mary

6   And the woman fled into the wilderness, where she hath a place prepared of God, that they should feed her there a thousand two hundred and threescore days.

Hail Mary

7   And there was war in heaven: Michael and his angels fought against the dragon; and the dragon fought and his angels, and prevailed not; neither was their place found any more in heaven.

Hail Mary

8   And the great dragon was cast out, that old serpent, called the Devil, and Satan, which deceiveth the whole world: he was cast out into the earth, and his angels were cast out with him.

Hail Mary

9   And I heard a loud voice saying in heaven, Now is come salvation and strength and the kingdom of our God and the power of his Christ: for the accuser of our brethren is cast down, which accused them before our God day and night.

Hail Mary

10   And they overcame him by the blood of the Lamb and by the word of their testimony; and they loved not their lives unto the death.

Hail Mary

Glory Be to the Father

Fifth Glorious Mystery
The Triumph of the Divine Mother

Jesus' I AM Lord's Prayer

1   Therefore rejoice, ye heavens and ye that dwell in them. Woe to the inhabiters of the earth and of the sea! for the devil is come down unto you, having great wrath, because he knoweth that he hath but a short time.

Hail Mary

2   And when the dragon saw that he was cast unto the earth, he persecuted the woman which brought forth the man child.

Hail Mary

3   And to the woman were given two wings of a great eagle, that she might fly into the wilderness, into her place, where she

The Glorious Mysteries

is nourished for a time and times and half a time from the face of the serpent.

Hail Mary

4   And the serpent cast out of his mouth water as a flood after the woman, that he might cause her to be carried away of the flood. And the earth helped the woman, and the earth opened her mouth and swallowed up the flood which the dragon cast out of his mouth.

Hail Mary

5   And the dragon was wroth with the woman and went to make war with the remnant of her seed, which keep the commandments of God and have the testimony of Jesus Christ.

Hail Mary

6   And I saw a new heaven and a new earth: for the first heaven and the first earth were passed away; and there was no more sea. And I John saw the holy city, New Jerusalem, coming down from God out of heaven, prepared as a bride adorned for her husband.

Hail Mary

7   And I heard a great voice out of heaven saying, Behold, the tabernacle of God is with men, and he will dwell with them, and they shall be his people, and God himself shall be with them and be their God.

Hail Mary

8   And God shall wipe away all tears from their eyes; and there shall be no more death, neither sorrow nor crying, neither shall there be any more pain: for the former things are passed away.

Hail Mary

9   And he said unto me, It is done. I am Alpha and Omega, the beginning and the end. He that overcometh shall inherit all things; and I will be his God, and he shall be my Son.

Hail Mary

10   And the Spirit and the bride say, Come. And let him that heareth say, Come. And let him that is athirst come. And whosoever will, let him take the water of life freely.

Hail Mary

Glory Be to the Father

It Is Finished!

VIII

Sign of the Cross

The Miracle Mysteries
Saturday - The Seventh Ray

Keeper's Daily Prayer
Jesus' I AM Lord's Prayer
Three Hail Marys
Call to the Fire Breath
Transfiguring Affirmations of Jesus

First Miracle Mystery
The Marriage at Cana

Jesus' I AM Lord's Prayer

1   And the third day there was a marriage in Cana of Galilee; and the mother of Jesus was there: and both Jesus was called, and his disciples, to the marriage.

Hail Mary

2   And when they wanted wine, the mother of Jesus saith unto him, They have no wine.

Hail Mary

3   Jesus saith unto her, Woman, what have I to do with thee? mine hour is not yet come.

Hail Mary

4   His mother saith unto the servants, Whatsoever he saith unto you, do it.

Hail Mary

5   And there were set there six waterpots of stone, after the manner of the purifying of the Jews, containing two or three firkins apiece.

Hail Mary

6   Jesus saith unto them, Fill the waterpots with water. And they filled them to the brim.

Hail Mary

7   And he saith unto them, Draw out now and bear unto the governor of the feast. And they bare it.

Hail Mary

8   When the ruler of the feast had tasted the water that was made wine and knew not whence it was (but the servants which drew the water knew), the governor of the feast called the bridegroom

Hail Mary

9   And saith unto him, Every man at the beginning doth set forth good wine; and when men have well drunk, then that which is worse: but thou hast kept the good wine until now.

Hail Mary

10   This beginning of miracles did Jesus in Cana of Galilee and manifested forth his glory; and his disciples believed on him.

Hail Mary

Glory Be to the Father

Second Miracle Mystery
Jesus Stills the Tempest and Heals the Gadarene Demoniac

Jesus' I AM Lord's Prayer

1   Now it came to pass on a certain day that he went into a ship with his disciples: and he said unto them, Let us go over unto the other side of the lake. And they launched forth. But as they

The Miracle Mysteries

sailed he fell asleep: and there came down a storm of wind on the lake, and they were filled with water and were in jeopardy.

Hail Mary

2 And they came to him and awoke him, saying, Master, master, we perish. Then he arose and rebuked the wind and the raging of the water: and they ceased, and there was a calm.

Hail Mary

3 And he said unto them, Where is your faith? And they being afraid wondered, saying one to another, What manner of man is this! for he commandeth even the winds and water, and they obey him.

Hail Mary

4 And they arrived at the country of the Gadarenes, which is over against Galilee. And when he went forth to land, there met him out of the city a certain man which had devils long time and ware no clothes, neither abode in any house, but in the tombs.

Hail Mary

5 When he saw Jesus, he cried out and fell down before him and with a loud voice said, What have I to do with thee, Jesus, thou Son of God most high? I beseech thee, torment me not.

Hail Mary

6 (For he had commanded the unclean spirit to come out of the man. For oftentimes it had caught him and he was kept bound with chains and in fetters; and he brake the bands and was driven of the devil into the wilderness.)

Hail Mary

7 And Jesus asked him, saying, What is thy name? And he said, Legion: because many devils were entered into him. And they besought him that he would not command them to go out into the deep.

Hail Mary

8   And there was there an herd of many swine feeding on the mountain: and they besought him that he would suffer them to enter into them. And he suffered them.

Hail Mary

9   Then went the devils out of the man and entered into the swine: and the herd ran violently down a steep place into the lake and were choked.

Hail Mary

10   When they that fed them saw what was done, they fled and went and told it in the city and in the country. Then they went out to see what was done and came to Jesus and found the man out of whom the devils were departed sitting at the feet of Jesus, clothed and in his right mind: and they were afraid.

Hail Mary

Glory Be to the Father

Third Miracle Mystery
The Feeding of the Five Thousand

Jesus' I AM Lord's Prayer

1   After these things Jesus went over the Sea of Galilee. And a great multitude followed him, because they saw his miracles which he did on them that were diseased.

Hail Mary

2   And Jesus went up into a mountain, and there he sat with his disciples. And the Passover, a feast of the Jews, was nigh.

Hail Mary

3   When Jesus then lifted up his eyes and saw a great company come unto him, he saith unto Philip, Whence shall we buy bread, that these may eat? And this he said to prove him: for he himself knew what he would do.

Hail Mary

4   Philip answered him, Two hundred pennyworth of bread is not sufficient for them, that every one of them may take a little.

Hail Mary

5   One of his disciples, Andrew, Simon Peter's brother, saith unto him, There is a lad here which hath five barley loaves and two small fishes: but what are they among so many?

Hail Mary

6   And Jesus said, Make them sit down by fifties in a company. Now there was much grass in the place. So the men sat down, in number about five thousand.

Hail Mary

7   And Jesus took the loaves; and when he had given thanks, he distributed to the disciples, and the disciples to them that were set down; and likewise of the fishes as much as they would.

Hail Mary

8   When they were filled, he said unto his disciples, Gather up the fragments that remain, that nothing be lost.

Hail Mary

9   Therefore they gathered them together and filled twelve baskets with the fragments of the five barley loaves which remained over and above unto them that had eaten.

Hail Mary

10   Then those men, when they had seen the miracle that Jesus did, said, This is of a truth that prophet that should come into the world.

Hail Mary

Glory Be to the Father

Fourth Miracle Mystery
Christ Forgives the Adulterous Woman

Jesus' I AM Lord's Prayer

1   And early in the morning he came again into the temple, and all the people came unto him; and he sat down and taught them.

Hail Mary

2   And the scribes and Pharisees brought unto him a woman taken in adultery.

Hail Mary

3   And when they had set her in the midst, they say unto him, Master, this woman was taken in adultery, in the very act.

Hail Mary

4   Now Moses in the law commanded us that such should be stoned: but what sayest thou?

Hail Mary

5   This they said tempting him, that they might have to accuse him. But Jesus stooped down and with his finger wrote on the ground, as though he heard them not.

Hail Mary

6   So when they continued asking him, he lifted up himself and said unto them, He that is without sin among you, let him first cast a stone at her.

Hail Mary

7   And again he stooped down and wrote on the ground.

Hail Mary

8   And they which heard it, being convicted by their own conscience, went out one by one, beginning at the eldest, even unto the last: and Jesus was left alone, and the woman standing in the midst.

Hail Mary

9   When Jesus had lifted up himself and saw none but the woman, he said unto her, Woman, where are those thine accusers? hath no man condemned thee?

Hail Mary

10   She said, No man, Lord. And Jesus said unto her, Neither do I condemn thee: go, and sin no more.

Hail Mary

Glory Be to the Father

Fifth Miracle Mystery
Christ the Bread of Life

Jesus' I AM Lord's Prayer

1   And Jesus said unto them, I am the bread of Life: he that cometh to me shall never hunger; and he that believeth on me shall never thirst.

Hail Mary

2   For I came down from heaven not to do mine own will, but the will of him that sent me. And this is the Father's will which hath sent me, that of all which he hath given me I should lose nothing, but should raise it up again at the last day.

Hail Mary

3   And this is the will of him that sent me, that every one which seeth the Son and believeth on him may have everlasting life: and I will raise him up at the last day. No man can come to me except the Father which hath sent me draw him: and I will raise him up at the last day.

Hail Mary

4 I am that bread of life. Your fathers did eat manna in the wilderness and are dead. This is the bread which cometh down from heaven that a man may eat thereof and not die.

Hail Mary

5 I AM the living bread which came down from heaven: if any man eat of this bread, he shall live for ever.

Hail Mary

6 And the bread that I will give is my flesh, which I will give for the life of the world.

Hail Mary

7 Verily, verily, I say unto you, Except ye eat the flesh of the Son of man and drink his blood, ye have no life in you.

Hail Mary

8 Whoso eateth my flesh and drinketh my blood hath eternal life; and I will raise him up at the last day.

Hail Mary

9 For my flesh is meat indeed and my blood is drink indeed. He that eateth my flesh and drinketh my blood dwelleth in me, and I in him.

Hail Mary

10 As the living Father hath sent me and I live by the Father, so he that eateth me, even he shall live by me.

Hail Mary

Glory Be to the Father

It Is Finished!

PART THREE

The Power Aspect of the Christ Flame

Fourteen Messages of the Word of Life
to the Children of the Mother

My soul doth magnify the Lord,
And my spirit hath rejoiced in God my Saviour.
For he hath regarded the low estate of his
*   handmaiden:*
For, behold, from henceforth
*   all generations shall call me blessed.*
For he that is mighty hath done to me great things;
*   and holy is his name.*
And his mercy is on them that fear him
*   from generation to generation.*
He hath shewed strength with his arm;
He hath scattered the proud
*   in the imagination of their hearts.*
He hath put down the mighty from their seats
*   and exalted them of low degree.*
He hath filled the hungry with good things;
*   and the rich he hath sent empty away.*
He hath holpen his servant Israel
*   in remembrance of his mercy;*
As he spake to our fathers,
*   to Abraham, and to his seed for ever.*   —Luke

Happy is the man that findeth wisdom and the man that getteth understanding. She is more precious than rubies: and all the things thou canst desire are not to be compared unto her. Length of days is in her right hand; and in her left hand riches and honour. —Proverbs

1

A Perpetual Vigil
Is the Requirement of the Hour

Out from the star fire of every man's being I come, bearing the flame of the World Mother, the flame that envelops planetary homes, galaxies, stars without number and worlds within worlds. I come bearing the chalice, and in the chalice a mighty flame—fire from the heart of the Almighty, from his altar. And the angels who accompany me, the mighty seraphim of light, have come afresh from his altar, where they sing, "Holy, holy, holy, Lord God, thou art holy!"[1] night and day with the joy of love for his flaming presence.

Now I dip into the chalice of fire and I take therefrom the fire of the heart of God, drenched with the rains of mercy, blazing the white-fire light of the Christ, and I pass it over the heads of this audience. Receive the fire from on high and be consecrated with the holy oil of consecration. For in this hour of great world need and travail, you must be clothed upon with the wedding garment,[2] the seamless garment[3] of the Christ, the armour[4] of the Lord and the fire of his consciousness, which is indeed thy armour, thy shield and thy exceeding great reward.[5]

I come, then, for the express purpose of charging you as representatives of the Cosmic Mother, of the Christ and of the Father Supreme to be in the world of form the representatives of the divine Trinity. The balance of the sacred fire within you, one and all, is the key to your divinity and the key to your service in the world of form.

Precious hearts, as I have spoken to you and written to you many times, the service of our final embodiment was not one where we were privileged at all times to dwell in the very Presence of God. We went through the necessary human confinements of the flesh, the human travail, in order that our testing might be complete and that the wonder of his glory might appear—that a great wonder in heaven might become flesh, that the Word might dwell among men.[6]

For you see, if we had been privileged or above all others, then our demonstration would not have been for all time and for all men. But it was, beloved ones, because we took on the forms that others wear, that you now wear, and we proved for all time that each individual can manifest the power of the Christ and of the World Mother and achieve his victory against all the onslaughts of the world.

For he who is centered in the flame of his divinity shall not be moved when the waves of mortal consciousness sweep across the sea and pound upon the forcefield of being and beat on the shores of human consciousness. What is the reason? It is because centered in the Christ consciousness and in the flame, the human is no more, the ego is dissolved and man finds his individuality in God—never lost but entirely merged within the flame. Thus the opposition of the world, the resistance of the carnal mind,[7] cannot touch that one.

But he who has withheld a portion of the self and hidden it beneath his garment and cloak will find that when the winds of God blow, that portion which has been set aside will be exposed, and man will go down because he will not have the immaculate wholeness of the perfection of the Deity.

Beloved ones, it is suicidal to reserve any part of consciousness for oneself. Is not your consciousness loaned to you from the Godhead? Can he not snuff it out at any given moment? Is he not the arbiter of the destiny of every cell of your being? Can a leopard change his spots?[8] Can a man by thought change his being?[9]

You are subject, then, unto the Deity who made you when

you give yourself unto him. But the vessel may be cast down and given to other sources, to an impure stream, and then it is also lost in that stream. But that stream is not the eternal fount, and it sweeps away the identity and all. And so you see, when you surrender to God, you know that you have eternal oneness, an eternal being in Christ. When you surrender to the flesh, you have nothing but a transitory moment of exaltation in the ego, and then there is nothing at all.

Beloved ones, the key to mastery, which was taught to us by the Great Hierophant at Luxor as we prepared for the final mission of our service—the key that he gave to us that so often meant so much in the hours of trial—was to impersonalize evil and the carnal mind, not only to impersonalize one's own frailties but also to impersonalize the invectives that are slung by others. If you can always see beyond the human to the Christ standing behind the mask, then you will never be fooled by the mask or cast down by it. And most of all, you will not react to the mask in yourself or in others.

How important this is! Mothers, teach it to your children. Fathers, speak it to your sons and daughters. Take them upon your knee and point to the world and the temptations within it. And explain to the precious little ones, even when they are small, that there is a mirage in the world that is not real. But beyond the veil and the mirage, there is reality, there is the true Christ in manifestation.

I have seen how little children are receptive to this truth, for they come recently from the etheric cities and temples of light where they have seen the beauties of creation. They are virtuous at heart. They are lovers of the Christ and of their divinity. And so they are flung to the lion's den at an early age by well-meaning parents who set them before the television sets and allow them to hear that music which will surely rend the garment of the soul and tear away all contact with divinity by the beat that causes a negative spiral to take them right down into the dregs of mortality.

O beloved ones, there is great wisdom in children. Withhold not the truth from them. Explain the Law to them in simple words, for they have great understanding. Those little ones who are coming into the world at this time especially have had exclusive training in our temples, for we have seen the need for an armour of light[10] to be placed around them when they come into such a place of discord as this world presently is. For we knew that their souls would not survive in the world and carry the light from the altars of God.

And so at the request of Lord Gautama Buddha, the Lord of the World, a program has been initiated for the incoming souls whereby they have learned on the inner a special means of insulating the consciousness, by the flame of purity and of protection, from all of the discord of the world. And you will see that these precious ones will have that filament of light around them whereby they will not take on the ways of the world, whereby it will be shed from them by the power of the Holy Spirit until the day when they receive the outer consciousness of the Law through the flame of the resurrection and they can tie into the God within until the age of reason when they can choose the godly way on their own.

I ask you, beloved ones, as I have asked you many times before, to pray for the little ones. For up to the age of seven, there is the great opportunity of sealing them in the fires of the Christ. Whatever is impressed upon the clay of consciousness during the period of formation and the first seven years is most important. Therefore, the protection of the angelic hosts can be invoked by you. And there are enough here in this room that if you would invoke daily the protection of the children of the world, that is all we need to step in with our angels to answer the calls. For you have the authority for this world, and until you ask we cannot come forth to do the bidding of the Father.

Therefore, will you pray for these little ones that they might be sealed in the immaculate concept, the design of the heart of God, and for their plan to be fulfilled in their lives? Will you call for the sealing action of the Sacred Heart of the World Mother around these blessed ones? Will you see them enveloped in purity?

So will a great service be rendered, for there are many souls coming into embodiment who are destined to be Christs unto all mankind, avatars of great light. They come with a mission and a high calling, and they must be protected, beloved ones. For in the past when we have sent forth such souls, many have been lost. Many have come to the age of majority and they have not known who they were, why they were here. And some have committed suicide because they could not stand to be in the consciousness of the world.

Precious ones, who knows but a mother's heart how difficult it is to adjust to this world when you have come from the octaves of light? To see the world in a condition of decay when you know how it should be, when you have seen the worlds of God that he designed at inner levels, when you have been shown the purpose and the plan and a latent memory rings true to come forth, is it not altogether understandable that these young hearts are caught up in the spirit of revolution that is led by the Antichrist, the laggards and the Luciferians to overthrow all that they see because it does not agree with the inner concept which they know to be true?

O beloved ones, there is a mainstream, a great tide, a great wave of energy that carries the souls of men down the path of mediocrity. And those who are not anchored to the divinity at an early age are swept away by this tide. Therefore, pray for the hearts of the youth of the world. Pray for people of all ages. For we see that even those in later years are also being swept by the concepts of the new morality, of the inverted sensitivity training and the evils of society that are a direct onslaught against the World

A Perpetual Vigil Is the Requirement of the Hour 233

Mother, against the image of purity of the All-Seeing Eye of God, of singleness of purpose and vision.

Above all, beloved ones, I admonish you: Do not withdraw from the world. Do not cut yourselves off from what is going on. For if you do, you will be like those on Atlantis who refused to see the decadence of the age, who remained in the retreats. And so Atlantis fell, and when the sinking came, the high priests who ignored the troubles of the time were also engulfed by the great wave.

Precious hearts, pray daily for world conditions, for an alleviation of world pain, for war to cease, and especially for the exposure of the manipulators who cause the wars in order to swallow up the sons of God in a great factory of death. It is a death factory, I say! And the astral entities desire the blood of the youth. Do you know why, precious hearts? Because in the blood is the atom, and in the heart of the atom is the Christ. And the astral entities must live off the blood of the youth because they have lost their contact with God. And therefore they create wars simply to perpetuate their own existence.

O precious hearts, a perpetual vigil is the requirement of the hour. I ask you to keep it with me on behalf of our young men, for the plot is now abroad to draw them into another war in the Middle East. And as the Karmic Lords have told you, if this war is allowed to continue, it could mean the greatest catastrophe to the planetary body that has ever been seen upon this earth.

I tell you, precious ones, you ought to be upon your knees daily for the angels of peace and the angels of victory to stay the hand of darkness that is about to break in the Middle East crisis. I tell you that those who are warring with one another there have been warring for centuries and centuries. Before they ever arrived upon this planet, they were warring one with the other. And I ask you, in the name of Almighty God, should the sons of God and the holy Christ children be drawn into their squabbles, into their battles, and lose their lives because they have not been able to settle their difficulties for aeons of time?

There are Christs and sons of God behind the iron curtain, in China and in Russia. Should these be pitted against the Christs who are born in America—all who have come forth from the same Father-Mother God, from the same temples of light, who have pledged themselves to the bringing-in of a great golden age of peace throughout this planetary home? I say, beloved ones, let the fervor of the World Mother rise up within you and let your determination be fed this night by the fire from the heart of God!

Determine, then, in the name of your own God Presence, that that war shall not come to pass! Determine it by action and by fervent prayer! I say it is important that you write to your congressmen, to your senators, to the president, to your state representatives and legislators that you do not approve of America or any other country being drawn into that war. It is antichrist, beloved ones. And I tell you that it is the greatest single threat to the Christ upon this planet today.

The Lords of Karma and your beloved Saint Germain expect a fiery resistance from those who are privileged to attend this conference and from all children of the light upon this planetary home. I say in the name of El Morya, it is time that the debacle of war be broken, that the beast of war be broken, that war shall be no longer upon this planet!

How long, O Lord, will mankind sit idly by and permit their sons to be taken as sheep to the slaughter? Will you permit it? I say no! You shall not permit it, because the Christ in you leaps forth in the center of your being to declare the victory and the peace of the Almighty. I trust, then, that you will go forth in the days ahead and not neglect to offer your prayer and not neglect to arouse individuals whom you know who can be trusted with this information to the seriousness of the hour.

The choice is the great golden age or a dark age such as the world has not known. For that war, becoming planetary in nature, could put this home back to the age of darkness where no man should know his divinity or the Christ, where the teachings would be entirely lost. This is the moment in the hourglass, beloved ones. This is the crucial moment in time where time can become eternity or where time can become no longer.

I come, then, this night bearing the fire from the heart of God. I remind you of the warnings which have been given through the visions at Lourdes and Fátima. I remind you that the pope has been given this information by cosmic dispensation. The need now is that all mankind should rise up, for I say that the Catholic Church has not fulfilled the promise of the Lord or his direction. It has not acted as a vanguard, as a protector of the Christ consciousness in these latter days.[11] It has compromised in great measure with the forces of darkness. But there are many great souls within the Church who are keeping the flame blazing.

I ask you, then, to unite with the body of the Lord upon this planetary home and to determine that no level of officialdom, either in religion or in government, shall stay the hand of the Almighty or of his plan for this age. Will you realize, beloved ones, that the earth is the Lord's and the fullness thereof,[12] that no representative, no one in any position of authority, has any more authority than you do? For one with God is the majority. And it is the children of light, the sons and daughters of God, who were sent by the Lords of Karma, by Sanat Kumara, the Ancient of Days, to rule the earth. And simply because the children of darkness and the fallen angels have usurped those positions of power, there is no reason why the children of light should feel that all is lost.

Beloved ones, they have no power! The names of those who are the rulers of the earth are written in heaven. The fact that they do not occupy public office or have not been elected or appointed by the councils of men does not mean that they are without that authority. For the rulers of this world are one thing, but the rulers of God are another. The divine right of kings, the authority of the sons and daughters, the authority of those who have self-mastery in the Christ consciousness—this is the authority that rules the earth! And therefore I say to you that your authority is given to you by God. It comes from on high. And there are more in this room this night appointed to office by the Almighty than there are in the legislature of this state.

And so, behold, I declare unto you that you are kings and priests unto God.[13] And you may decree, by the authority of your I AM Presence, by the authority of the Christ and the office which you hold, for a change in world conditions, for a change to all human nonsense and a complete reversing of the tide. It can be done, I say! It is not too late! From a mother's heart, then, I plead with you. Realize that the hours are short but that you have the time locked in eternity to accomplish your mission.

Rise, then, as sons and daughters of the flame [audience rises] and be anointed of the World Mother. I come in her name, in the Spirit of Omega. And I bring forth the OM—E—GA [chant]. From the heart of the sun, receive, then, the fire within your heart. Let it *expand*! Let it *expand*! Let it *expand* and take dominion over the earth![14] Take dominion over the earth! Take dominion over the earth! *E pluribus unum.*

Mary

Santa Barbara, California
October 9, 1970

She is a tree of life to them that lay hold upon her: and happy is every one that retaineth her. The LORD by wisdom hath founded the earth; by understanding hath he established the heavens. By his knowledge the depths are broken up, and the clouds drop down the dew.
—Proverbs

2

A Cup of Freedom in His Name

Every manchild that is born of God is sealed with the flame of the Christ, the holy Christ Child, whom I salute in each one of you this day. And I speak to the babe in arms and I say, expand thy light and let it encircle the globe! Let the child of thy divinity come forth! Let the threefold flame be expanded within you! Receive the impetus of thy mission this day, and respond to the call of old "Go forth, my son, to do my will!" And hear the answer of the Christ, "Yea, Father, I AM come to do thy will!" The perfect circle of Father and Son and Holy Spirit—Holy Mother of Fire—this Trinity is the key to your divinity from whence you were born.

As a representative of the World Mother, I come to you this day to remind you of the great world need. The drum of the noise of the world often becomes a din, a roar so loud that soon you seem to ignore it. You become accustomed to the jangle and the discord. You become accustomed to the encroachments upon your freedom. You become accustomed to the half-light that obscures the night of illumination.

I say, be not content with mediocrity! Be not content with compromise! Be not content with the restrictions that the manipulators have imposed upon you, beloved ones. Assert your God-dominion, the authority of your divine perfection, and go forth and accept nothing less! Claim your divinity! For I tell you, the world will not claim it for you, and the ascended masters are forbidden by law to claim it for you. Therefore you are the only one who can claim your divinity, and you have a responsibility on behalf of all life to do so.

I remember, during the days when Jesus was a little boy and he played among the children in the town where we lived, he would come home sorrowful to me and tell me about the coarseness of the children and how they were selfish and did not think of their heavenly Father. At times they were jealous of his light, for even then his light was a rebuke unto their darkness. And so I counseled him to understand that their attacks and their cruelties were never against the person but against the light. Then he understood and was not hurt or offended by those little ones. But he learned at an early age to recognize the Christ within men and yet never to be deceived by the carnal mind,[15] the outer consciousness with all of its frauds and deceits.

This is the training that is necessary for the children of the light. Won't you remember to train your own consciousness in this understanding that the powers of darkness and of Antichrist ever attack the light that is within you and that the light that is within you is adequate to reverse all opposition to its glorious fulfillment. You need never be concerned, then, if people do not like or appreciate your ways or your devotion. If on the instant they are offended by the mission that scintillates in your aura, you may understand by their antagonism that you are indeed a pillar of fire in the world and that the world is sometimes singed by that fire that you bear. Be not dismayed, then, but go forward in your appointed way. Go forward in the calling, and do not allow your consciousness to be scarred by these unfortunate contacts with the world.

As I gaze upon the children in this age, some of the same ones who played with Jesus are now in embodiment again. And the holy Christ children who have come forth and who dwell among them to be the future leaders of mankind must often come to grips with these unfortunate situations. Sometimes it tears their very hearts that they are left out of the group, of playtime, of parties and activities, and they do not understand what is wrong with them. But I say, the wrong is entirely in those who reject the light and the Christ. So has it been for thousands of years. Therefore, be comforted in the love of the World Mother, in the Holy Spirit and in the knowledge that many have gone before you to hold the torch of the light. And now the torch is passed to a new generation who must carry it nobly and well lest freedom perish from the earth.

In the name of freedom, then, and in the name of the freedom which was brought by my Son, let us hold the banner high and the torch firmly, and let us extend to all a cup of freedom in his name. The fires of freedom that are descending now to the planet earth are a whirlwind action of the sacred fire of the Holy Ghost as on the day of Pentecost.[16] For this freedomtide, the masters of light and of cosmos and the Lords of Karma have been given the authority from the Most High to authorize a dispensation of light and of freedom to the earth that the world has never known. Indeed it is required in this hour, for they have built a monolith of power so high that it seems that it ought to crumble of its own weight, and yet it has not crumbled.

Therefore, retain vigilance. Be wise. Be on guard. Be on guard, beloved ones. For at the time of the toppling of that great Babylon,[17] that city, you will see a great stirring in the elemental kingdom. You will even see forces of cataclysm as mankind have to adjust to the incoming currents of freedom—as they are forced, almost suddenly, to break the old matrices, to tear down the walls of partition that separate them from the Holy of holies. And when those walls are broken down, they will have no protection against the great heat and fire of the sun of their own being. And some will fall and faint, and there will be weeping and gnashing of teeth.[18]

Nevertheless, fear not, beloved ones, for the goal of life is the ascending spiral. To that end came forth the Christs of old. And if by cataclysm, if by no other means, mankind will be catapulted into the ascending spirals, then is not cataclysm a blessing? A blessing is an experience by which we ascend. Therefore sometimes sorrow and pain are a blessing. For the goal of the light of the soul is to rise, and that purpose must ever be served and the Brotherhood is ever mindful of it.

We do not look to spare suffering where that suffering can bring forth joy as a blossom, as a rose which comes forth from the marshes of life. You yourselves must not see life and its goal as merely pleasure and happiness from day to day. But you must see that service, the doing of the will of God, the pursuing of the high calling, is the goal. And if it requires sacrifice, if it requires some pain in order that the end might be forthcoming, then so be it. What is that to thee?[19]

It is not God who sacrifices, but it is the ego which must be sacrificed. Let us lay it upon the altar this day. I ask you, in the name of the Holy Mother, to lay upon the altar your sacrifice, some pleasure or pain that you desire to give up in order to be free—something of the world, some attachment, or it might be a detachment. For all must come to the center, the Middle Way, and draw in the fragrances of Being, the energies of perfection, to the central theme and calling of the resurrection spiral.

I was there when he rose. I saw the inner momentum of light expand from within the tomb. I saw the initiation passed. I breathed a sigh of relief. I knew that my Redeemer lived. And as he lived, so too should all men live, for what one can do all can do. This is the great victory of one life—that all can go and do likewise. This is the victory of one nation dedicated to freedom. And so this nation was selected by God to be the representative of freedom, to show mankind the way on a national level even as Jesus showed the way on an individual level.

Let men, then, not seek to tear down that which has been built by God, but let them transmute all that has set itself in opposition to the Father and to his noble purposes here. Let them judge according to the plumb line of truth, according to the knowledge of cosmic law. Let them expose, then, the manipulators, the spoilers, the deceivers, the Antichrist in their midst.

And let us get on with freedom. Let us get on with the banner. Let us get on with the march. For the hosts of light are coming. They are coming in grand array. And they will not stop or wait for a nation that is not ready. They will continue to march. And they sing the anthem of the free. They sing the anthem of victory.

They come bearing swords of flame, banners of triumph, instruments of glory. You hear the trumpets. You hear the calling. You hear the declaration of peace. And you know that in a very short time, mankind will have to make the decision between freedom or a long night of chaos. For the hosts of light will continue to march. And those who do not follow the upward spiral, the cycle which they bring, must be left upon the shores of life to go into a downward cycle of darkness like prehistoric times. The choice is in the individual. The choice is in many individuals united as one—one body of free men dedicated to the preservation of the noble ideal of the Christ, the child in arm, in every heart.

I say, come forth! Come forth, the Divine Manchild, and overshadow the outer consciousness! Come forth and break the bonds, and let mankind be free! Let them be free by the power of that flame within—indomitable, invincible, victorious now and forever! So it is written in heaven; so let it be written upon earth! So write it, beloved ones. You are the writers in this age. Write it with the sword of truth, with a pen of fire, with the power of the spoken Word. Let it be written, and let it be penned in faith, in hope and in charity! Let it be written so that all the world might see. Let it be inscribed upon akasha* that all men are free in

---

*A substance and dimension upon which the recordings of all that has taken place in an individual's world are "written" by recording angels. Akashic records can be read by those whose spiritual faculties are developed.

Christ, in God. And there is no other purpose, no other reality except that which men may choose by the darkness which they also choose.

Out of the light and down the centuries I have come nurturing the Christ in you all. I remain ever watchful, a guardian of the flame. And I ask you to take up that high calling so that it might be written in the pages of history: "These are they who loved not their lives unto the death. These are they who overcame by the blood of the Lamb,[20] by the essence of the sacred fire." So shall the earth be free. So shall the earth ascend even as free men pledge their lives, their fortunes and their sacred honor[21] unflinchingly with devotion and high courage. For this indeed is the need of the hour.

Men, women and children of the Spirit, I say, arise and accept the high calling as sons and daughters of God. I anoint you this day with the balm of Gilead[22] from my heart flame. It shall ever be a comfort to you in this battle as you recognize that carrying the banner at the head of all the legions of light is the World Mother, who comes to claim her children, who comes to take her children home. She moves forward. And none can stay her hand. So come the legions of light. So join in the glorious array.

In the name of the World Mother, I AM Mary in the service of your light.

Mary

Colorado Springs, Colorado
July 2, 1970

Get wisdom, get understanding: forget it not; neither decline from the words of my mouth. Forsake her not, and she shall preserve thee: love her, and she shall keep thee. Wisdom is the principal thing; therefore get wisdom: and with all thy getting get understanding. —Proverbs

3

The Chalice of My Heart

In the heart of the lily is the resurrection flame, and in the heart of the flame is the Christ risen and ascended. He is not here: He is risen[23] into the domain of consciousness that is in the center of the God flame. What rejoicing that one son of God is raised into the stature of immortality! What rejoicing when a million sons and daughters of God are raised into their own immortal identity!

We set the pattern of victory, we set the pattern of purity on behalf of evolutions whose time has come, and nothing can stop an idea whose time has come. Ye are all ideations of the one God flame sent forth, and now it is time to rise into the maturation of your own God flame. Let us invoke, then, the resurrection flame from the base of the pyramid and in the center thereof. And let it swirl around the body holy, the temple foursquare of man and of God in man. Let its pulsations now curl through the four angles, the right angles, and the sides of the tabernacle of being. And let the wedding garment[24] be placed upon these ones, precious heart flames from the center of the lily.

And so, my angels, place upon them the cape of immortality, and let them feel what it is to know that one is well clothed in the wedding garment. And let them wear these capes throughout this dictation, and let them know that they might go forth to weave their own wedding garment, the seamless garment[25] of the living Christ. Know ye not that ye are naked? I counsel, then, that ye come forth this day and be clothed with the fine raiment and gold of the Holy Spirit.[26]

Let us put off the old man with his deeds![27] Let him go down.

Let the ego go down. Let the human consciousness go down that the Christ may arise. Into the arms of the All-Father comes the Son of God prepared, purified, whole. Draw nigh unto me and I will draw nigh unto you.[28] The triangle of the lower self merges with the triangle of the Higher Self and a star is born—the star of your own victory and of the immortality of the divine design within you.

I am Mary. You call me Mother, and some have called me the Mother of God. You are all mothers and fathers of God, of the God flame aborning within you. And it is not sacrilege to so deem yourselves; for God must be born in man, God must be nurtured in man. And it is the flame of the Father-Mother that draws forth and expands and magnifies and intensifies that flame until a God is born, until a Christ is become one with all life.

O Holy Spirit of the Most High God, descend as upon the day of Pentecost,[29] and let the whirlwind action of the sacred fire be established upon this altar, in this room. And let the mighty surging power of the wind of the Holy Spirit draw all that impedes the flow of the light from these blessed hearts! Let a whirlwind action now occur! I call to the mighty seraphim and the angels of my band: Angels of the Holy Spirit, let the dove of peace be upon their shoulders, and let the perfect power of the peace of the whirlwind be known by these hearts this day!

O Most High God, O beloved Alpha and Omega, I plead on behalf of a wayward generation! Almighty One, descend this day into the chalice of my heart, which I place above this focus. And I call for the cup of crystal fire mist in the heart of the City Foursquare to be poured into the cup of my consciousness that I have held these many years on behalf of the Christ aborning in the precious children of God upon Terra. Let it pour now, O Alpha and Omega! Let the contents, then, be lowered into this octave.

And now I say: Angels of my band, place a miniature replica of my cup around the hearts of those gathered here so that they might also contain that elixir that cometh down from the Father of lights, in whom there is no shadow of turning.[30] So let the sword keep the way of the tree of life[31] within them. Let the Almighty appear within the heart flames, and let that essence circulate through their four lower bodies until the cosmic cube is established. Let it also go forth as that cup of cold water[32] extended to hungry hearts in time of need. And so I, Mary, have invoked the cup that I might give unto you that cup, that you might give that cup unto each precious one that comes and knocks at the door of your heart flame.

Roses from the World Mother are tumbling into your midst. Receive the fragrance of her heart's love. Receive it into your heart, and let it be carried as a torch of fire, of living flame, of the essence of the Spirit Most Holy. Consider yourself a rose in the heart of the World Mother. And consider that that rose has an infinite number of petals ever replacing themselves by the power of the resurrection flame so that often you may take from your heart a petal of the rose of the World Mother and give it to one who does not know her fragrance or her love and say unto them, "Tarry here that I might tell you about the petals of a Mother's heart, about her love that is given freely to all." And then tuck that petal in the heart of that one and promise him that if he waters the petal, that petal will also become a rose like unto the one you wear.

Let the multiplication and the fragmentation of the World Mother appear this day by the power of her love anchored now within you! The elixir of the Spirit Most Holy is yours. The tangible materialization of that elixir in the rose is also yours. And so Alpha and Omega have come unto you this day through my intercession. I go, then, to prepare a place for each one of you.[33] I go to intercede on your behalf and on behalf of a planet and all lifewaves. On behalf of elemental life, I intercede for you daily. I AM the Mother of the God flame within you. I AM the Mother of the God flame within your heart—in the heart of a lily, in the heart of a rose, in the center of the crystal and the star that is born.

Angels of my band, take now the capes, but leave the remembrance of the electronic pattern of those capes within the etheric bodies of these precious ones that they might follow the pattern in weaving the immortal garment that they will one day wear as immortelles, as flames of God. I give you the thread from my heart flame that you might begin to weave the seamless garment. And so all hearts are tethered to my heart even as I am tethered to the heart of the one God. This is the meaning of hierarchy. This is the meaning of coming down from the cross and raising the consciousness from death unto life.

So is Victory's flame given unto you. So is the resurrection your own even as it belonged to my Son in that glorious moment when the angels came and assisted him to magnetize the full-gathered intensity of the resurrection flame from the heart of the eternal One. None shall take from you the privilege of drawing forth your own momentum of the resurrection flame from the base of the pyramid to the apex of your ascension in the light.

I have come to give you an understanding of how you might also do as he did. And all of heaven stands waiting and watching your invocations to assist you. But none will ever do it for you, beloved ones. For the joy is so great to do this oneself that no angel or cosmic being would be so selfish as to deprive you of that opportunity and that joy. Therefore in rejoicing we cheer you on as though in a grandstand, a cosmic amphitheater. And so it is your time, it is your place. You are the ideas that have come full cycle, ready now to stand in the heart of the flame and to experience your own resurrection.

So be it. The power of God is within you, precious hearts, mothers and fathers of the God flame.

Mary

Colorado Springs, Colorado
April 9, 1971

Exalt her, and she shall promote thee: she shall bring thee to honour, when thou dost embrace her. She shall give to thine head an ornament of grace: a crown of glory shall she deliver to thee. —Proverbs

4

Create the World Without That Is Your World Within

    I come to you in the spirit of Elijah, and by the power of his cloak[34] I place upon you the benediction of the Most High God. The whirlwind action of the sacred fire that drew him into the Presence of the Almighty[35] can also draw you, each one, into the Holy of holies, the seat of the Christ consciousness.

    If you would enter there, then come with me this night. For I take you into the arms of the World Mother, and I show you a mighty scene of worlds within worlds and worlds without where there is being born a star of wonder, a star of wonder in the sky, the birth of your own mighty I AM Presence, the I AM I. In the center of the being of every man is the seed of fire, the potential of the Christ, and within the seed is the immaculate conception of your fiery destiny.

    I come, then, from the heart of the sun, where I have perceived the fiery destiny of many worlds, worlds within and without. Do you know whereof I speak? The worlds within are those which will not be born in this *manvantara*. The worlds without are those which come forth for the expansion of God's consciousness, gathering more of their kind, more of the flame, more of itself unto the glory of the kingdom. By the power of the four beings of the elements, by the power of the cosmic cube, so is creation ongoing, expanding, flowing outward as a billowing sea of fire, curling under and moving outward again in another cycle.

    You are a part of the sea, beloved ones. For you are the worlds who have gone forth, gone forth from the heart of infinity to the periphery thereof. You have gone forth carrying the mighty scepter

Create the World Without That Is Your World Within 251

of power. Do you know that your own destiny, as a blueprint, is a scepter of power? Do you know why that is? Because it is a complete plan, complete in the mind of God. And wherever you have wholeness, completeness, a reflection of the Almighty, there you have power. And therefore I say to you this night, invoke the power of the fire within the seed, the pattern of your divinity. Claim it. And by its authority, go forth to conquer the world without which is yours to command in the name of Almighty God.

How can you go forth without a map of life? How can you go forth without the rules of the game? How can you go forth without a sense of mission, of purpose? These three aspects of the threefold flame are locked within the seed.

There is a saying "Fools rush in where angels fear to tread."[36] When we look upon the children of God who come anew into a focus of our teachings and we see how their hearts are joyous at the treasure that they have found and we see others who have been here for some time, we see that there are some among them here and there who would go forth and conquer the world without first having the scepter of dominion, the plan, the knowledge of the Law and the sense of mission. Do you understand, beloved ones, that when you try to accomplish these things without the proper tools, you are rushing in where angels fear to tread?

Do you know that not an angel leaves the throne of the Almighty to go forth to bless and heal a segment of the evolutions of God without his plan of purpose? They carry, as it were, road maps. They know where they are going because they know that the detours and pitfalls are many. Even on the heavenly highways there are detours of such great beauty that it takes great discrimination even for the angels to keep upon their appointed rounds. How much more, then, do you think that the temptations of the world are apt to take the new disciple from the Path when he is not fully armoured in the love of God, the wisdom of God and his power.

Therefore I say, come and sit at the feet of the masters. Put on the garment, the cloak of Elijah, which is the cloak of your own divinity, the robe worn by your own beloved Holy Christ Self. And when you have worn that robe for many a month and absorbed the consciousness of the Christ from the tapestry that is woven therein, then think about going forth in the full power of Elijah, of the priests of the Order of Melchizedek[37] and in the footsteps of my Son, Jesus.

Do you recall that he himself was tutored for thirty years for a mission which lasted only three years? It is not, then, the time which counts, of which so many feel that they have so little, but it is the mastery which counts. For he who has self-mastery can work all miracles, not in time but in eternity. Jesus' mission was a moment in eternity never banded by the bands of time. It was a cosmic moment. And in the full dress of his mastery, he set the example for the age.

It is our desire to see you, each one, go forth and do likewise to perform the seeming miracles which are but demonstrations of the science of alchemy. It is possible for men and women in every age to do this, beloved ones. Is not the Law written within your inward parts, in your very heart?[38] Therefore why go here and there seeking the Law when it is within? Go only where you are taught how to go within, how to find the Law, how to bring it forth and create the world without that is your world within.

I, Mary, come to you on the eve of the *Harvest Festival of Light and Gratitude*. I come to you bearing the radiance of the World Mother. And the intensification of her power upon the planet is felt in the blue ray, in the will of God, in the healing of God and in the white-fire core. I AM expanding my consciousness from the heart of the white-fire core of your blessed planet, and I can feel it as a mighty sphere of light expanding through all the strata of the rock unto the very surface. And this is the way to self-mastery—from within without.

Know ye not that ye are spheres of light, manifestations of the ultimate power of the Deity, still in potential, still in embryo, as it were, yet so powerful? And the release that shall come forth from each one of you—if you are diligent in your application of the Law, consecrated to surrender, loyal to the heart in all life—that power will be comparable to the power released when the atom is split. It is the power of Alpha and Omega, beloved ones, right within you—within each cell and atom. When you think upon the mysteries of the universe that is right where you are, is it not a marvel, is it not a great wonder how God has condensed into the form of man a starry being within a sphere, all of the light of galaxies yet unborn?

And so as we watched the star that night, we also knew that the star was within us, the star within cradling the king to come—to come into every man throughout all ages. And by the knowledge that was given to us from on high, we followed the way to the place where Jesus was born. Oh, what a holy night! Oh, what promise! Oh, what promise when each son and daughter of God descends from his throne vowing to do his will! Oh, the mysteries of the kingdom locked within the heart of flowers, of children smiling, of the aged coming to a newness of life, to a resurrection in the twilight years of their endeavor! No matter what the age or the face, God rejoices and is reflected in the smiles of those who rejoice to find him.

Many shall come to this focus of the World Mother as they came to the place where Jesus was born. And they shall follow the star of their own divinity, for it is the only star that can lead man to the place where the Christ within him is reborn. Let this focus, then, be a cradle for the incoming children of light, for those who are being born again, for the emerging Christ consciousness. Let it be the cradle, the arms of the World Mother. And let none who will cross this threshold forget that the hand that rocks the cradle is the hand that rules the world. The world is ruled by the Mother principle, for the Mother principle is that portion of the Deity which has gone forth into form. And did the Spirit of the Lord not say unto man and unto woman, "Take dominion over the earth"?[39]

Beloved ones, the fields are white unto the harvest.[40] Go forth, then, with the implements not of war but of the harvest, and gather the Lord's children into the fold. And let the storehouse be filled with the sparkling light of the Christ consciousness in every man, woman and child who enters here. For you shall see mighty works performed in this age. Therefore be not surprised nor wonder, for the ascended masters are walking and talking with men even now. And it will take, beloved ones, by comparison to our octave, only a very slight raising of the consciousness of the earth for mankind to reach the place where they can behold their teachers, where their teachers shall no longer be removed into a corner but they shall see their teachers face-to-face.[41]

As the angels of his Presence and of my band, as beloved Raphael surrounds this focus with the healing angels, remember that there are many more angels in the sky than there are people upon earth. For each one of you there are thousands. Therefore live in their consciousness, and develop the feeling that as you go about your seemingly mundane duties you are walking and talking with angels and entertaining them unawares.[42] As the holy saints of the ages have done, so may ye do also. With reverence for life, for the Christ in every man, with reverence for the unseen guests and the dawn that is coming, so go forth to do a perfect and mighty work for the Lord.

In the name of the World Mother, I bless you with the love of my heart, with the healing flame from our retreat, with the wholeness of your own divinity. Take the flower from my heart and let it be anchored in your own to assist you in unfolding the heart chakra for the love of all mankind and for their return to the Sun of Being. I thank you.

Mary

Santa Barbara, California
October 4, 1970

Hear, O my son, and receive my sayings; and the years of thy life shall be many. I have taught thee in the way of wisdom; I have led thee in right paths. When thou goest, thy steps shall not be straitened; and when thou runnest, thou shalt not stumble. Take fast hold of instruction; let her not go: keep her; for she is thy life.

—Proverbs

5

The Prayer and the Warning of the Universal Mother

Gracious children of the one God, I come to you tonight in manifest awareness of the holy Angelus, at which time, as the pause honoring God and heaven occurs, mankind may feel the celestial carillon pulled by angelic hands, signifying the end of the day's work at every hour. Have you thought upon this, that every hour is the Angelus somewhere upon this earth? Well, then, beloved hearts of light, will you think also of the great human need for healing? How mankind continually, because of the misalignment of their precious energies, do carry burdens, both of mind and body!

I thought before I came to you this night as to how, by your faith, I could assuage some level of human grief and bring greater peace to all. When my Son, Jesus, was touched by the woman who had spent all that she had in search of a physician to dry up the issue of blood with which she was plagued, it came to pass that as she touched the hem of his garment, the issue was dried and healing was bestowed.[43] As I came, I spoke also to those angels that together with Lord Raphael do so much concentrated service to mankind, and I asked them, one and all, to come with me. This they agreed to do.

And so the trailing garment which I wear tonight is one charged with healing for body, mind and soul. I do not say that all can summon those vestiges of vital faith that will produce the cosmic miracle in action now. But if your faith is large enough, I can assure you that you will be healed by the touch upon the trailing garment which I wear, thus producing in effect that which

The Prayer and the Warning of the Universal Mother 257

El Morya pleaded for in his initial application to the Karmic Board as the class was convened and before. He asked that in honor of Saint Germain, who was my own blessed protector, Joseph, mankind should receive the touch of the miracle hand of God to give some another chance and that they might perceive the great love heaven bears simultaneously with the hand of chastening warning unto mankind.

Long ago, when I spoke unto the children of Fátima in my appearance there,* it was to speak of diverse conditions coming upon the earth. O beautiful garment of cosmic loveliness, O fruitful abundance of the sacred laws of God, how thou hast been trampled upon again and again by human feet until the sands in the hourglass of mercy seem to be utterly depleted! And now in the midst, toward the end of the cycle, we wonder how we can avert the return of man's recalcitrant energies upon his own head.

Yet we still pray for mercy and forgiveness for those hearts that have so carelessly trampled upon the very garments of cosmic loveliness which are the fabric woven with angel hands and endowed with the sense of the eternal womanhood of God. You have thought of him as Father; think also of God as an immaculate Mother. Of old and in previous ages, this was called the *cult* of the Mother because it represented in the children of men the *cult*ivation of those beautiful spiritual energies which are your own blessed forte.

Never in the heart of the immaculate image of God has he desired to see harm come to any of his children. Oh, how through the centuries heaven has worked while the callousness of men has continually caused such sorrow to those of the angelic hosts and to those who are the true servants of God upon the planetary body.

When we pray the great prayer for all souls, it is a prayer of infinite compassion, it is the prayer of the universal Mother, it is the call unto God that compels the answer. And when mankind

---
*In 1917 Mother Mary appeared to Lucia dos Santos and to Francisco and Jacinta Marto in Fátima, Portugal.

do not heed that call, the return of mankind's negative energies upon them appears as a chastening that cannot always be averted. Thus the great drops of cosmic mercy that are the passions of the living God for his children—that they remain not ever in the vale of human tears and sorrows—is one aspect of the flame that is very near and dear unto my heart.

Tonight I have been selected by the hierarchical masters of the Karmic Board to present to you a solemn warning that upon all mankind will destruction come. In some cases even the good will suffer side by side with the evil, for it is not always possible to exercise cosmic discrimination. When the grossness of darkness manifests, all are subjected to the vale of darkness. Only the light of the heart remains to cheer those souls who recognize with full devotion that tremendous eternal love-ray concept that connects their heart through the darkest night with the heart of God.

And, oh, how in reality, through the avatars, the angelic hosts and those stars of light that shine in the world, God himself has flashed forth tears for humanity because humanity's concepts have become so gross! The land is plagued with darkness upon the screens of the invention of the motion picture. The land is plagued with darkness over the churches devoted to honor my Son's name. The land is plagued with darkness as the political candidates struggle among themselves, seeking a temporal crown. And how few are the leaders who are pledged to give to mankind a divine equity upon which men can rely.

I am Mary. And focused within my heart is the offering I long ago pledged to God—to be a representative of the universal Mother. Thus have I found and apprehended that entrance into human struggle which is aware of the darkening clouds gathering over the world community and seeking to obscure the sun shining in his strength,[44] the cosmic Christ consciousness. Thus I have the blessed awareness of the pains of mankind, which are so unnecessary.

The Prayer and the Warning of the Universal Mother

Had the world, in pure truth, long ago chosen to hew out the manifestation of their lives as though they were a cosmic statue of eternal grace and loveliness endowed with the vibrancy of immortal life, all could have been averted in the triumph of heavenly reality, as today, now in time, all the world would be singing the song of universal redemption. Do you see, O mankind, how fruitless is the present struggle—and how it always has been?

Through the ages human struggles are so unnecessary. They are only a vying in and among mankind with one another for those trophies of human desires that in reality are as straw cast upon an altar to be burned. Those things that are worth living for are eternal things, values which are cloaked in part in the manifestation of abundance upon earth but that in reality, O blessed ones, may become your own as you yield your blessed consciousness to the light patterns that emerge so victoriously in such a magnificent parade of cosmic values.

It is never enough for mankind to simply have appreciation. Heaven will be satisfied only with your manifestation of light. To appreciate the value of light without distributing its great tributaries of light into your consciousness is an error of humanity. It fulfills that ancient scripture that mankind draw nigh unto God with their lips, whereas their heart is so frequently far from him.[45] This is because the education of human values concerning divine values is somewhat nonexistent in the world community. They do not understand just what heavenly values are, for they do not allow the screen of the mind to reflect those values and thus feel the magnificent passions which are the nature of God.

Long ago in coming to Bernadette,* I saw the heart of a child. And how this child suffered because the crassness of mankind would not receive her thoughts! The revelation of universal grace that has poured out from heaven to so many souls not always known among men has in so many cases not ever been seen by

---

*In 1858 Mother Mary appeared to Bernadette Soubirous in Lourdes, France.

them. And only the heart of a World Mother can feel and see at inner levels—if necessary, even through my angel representatives. Think about this, O mankind. For each angel peeping through the veil betwixt heaven's experiences and the experiences of earth is in reality my vision and the vision of the Mother of the World. Her cherishment for God's children does not exclude any but is given to all.

Tragic, then, is the impending doom hanging like a sword over the heart of the world, for the elementals have communicated recently with one another and they are preparing to execute cataclysmic strands of destruction that have only begun in the world order. And this shall come to pass unless the teachings of God shall be fulfilled in the hearts of many men and women presently totally dedicated to their own selves without understanding the great needs of humanity.

I am Mary. And as I come to you this night, it is to suggest to you a plan, that perhaps the Lords of Karma may hear, whereby through the acceptance in your heart of the burden of the world, you may be able to pull and create a little tug upon the heart of God through the Lords of Karma, that mankind may be at last relieved of some portion of their burden. And so the Great Law may be assuaged and those universities of the Spirit be established where mankind can gather to learn the laws so beautifully taught by my Son, Jesus.

O mankind, let your faith not be in that which condemneth, that which is of the carnal mind, but let it be that faith which valiantly succeeds. Otherwise, that which is coming upon the earth will not be pleasant to relate, nor will it bring joy or delight to the heart of God or any of the angels of heaven who will, of necessity, avert their gaze from the destruction mankind have wreaked upon mankind.

Now, then, as a cosmic mother, I come to you in that fond hope still that you will think as to how you may unify, how you may create greater faith among the multitudes. What difference does it make, when so many hearts are seeking, what they think of you or your opinions? One hundred years hence, how many of you will remain in physical embodiment to behold whether or not you have exercised your cosmic trust properly? Do you see how important it is, then, to act now? Do you see that the torch that must pass to the ages may well come to some of you with the flame extinguished, because the woes of mankind have grown very great and those who are heirs of this age will find themselves bereft of much of the intended reality that ought to be conveyed?

I stand today at the Good Friday concept of man's destruction of Christ-values to plead with you before it is too late. In the name of heaven, blessed ones, do not think that my voice that is crying to you tonight is crying in vain, for surely some among you and among mankind will see the reality of the Christ-crucifixion continuing through this present age. Even at Christmas they have only commercialized upon the value of the love of my Son, intended to bestow the crown of life upon the ages. They have sent gifts to one another, they have made merry, and they have manufactured destruction rather than construction.

The plan I bring this night is one of cosmic construction through the hands of men in whom I have vested a sacred trust. Will those of you who will accept my trust this night, the trust of the ages, to preserve the Christ-values within your hearts and the hearts of all mankind stand at this occasion [audience rises] and recognize that only by a pact of pure love fulfilled among men can we now preserve intact in the world community that undying love which will not crucify my Son afresh nor put him to an open shame[46] but instead will exalt his name and the name of God and its values high upon the pole of life, that now the brazen serpent may be raised in the wilderness anew,[47] a symbol of man's victory over death and over mortality.

Must your little self triumph when your giant God Self may

find its winged victory in the world community and the triumph of every heart will sob unto the victory of life?

> I AM victory over the defeat
> Of human thoughts and feelings.
> I AM victory over all distress
> That has brought to mankind those reelings
> That bring to his heart awareness
> To confess his failures to start
> In this moment of world turmoil
> To reverse the process
> And gain for all
> That cosmic coil,
> Serpentine, caduceus action
> Up the spinal ladder of cosmic progress
> To where the winged victory of the mind
> At last represents the Law
> And the Law in all its kindness,
> Fulfilling the brotherhood of man
> As design most holy and sign most pure
> That enables all mankind to endure those tests
> In all their ageless purity and righteousness.
> For all can triumph
> Through the light of the Eye of God,
> Through the light in the mind of Christ.
> The radiance of my Son
> Establishes this night
> The unity of the One.
> He who rides the white horse to victory,
> Ruling with the rod of iron[48]
> Shall unify the nations,
> Triumphing in all
> As the Christ-pattern of all ages.

The Prayer and the Warning of the Universal Mother 263

I, Mary, salute you.
I, Mary, salute your soul.
I, Mary, pray God to make all whole.

Mary

Colorado Springs, Colorado
July 3, 1972

Doth not wisdom cry? and understanding put forth her voice? She standeth in the top of high places, by the way in the places of the paths. She crieth at the gates, at the entry of the city, at the coming in at the doors.

—Proverbs

6

The Law of the Transposition of Energy

    Children of infinite peace, I am come this night to enfold you in the all-powerful love that flows from the heart of God imparting wisdom to those whose ears are attuned softly to the gentle vibratory action of the voice of God speaking within the silent recesses of each man's heart. I would speak to you tonight briefly upon the law of the transposition of energy, that you may have imparted to you in this holy wisdom the tranquil knowing of how the being of you, the consciousness of your identity, was transferred by the power of love from those higher octaves into this present one.

    Your consciousness, beloved ones, is the key to all perception, to all knowing. Your consciousness is unique unto yourselves, for with it you are able to perceive all outer conditions. Yet all inner conditions are not always made known unto you, and the mysteries of life on the inner planes remain successfully veiled from the eyes of mankind embodied here. This unique you, this consciousness transferred at the hour of your birth to mortal form, manifests, then, in that form. And so it is as though you were anchored there and could not depart therefrom.

    Like unto Ruth and Boaz, the soul and the body remain wedded, and the words "Whither thou goest, I will go"[49] are truly spoken of body and soul from the hour of man's birth. And yet it need not be so—it need not be so that the body house become a prison to confine those precious energies therein and keep them from tasting and having a foretaste of that divine glory which will be so sweetly imparted to mankind in due course of time and evolvement.

By the transposition of the energy of self, you will find that you are able to skillfully escape the body prison without disturbing the beating of your heart. You will find that without creating a condition of rigidity in the body parts, you can leave the body quietly sleeping, as my Son so often did in the back of a boat on the Sea of Galilee, and fly afar to become a part of both the natural kingdom and the spiritual kingdom of God. How this is accomplished can be so easily revealed to you by the Holy Spirit.

While it is always desirable to have a guru, a spiritual teacher, one who will impart this knowledge unto your waiting heart, it is also possible, beloved ones, for you to be divinely taught, to be God-taught, in the quietness of his Presence, to extract that sacred knowledge of the sacred fire which will make you, as my Son, master over the law of the transposition of the energy that is you.

As you have gazed at night upon the silvery light of the moon, as you have gazed upon the softness of the billowing clouds, has it occurred to your blessed hearts that you could as easily blend with the soft texture of the clouds as with the body form you wear? Has it occurred to you that while your body rested quietly, you could rise with the full power of perception into the heavens before your physical ascension, before your spiritual ascension, even in your present condition, through the knowledge of the great law of life? Has it occurred to you that you could blend with a single moonbeam, climbing upward on that gentle ray of light to enter into the heart of nature, to behold the sweetness that rests like a mantle upon many a quiet country town, upon a mountain hamlet?

You, then, rising apart from the body, could behold the trouping children returning home from school. You could behold the beds of pain where grief fills men's cup to overflowing. You could behold the miracle of birth and rejoice in the unfoldment of a rose, witness the dancing of the elves in an Irish glen, observe

The Law of the Transposition of Energy

the spirits of nature at work in the chemical laboratories of God. As a part of that elemental life, you would find no frustration; for you would recognize that there is a free flowing of spiritual energy, the energy of your life. Oh, that precious energy is balanced so delicately within the golden goblet of your heart, and the shimmering cord of silver* descending from your precious Presence is so wondrous to behold!

Yet it is a very easy thing for a trusting one to rise out of the body form with sweet simplicity, as one might lay aside a robe or a garment and in spiritual likeness behold the beauty of the world. And yet if one would speak truth, one cannot help but also witness the sorrow of the world. And as the sorrow of the world is witnessed, the power of the great love of God, the power of the holy Mother of the World must seize upon the consciousness of those devoted to truth and generate therein a desire to render assistance, to reshape the destinies of men according to a more perfect pattern, and to weave in the individual forcefield of man's own identity a greater awareness of the presence of immortality within the temple of consciousness.

I recall so much of life, for to hold the image in the immaculate chalice of memory century after century after century is indeed a cup that runneth over with a flow of life's wondrous energy. The energies of life are precious not only to me; they were most precious to my Son. And when he mounted Golgotha's hill, it was with a sense of completion of a journey into being in consciousness. The example which he set, although I must confess it tore somewhat upon my heart, was also cause for great rejoicing. For both Joseph and I knew so well, so full well, the meaning of that mission and that across the seas and through the years that would come, men would be drawn closer to that consciousness that is life within them.

Precious ones of the light, strip all the doctrines of the world

---

*Also known as the crystal cord.

of all of their words. Divest them of all of their ritual. And in the sweet simplicity of spiritual oneness, they reveal God, God, God to man. In the revelation which they speak in truth and knowing, man is able to absorb a greater sense of knowing, of our Father who art in heaven, until in that knowing the cords of love bind together mankind. And in binding mankind together, they free mankind from those divisionary creations, thoughts and feelings which have produced so much imperfection and created so many thorns and thistles upon life's pathway.

Most of you heard this evening last the address of beloved El Morya, who has so long been my knight champion, and you are aware of the intensified action of light. You are aware that light continues to pour forth and draw the planetary body together, knitting heart with heart.

We expect rebellion from mankind, O sons of light. For we recognize that rebellion is a result of mankind's ignorance, and because all men are not fully illumined rebellion arises within their hearts. But it is an innocent rebellion in most cases, and there are few that truly would, if they could, inflict a wound upon the body of God. For that is exactly what mankind do when they strike one of these little ones that God has created.[50] The wounds are not inflicted upon the body of man; they are inflicted upon the body of God. For ye are the temple of the Father, and the Holy Spirit abides in each one of you.[51]

Deny, if you will, the presence of life; this presence will not deny you upon earth. But it would not be wise to continue to deny the Father. For to deny the Father continually while yet in physical form is to create a set of the sail of your identity, which when you are no longer occupying a body, might cause you to deny God outside the body. And then, by reason of your denial, he would be unable to establish contact with you and bring you safely into his heart.

All is the result of cosmic law. All is the result of the law of perfection. So often the children of God upon this planet, in their state of unknowing, have the idea that many things occur haphazardly. They do not, beloved ones. All works as do your clocks and watches when they work with precision. All is the result of precision and perfection. My Son said long ago, "Heaven and earth shall pass away, but my words shall not pass away"[52] and "Till heaven and earth pass, one jot or one tittle shall in no wise pass from the law, till all be fulfilled."[53]

There are times that mankind, in their state of ignorance, seem to feel that they have avoided all forms of punishment for the inequities which they have manifested. Let them not feel so, for the Law does not intend to chastise mankind. The Law intends to exalt man. The chastisement is the result of man's own wrong reactions to the tides of life. For while life would lift mankind by showing them how to balance their ignorance and resentment and rebellion by the power of Christed love and wisdom, mankind turn everything upside down. And in place of perfection, the lash of karma manifests in the human consciousness.

Precious ones of the light, I am so aware of each one of your hearts that are here. I am aware of the devotees of God who love him without ceasing. I am aware of those who are confused here and wonder just which way they ought to turn. I am aware of those who have doubts and who do not understand how I am contacting you this night. I am aware of everyone in this room and upon the planetary body. For I am, by God's grace, known as the Queen of Heaven, the Queen of the Angels, and this is but my holy office. My office is to serve the great Mother of the World. Although I have become, in sense and in essence, the Mother of the World, this is as much a part of your life, each one, as it is a part of my own.

Every woman, every man is, in one sense, a part of the heart of the Mother of the World. Your destiny is so closely linked, it is like the garments which you wear—the warp and the woof, the passing through of all, link together your blessed consciousness in a perfect fabric of identity. Oh, there may be holes in your consciousness, blessed ones, but they are very small and tiny. And one day the spiritual light will flood through the grid of the cloth and weld it all together into a seamless garment as my Son wore.[54] When you wear that seamless garment, you will know the meaning of the all-enfolding flame of life, of the all-enfolding flame of the Christ, of the all-enfolding flame of the Mother of the World. You will understand the mystery of birth, of life and of passing from the screen of life to another dimension in order to bring to you progressive spiritual evolution until you, too, return to that God-estate for which you yearn.

I shall leave tonight dissertations concerning the Great White Brotherhood and its desire to bring about certain changes in the evolutionary status of mankind. I shall leave intellectual comprehensions, and I shall speak from my heart to your heart. Throughout this class there has been released into your world a great deal of energy. Therefore I decided tonight, long before I stood upon your platform, that the words that I should speak should be gentle words.

It is my wish to convey to your hearts that God is near. It is my wish to convey to your hearts that you must not generate in your consciousness or your mind the idea of God as far away. You must not be confused because you do not see with your eyes the transposition of your consciousness.

You have wonderful faculties, blessed hearts. Your eyes, so luminous and bright, reach out to the stars and behold their light. Your ears hear, when rightly tuned, the melodies of the angelic hosts and the music of the spheres. Your consciences, developed through millions of years of evolution, are so gentle that ever so frequently you respond to a mere thought upon the reins of life and you turn back, as a child would recoil from a hot stove, when you realize that you are making an error. This is so blessed. It is so sweet. It is so gentle, so godlike. This is divine meekness.

You have heard it said, some of you, and others of you have read, the words of my Son "The meek shall inherit the earth."[55] Yet so few have recognized the meaning of those words. So many have felt that by strong will, by drive or by service or by other methods, achievement should be made—and it is.

But those who are meek themselves but are strong in their divinity are holy men and women of divine character who can express upon this planet the noble lineaments of divinity before mankind. These are they who can be relied upon when the widow's son[56] is smitten with the pangs of death to reach out a hand of immortal comfort and say, "Arise, return to life." Those able to recall the dead from the halls of death back to the scene of life are those Christlike beings, no different than yourselves, who have faithfully, embodiment after embodiment, pursued the path of righteousness for the sake of God's holy name, I AM.

This means, beloved ones—and I urge you to watch this carefully—*Being*. I AM is Being—the Being of God identified with the being of yourself. And it is in this recognition that you speak his holy name, and it is in this recognition that your acts become his holy will. To identify with the will of God is not unhappiness. It is supreme happiness, it is supreme courage, and it is supreme mastery over the electronic structure of your forms, over the thoughts that flash across the span of your minds and consciousness. And as a spiritual endowment, it is grace without limit.

O gentle angels of love who have accompanied me wheresoever I go, I call unto you now and ask you to descend with a gentle rushing wind. I ask you to saturate the consciousness of these holy children with the divine comfort that was extended to the Hebrew children as they were thrust into the fiery furnace.[57] I ask that these, thy children, may receive some bond of faith this night that shall help them throughout the balance of this embodiment and unto their own glorious ascension in the light.

I ask that there be wedded to them, O All-Father, the supreme bestowal of divine grace. May it rest as a holy mantle upon their brow, a mantle of perfection. May it drape and enfold their shoulders. May the spiritual cape of service of my beloved consort, Joseph, now your precious Saint Germain, rest upon each one of you who are willing to be a part of divine grace and holiness. And may you feel no shame in acknowledging God and his grace, but only that divine delight which will be your comfort through every moment of pain and sorrow and trial and anguish until you develop that character which can face the world with the light of God that never fails.

To visit the sacred retreats is a blessing, to be able to raise the dead is a blessing, to be able to heal the sick is a blessing. But the greatest blessing of all is to completely unite with God; for when you do this, you can do all of these things and more. And nothing in heaven and earth can be denied you. For you can stand with my Son upon the hilltop of life and you can say with him in God's holy name, "I am the resurrection and the life;[58] all power in heaven and in earth is given unto me,[59] and to whomsoever I will I may give it, and it shall be so."

But you will do as we do. You will impart the all-power by an action of the divine law to those hearts that will cherish your words, that will cherish your love. For seed planted there is not planted upon stony ground or upon barren earth, but upon fertile soil where it will flourish and magnify the presence of life until you and the angels and mankind and God our Father will simultaneously rejoice in the attainment of the great planetary chain of human relationships extending across the planetary body in the service of light's unfolding perfection and immortality.

Gracious ones, some of you are familiar with the fact that on Long Island there is an image erected in honor of me. Many of you are aware of the fact that the earth is filled with graven images

The Law of the Transposition of Energy

of my form, that millions pray to me daily, that millions speak a rosary to my name. I ask you now to think yourselves how it would be to wear my mantle, to wear my garments, to be myself in action. It is a great responsibility. And I am most grateful that his love has been sufficient to fill the matrix of my heart with a compassion from the great cup of universal life, and I am grateful that this cup has been sufficient to supply the needs of all that have called upon me.

Some are aware of the fact that the Madonna upon Long Island has ever so frequently shed tears and that no man has been able to solve to this present hour the source of those tears, and so it is called the weeping Madonna. I tell you, beloved ones, far more of my time is spent in rejoicing than in weeping. And yet the sorrows of the world do frequently fill my heart when I realize that if men would but be true to themselves, they could end all of their pain and suffering. They could assuage all their grief and do it quickly. I therefore remand you to the precious words of my beloved Joseph uttered to you through that great soul Francis Bacon, "This above all: to thine own self be true, and it must follow, as the night the day, thou canst not then be false to any man."[60]

I close now with a plea for spiritual integrity, that each of you shall recognize that in this gentle ministration, more good shall be accomplished than is ever dreamed of by man as he presently contemplates my words. My words in action are the greatest gift. My words merely heard are a temporary blessing to those able to assimilate them. To those not able I say, abide in God and all things shall be fulfilled in due time, regardless of the state of your consciousness. Whether or not you are aware of all of God that you ought to be, be patient until it is revealed. For when it comes, it is worth more than gold, worth more than garments, worth more than houses and lands, flocks and fields. It is all.

For as the foxes have holes and the birds of the air have nests, the Son of man hath no place to lay his head[61] save in the heart's open door.

Thank you and good evening.

Mary

Los Angeles, California
September 9, 1963

Unto you, O men, I call; and my voice is to the sons of man. O ye simple, understand wisdom: and ye fools, be ye of an understanding heart. Hear, for I will speak of excellent things, and the opening of my lips shall be right things. —Proverbs

7

Sons and Daughters of the Dominion of the Water Element

I am called the Queen of the Sea because I manifest dominion over the emotional bodies of mankind. When Jesus spoke to the raging tide and said, "Peace, be still" and the waters were calmed,[62] it was the manifestation within him of the power of God-dominion over energy in motion, *emotion*.

I come to you this day as the representative of the Divine Mother in the heart of the resurrection flame to bring to you that Christ-mastery—the power over self-condemnation and self-belittlement, over fear and tyranny and self-love. And so I come to initiate you in the Order of the Sons and Daughters of the Dominion of the Water Element.

These are they who have overcome, as it is written, "by the blood of the Lamb."[63] The blood of the Lamb symbolizes the sacred fire of the Christ, the pulsation of the essence of the Holy Spirit in the body of Jesus. This is the flow of fire that becomes the flow of water, liquid light. Liquid light within you, in order to expand, in order to spiral into a magnification of cosmic victory, must have the power of God-control.

God-control, then, is the key to self-mastery and to the resurrection. If you would become the Christ, precious hearts, then I say, become the masters of energy in motion. Let not one erg flow through the mind or the feelings, the motives or the body over which you have not conscious control. Also, you must have control of that which is beneath the level of your awareness. And so you must test your control, not by observation but by vibration. You must develop the sensitivity in the center of the Christ to know when there is turbulence beneath the surface and when there is calm, for only by that omnipotence can you go forward in the action of becoming the Christ.

The transfiguration is yours, the resurrection and the ascension. The tests will come to you surely if you have shown the willingness to master the power of God's love as it expands within you. For when the flame expands to cover the earth, you must have the consciousness that can travel with the flame, with the rays of the flame and the light that shoots forth. And so you must be present in your body and also present with the Lord, or the law of Being that is within the light that is emitted from your chakras.

Do you see, precious ones, to be the fullness of the manifestation of the Divine Mother requires that you be with God omnipresent, that is, everywhere present. You must be as conscious of yourself in an atom in a tree that is growing on an island in the South Seas as you are conscious of yourself here in this form in this place in time. I AM here and I AM there and, lo, the victory of the Christ is manifest within you.

Let, then, the borders of your consciousness expand to include the universe. For even as I AM everywhere, so you can be everywhere if you will let yourself. You are not confined to your physical body any more than you are confined to your emotional, your mental or your etheric body. But you use these as the platform for your evolution and for your expansion. The light of ten thousand suns may be upon you and you may be in the light rays and also in the heart of the sun, but you must practice. Practice makes perfect.

And so the Mother teaches her children to exercise daily in the rituals of soul expansion, of solar awareness. For only thus can you go forth to heal, to raise up the energies of the Christ in your fellowman. And this is what you would do after all, this is what you have longed for—to be healers of nations and of children and of men. If this is your heart's prayer, then realize there is a science, an alchemy to healing. You must know that science and not rush forth blindly to focus a power that is greater than yourself until you have become the master, the peace-commanding presence from your own God-awareness.

You must remember, precious hearts, that as you rise in the stature of the Christ, people will come to you for assistance and you will give it gladly. But they will attribute the help they receive to your person. And if you are not careful, you, too, will come to identify with your outer person because all around you identify with that person. And then you will find that that person is not adequate to meet the tests that increase in difficulty and in complexity. You will find that the outer personality, then, will fall if you identify with it.

And so you must conceive of your consciousness as a grid, a latticework through which the fires of the Holy Spirit flow and the winds thereof as the rushing of the sound of many waters. And when individuals look to the latticework and say, "I have been healed by that latticework," you will know that it was not the latticework but the wind that flowed through the lattice.

Do you see, precious hearts, if you do not have the correct awareness of your God-identity, you cannot go forward. You will not master the tests of the Divine Mother. You will not understand the personality of God—how God can be a person and yet be a flame at the same time, how you yourselves can manifest in this physical world as a person and yet not a person, as a flame that is personal and made tangible and real to those around you.

It is almost like playing a dual role, for you know that those who are on lesser rungs of the ladder of attainment will not know how to identify with the flame. It is not necessary that they do so. This is why the Divine Mother has provided you with the form— to give some semblance of association and relevance to those in the world around you.

And so the form is there, and as long as you yourself do not become attached to it but only to the flame, you will not be scarred in your service or hindered by other people's opinion of what you are. For you know that I AM the flame and I AM the power of God in the heart of the flame. I AM the love of God in the heart of the flame. I AM the wisdom of God in the heart of the flame. And by the power of that flaming consciousness, that flaming awareness of life, you will go forth to heal as the fullness of the manifestation of the Divine Mother. This is God-control, this is God-power, this is God-harmony, this is God-reality, and this is your victory. This is your natal day when you are born of the flame, to the flame and in the flame, and there you remain.

If you can comprehend this mystery, you will follow in the footsteps of Jesus all the way to Golgotha, and you will experience the mortification of the ego as a ritual of the Brotherhood through which all must pass. And you will come down from the cross. And when you are in the tomb during that period that is required, you will descend into the astral realm to preach unto the souls that are caught there, even as Jesus did.

And because you have mastered the waters of the earth, the waters of the sea and the waters under the sea, you will come forth from that final trial victorious, and you will rise. Having dominion over death and over form, you will command the atoms to coalesce. And standing in the flame, the resurrection of all that manifested in the planes of Matter will take place, and your identity will be secure in the plane of Spirit form. And so you rise to meet your God, and so your God descends to meet you. And in the center of the six-pointed star, there the victory will manifest, and you will be master over Matter and over Spirit. This is your reason for being and your divine calling.

I, Mary, will remain with you as I did with Jesus to hold the immaculate concept for you. And I will remind you of this key and this mystery, which I gave you this day, of identifying with the flame. I will remind you of your dual role, and I will remind you of the permanent atom within the heart that is your true personality, your true identity.

I leave with you the fragrance of the resurrection lilies and of the white rose from my heart. May the lily of the valley, which my angels bear, also rest as a garland in your hair, that you may know that the fragrance of the love of the Divine Mother is upon you always. I hold you close to my heart in a divine embrace, and I place upon your forehead the kiss of the Divine Mother.

Mary

Santa Barbara, California
March 31, 1972

Receive my instruction and not silver, and knowledge rather than choice gold. For wisdom is better than rubies, and all the things that may be desired are not to be compared to it. —Proverbs

8

The Beckoning and the Call of the Cosmic Mother

With a mantle of cosmic beauty and perfection, I am come this night in the memory of my beloved Son and the glory of his nativity. As I ponder the magnificence of that perfection gathered and solidified within the tiny form which I held in my arms, I am aware now of the expanding glory that comes through the portal of birth to every child held in every mother's arms and clasped to the heart of every mother.

I am a cosmic mother, and my infinite compassion in the holy name of God enfolds the world this night as it did that night so long ago when the glorious child laid within my arms was yet the fulfillment of a promise—the fulfillment which had not yet come to fruition but which was destined to make its mark upon the annals of eternity—to chronicle for all mankind the beauty and the perfection of the eternal spheres of happiness and God's love.

The aura of the Christ which surrounded my Son is the aura of the Cosmic Christ of everyone, for in no way was his life unique in the sense that it was separate and apart from that of every other lifestream whom God hath created. The only begotten of the Father, my beloved ones, is the Cosmic Christ, the light of every man who comes into the world.[64]

Therefore, as I come to you in this hemisphere and area this starry night of beauty and loveliness, I come carrying in my heart the memory of the eternal songs which the angelic hosts sang together that night in a magnificent oration of light to the sons of light, the sons of the morning, the sons of the dawn, and the glory of the spheres of ever living perfection.

Tonight as I am speaking to you, this light of the Christ has not bedimmed itself in any way, but it shines evermore toward that eternal perfection. The open heart's door beckoneth this Cosmic Christ light within to the portals of each lifestream. And therefore the enfolding of each one in the swaddling garments of their great cosmic Be-ness is dependent upon their acceptance of the momentum of life's perfection, which can never be requalified by the human. This is a mantle of God-design, the perfection of those spheres of love which are and exist and shall be forever.

Beloved ones, I recall in the subsequent days that this child grew and waxed strong.[65] And as the magnificence that is the God within him came to full stature of devotion and perfection, I, too, took courage and I came to magnify the Lord more each day. As I stood in adoration at the ritual of each dawn, I was thankful with a gratitude to the Eternal that my Son was a reflection of the golden aurora of each dawn.

I was thankful that in him and around him was the light of perfection and that those people who sat in darkness might see this great light,[66] that the perfection of the Christ might be made known, that the historical drama might come to have a personal and real meaning to the hearts of mankind. It does not matter whether it was this child, this Son of mine, cradled in life's perfection in the manger of Bethlehem, or whether it was a manchild born to a mother upon the Mayflower when it first journeyed across the ocean to the shores of this land of America. It is still a manchild destined to be a son of light, a son of God, a person destined to accept all that the Father intended that one to accept.

And therefore, little ones of God, consider the destiny of yourselves. Ponder how you also were held in a mother's arms; and this mother, in her inner vision if not in her outer concepts, was able to perceive as I did the great glory that you should be. And thus in each fresh reembodiment, a soul is once again clothed with the rite and the ritual of a mother's love. And so the great all-enfolding, all-surging glory of the eternal Mother comes into manifestation, and the light and life and love is expanded without limit.

And so my soul tonight doth rejoice in God anew and I sing again with those hosts of my beloved Raphael the song of newness and the song of perfection, the song of love and the song of hope that is instilled into a mother's heart by her own latent divinity. Blossoming like a rose or an unfolding lily, the perfume of its fragrance spreads across the years. And that manchild comes to a destiny at last whereby the eternal Father stands there in the seal of great cosmic approval to bless that one with the anointing of the Whole-I-Spirit, the fullness of its own immortal perfection and cosmic destiny.

Can, then, anyone place a blot or a mark against that perfect soul? I think not. All blots and all marks, beloved ones, are placed there by mankind and by their criticism, their condemnation and their wrong judgment. Did not my Son declare, "Let him that is without sin among you first cast the stone at her"? And did they not all, vanquished within themselves by the conviction of their own wrongdoing, turn away with great sorrow and realize they could not condemn this woman? And so my Son spake to them and said, "Woman, where are thine accusers?" And she said, "There are none, my Lord." And so he said, "Neither do I condemn thee: go, and sin no more."[67]

And therefore, in the perfection of a mother's hope, there is this cosmic desire to see the Son of God manifest within the heart of every being brought into existence, whether that birth be a physical birth or a spiritual rebirth or a regeneration of the power of light and the power of love and the power of the sacred fire.

Here upon Long Island the Madonnas have wept. Why? Because they outpicture the great cosmic life and love and yearning and compassion of my mother's heart that pours out to the world and desires to give the world an eternal compassion that heals.

I am beckoning! I am calling! I am enfolding all in my love and light! The nativity is repeated oft, the scene wherein I envision the same aurora of the dawn wrapped around the enfolding head and encircling that glorious sphere intended to be a sphere dominated by love and love thoughts. And I see and envision in each tiny lifestream the glory of the risen one, the glory of the ascended one, the perfection of the immortal intelligence of God come to maturity of expression in each lifestream. This is the intended perfection. This is the glory of life—no domination by lesser qualities, no submission to the fiats of mere mortals, but a recognition of that cosmic intelligence, that discrimination, that beauty, that perfection which is God.

In this, O my beloved ones, is your hope and mine. It is the hope of the world. It is the hope of life in its eternal longing for itself. Come, then, in your hearts. Kneel at the manger of perfection. Express the qualities of adoration to the God within yourself as the Magi of old. Know that in the magnifying of your cosmic virtue, you are expanding the cosmic virtue within all mankind. How can you serve better than in the pattern established by my Son, revered by myself and adored by beloved Saint Joseph, who is your own beloved Saint Germain?

Come, then, beloved ones. Accept the power of love. Accept the power of love to sweep aside from the world all lesser conditions, to enfold the world in its perfection and purity, to accentuate the greatness of divinity in essence and in expression. Accept all of this and be free in the immortal perfection, the immortal beauty, the immortal establishment of God-immortality among men. How else can the earth escape? How else can men be free? How else can the glory of God be amplified?

As I take my leave of you now, I wrap around this place a robe of Cosmic Christ purity—a robe woven by the angels from eternal substance and made of light, woven of the love from the flame that burns on the altar of God's own heart, in the heart of the Great Central Sun. As I wrap this substance around you, I pray that it expand throughout the earth and bring comfort to everyone. I pray that in every heart that beats with the power of Almighty God—in whom manifests a tiny expression, a threefold flame of life's immortality—there shall blaze forth now an added pulsation, a rising beat of hope.

This men hear, though from afar. And yet they hear the echoes that come from our shore and our octave, and they know that there beats within them a call to light, to love, to purity, to perfection, to a divine strategy that will free them from all the wiles of iniquity and bring the perfect divine balance into manifestation. This the angelic hosts use, by the power of light, for the precipitation of all good to all mankind in every hour of every moment—until in the dawn of the cosmic light, the portal of eternity shall enfold every lifestream at birth, and all shall know their own God Presence, from the least to the greatest.

Thus shall the Cosmic Mother rejoice. Thus shall our Father who art in heaven manifest his glory among men. And the rolling spheres everywhere shall express those paeans of praise and adoration to God which make one vast harmony, one great heart of light and love, one eternal Christ-sphere of perfection. One, one, one! O God, make all one!

May the Christ Spirit of light and purity bless you this night, and may the earth know that I am praying. I am an ascended being and I am praying for the world, for the perfection of men's hearts, for the establishment of their love in the spirit of divine liberty, and for the liberation of all who are bound that the captives may go free.

I thank you in the name of the ascended Jesus Christ and I bless you with his blazing light. May this Christmas season be a blessing of eternal Christ Mass. Peace in God's name, my little

ones, children of eternity's light and love.
  Goodnight. God be with you ever.
  Mary

Long Island, New York
December 16, 1961

I, wisdom, dwell with prudence and find out knowledge of witty inventions. The fear of the LORD is to hate evil: pride and arrogancy and the evil way and the froward mouth do I hate. Counsel is mine, and sound wisdom: I am understanding; I have strength. By me kings reign and princes decree justice. By me princes rule, and nobles, even all the judges of the earth. I love them that love me, and those that seek me early shall find me.
—Proverbs

9

It Is the Father's Good Pleasure to Give You the Kingdom

"Fear not, little flock; it is the Father's good pleasure to give you the kingdom."[68] How oft have these words of my beloved Son comforted the weary traveler upon the pathway of the ascension.

I bring to you this night the magnetization of the fires of the Holy Spirit, which I held in my very heart. As the time approached for the birth of the Christ, the descent of the magnitude of his love was, oh, so wondrous to behold. And I saw in the heart of the universe, even in the heart of my own beloved Presence, his star approaching in the East.

As you also approach the advent of the Christ Mass, remember the flame of the Cosmic Mother. Take them in thine arms; take these precious ones who long for the Christ and yet know not even his name—Jesus, Immanuel, God with us. Indeed he is with us. The divine union, the supremacy of the Holy Spirit, can be reached by all, but it is a special gift to the mothers of the world. For only a mother knows the inbreathing and the outbreathing, the special flame-focus of the Christ who is appearing.

I count you all as mothers and fathers of the incoming children, and I charge you all by my flame that simply because you do not have your own flesh-and-blood children is no excuse for neglecting this so important responsibility of nursing the divine flame in each lifestream. How the angels dote upon the incoming children. You think that mankind squander their attention and their love upon the children newly born, but I tell you there is no comparison to the love of the angelic hosts. From the mighty archangels to the tiniest cherubim, they stand almost with bated breath awaiting the fullness of their appearing.

My beloved Raphael, who ministers unto the flame of life, who assists the birth, also assisted me in holding the pattern of divine truth for the Christ, even as the archangel Gabriel did appear unto me and does appear to this very hour to every mother with child. If they could but know him as I did, as I do! Would it be so, that all could stand in the presence of Gabriel and see him declaring the ringing truth of the perfection of man, of every son and daughter of God! This is a ne'er-to-be-forgotten experience, but the angels of annunciation are announcing hourly to the very chimes of the church bells the divine union and the perfection of the pattern of every man, woman and child upon this blessed planet.

Do you know the meaning of hearing the annunciation of your own divine perfection, the power of the Word of God that utters unto you, "This is my beloved Son, in whom I am well pleased"?[69] Is it not so, that the Lord of Creation is well pleased in the offspring of his heart? Accept, then, the praise of the Most High God and give it unto him also. Rejoice daily in the perfection that the Creator has given unto you in the beginning. Rejoicing! Rejoicing is such a great part of the love of the mothers and fathers of the world—rejoicing at each tiny step, at each moment of progress, rejoicing each step of the way, believing in the Son of God.

Do you believe in the Son of God within your own heart? I say unto you, believe as you have never believed before! Believe in him! Believe in the power of the divine example of the Word in you, and then you will believe in your fellowman. No more the cynicism—the veil of doubt and fear! Believe in man! You have been taught to believe in God. I say, believe in man! Believe in his creation. Believe that God can raise up in mankind those noble souls who shall deliver this planet in her hour of trial!

There is no doubt in our consciousness that the Christ is victor in all and that the divine compassion of the Holy Spirit, the tender love and warmth of the Maha Chohan, is with each one. I say, down with this creation of mankind that has dethroned man, that has made of him an idol and then cast down that idol for want of faith and vision! How important the vision of the Christ is, and that immaculate concept is based upon faith. You cannot see what you do not believe in. If you would love God, you would love him because you have faith in him; and you would have faith in him because you love him. And so it is true with thy brethren.

Mankind do not believe in themselves. How can they accept those whom they have appointed to public office? Their teachers, those who should command the respect of the world, all have fallen! Mankind are fallen idols one and all, and there is chaos and confusion where the broken statues lie midst the corruption of the age. It is time to resurrect! It is time to raise up in the consciousness of mankind the Divine Image that cannot be torn down. It cannot be broken, for it is a unified whole—the perfection of the Manchild of God. This cannot be torn down because it is not based on the outer consciousness. It is not based on the comings and goings of human consciousness, of human emotion, of intellectualism, of pride, of ambition. Nay, the Christ remains! The Christ remains always just behind the veil.

Would you admit your lack of vision with condemnation of the human identity when there standing before you is the Christ in all men? Do not give voice to your own ignorance. Be ashamed to utter a word in defeat of thy brethren, beloved ones. Do you think that any son of God could return to the heart of the Father if someone somewhere did not hold faith that he would succeed? Who do you suppose is holding the faith for mankind in this hour of trial? Who do you suppose? Not mankind! The students of light, it is our hope.

But I tell you, the greatest focus of faith that is held for mankind comes from the very heart of the Christ himself and from the hearts of the angels who have never descended into the world of form and therefore know not human consciousness. Yet they are aware of its degradations, and still they plight their faith. And this is the beauty of God in manifestation—that the faith of God as a ray of light descends to the very heart of the earth to uplift and to carry child-man back to the heart of the Central Sun.

I AM a cosmic mother. Those who share with me the ministrations of a planet, of a system of worlds realize that it is the humble of heart who reach most quickly the heights of spiritual victory. But we hold for all the vision of perfection. And because we hold that image, there are some among mankind who make the grade, who do not fall short of the mark of the high calling in Christ.[70] These come home, for our arms are outstretched.

Will you not hold with us for them the Christ-design? Will you not *determine* in the face of every form of density and opposition to call forth in your fellowman the manifestation of the Christ? Say in your heart: "I will not accept aught but thy perfection, O God, and I know that thou art ever present in this beloved one. So be it." Accept it, beloved ones. Become a cosmic mother, for one day you, too, shall share in the creation of systems of worlds, of spiral nebulae, even as the universe expands the Father's plan for his creation.

Many things are held in promise for you if you can but go beyond the simple manifestation of the holding of the immaculate concept. But part of the test, part of the trial, is that you know not what lies ahead. For if you could see the reward, you would work for the reward rather than work for the blessing of service in and of itself, which is a great fruit, beloved ones. To us who are ascended, the rewards of the ascended state of heaven seem like a gift, like something extra. For our reward has always been and will always be in the joy of seeing those whom we assist overcome.

And so the reward for that service, as beloved Morya has said, is greater service. Rejoice in service and weary not in well doing.[71] For you are indeed Christs in the making, walking the earth, leaving your footprints upon the sands of time. And the children of men will follow in those footsteps. Take care, then, that what you leave behind is what you yourself would like to find before you—guiding lights along the pathway to the ascension, not stumbling blocks in the road.

Above all, I would counsel you, beloved ones, to remember that all whom you meet are babes in Christ. If you can remember Jesus in the manger each time you see someone who seems to misrepresent his God, you will have greater compassion. For somehow in the harmlessness of a child-man, there is no competition, there is no pride, there is no defense mechanism that is stirred up. There is no need to react to a babe, and therefore will you find it easier to carry the burden of thy brethren along the pathway of life. Remember that divine matrix, then—the image of a child in cradle.

There is more to the celebration of the Christ Mass than mankind understand, for much is symbolism that involves the mysteries of creation and of the Christ. The thought patterns that appear to mankind each Christmas are intended to invoke in them the divine memory of the Logos itself, of their own immortal creation. Take only, for example, the three wise men. Mankind who do not understand the power of the threefold flame and who cannot accept the divine kingship of their own identity can accept this as outpictured in the world of form in three individuals. But in reality, these beloved ones who carried the flames of love and wisdom and power are intended to represent to everyone who kneels at the altar of the Christ the Holy Christ Flame within the heart.

And do you know, beloved ones, that the soul of mankind recognizes this fact? It is only the thin veil of the outer consciousness which continues to see this pageant as an outer, objective manifestation, when truly it is the representation of the trek of the soul to the altar of the Most High God. The star appearing is the mighty I AM Presence; the shepherds who watch their flocks by night the four lower bodies of mankind, who must be vigilant over the human emotions and thoughts that trample upon it in order to be ready when the star does appear. And those shepherds were ready, and they saw the star and they followed it too from the East. This shows the necessity of the alignment of the four lower bodies, the control of the Christ and the perfect identification of the lower self with the Higher Self.

And even as the Holy Trinity was carried by beloved Joseph, the Christ and myself, so is the Holy Family the divine union, the triangle of God upon earth. And that family must be kept intact as a social means of bringing mankind to the feet of the master—and also individually in each one. For each of you is the divine Trinity of the Holy Family. And at various times in your calling, God demands that you manifest the aspects of Father and then of Son and of Holy Spirit. And you know not at what hour you will be called upon to manifest the offices of God upon earth, but you know that you must be ready. And every mother must be ready to be not only mother but father and son. Do you understand, precious ones? And the son must become the father and embrace the Motherhood of God.

So is life one, not separate. And so do the various players in this scene of the pageant of Christmas bring home to mankind the calling of the Father. May your life be a pageant also of divine victory! May mankind remember your triumphs, your overcoming! May that pattern be so clear that the soul, too, may learn from that drama. For ye are all players upon the stage of life, and to bring the knowledge and teaching of the Presence of God is your calling. This will you do by the power of the Holy Spirit, by the Motherhood of God and the Fatherhood of God, by divine Sonship.

Precious ones, approach, then, this Christ Mass with reverence, with renewed dedication. You have witnessed year in and year out the songs and hymns of mankind and their prayers. Their attention

It Is the Father's Good Pleasure to Give You the Kingdom

to the Christ has drawn to this planetary body angels from out the Great Central Sun Star, from Sirius, from the Pleiades, from the heart of Helios and Vesta, angels serving other systems of worlds. And you know, if that momentum could be sustained throughout the year, what a blessing of victory! How peace would reign upon earth! It requires only the extension of the flame. Therefore extend, expand and learn to flow in the wisdom of God that shall draw all mankind to the Divine Presence.

There is no stoppage to evolution, beloved ones. The Christ shall ever expand. Therefore be not concerned at the rumblings of the outer world, but realize that life shall go on and shall be found victorious over every outer manifestation. If the worlds crumble, if earthquakes come, if cataclysm comes, realize that life continues to expand. Our only request is that you be found with your lamps trimmed,[72] that you not be found unprepared, that you be ready to hold the chalice of victory for those who will tumble in the tide and be swept off their meager moorings. For they need the hand of righteousness extended unto them; and in that time of trouble, many will be needed to extend that help.

Be Prepared is the motto which beloved Saint Germain gave when he founded the Boy Scouts of America, when he placed the insignia of the holy threefold flame upon every heart. Be prepared, then, for whatever comes, and know that thy forward victory shall take place—even unto the conquering of worlds and the ascension in the light.

I close once again with the comfort of my Son: "Fear not, little flock; it is the Father's good pleasure to give you the kingdom!"

Mary

Colorado Springs, Colorado
October 13, 1967

Riches and honour are with me; yea, durable riches and righteousness. My fruit is better than gold, yea, than fine gold; and my revenue than choice silver. I lead in the way of righteousness, in the midst of the paths of judgment: that I may cause those that love me to inherit substance; and I will fill their treasures. —Proverbs

10

The Light That Shines in the Dark Streets of Jerusalem

The light that shines this day in the dark streets of Jerusalem is the light that you bear—the light that you have carried here in the name of my Son, in the name of Christ Jesus, who also has walked with you these days. And as you have called to him, so he has said in your midst, "I and my Father are one."[73] This oneness, blessed hearts of light, is the oneness which we share.

Throughout the ages people have always thought that their era was the modern time. Each successive decade considered itself to be more modern than the previous one, and so we say "in these modern times." Times have always been modern, for the modes of the human consciousness have changed little. You understand this—you who are the perceptive ones, who know that the Christ lives in all whom you meet, you who know that the light must be borne in the physical octave that the physical octave might be healed by the power of the Divine Mother and the Divine Son.

The light of God does not fail to raise up the human consciousness until it is brought to that level where it must either become divine or be consumed and be no more. The raising of the planetary body by the power of the light of the Christ—that cycle was begun in this very place in time and space, in this very forcefield two thousand years ago as the little band of the followers of the light came together for that holy demonstration, the drama of eternity which was to portray the victory of the light in every man, woman and child.

The challenge of the two-thousand-year cycle which has followed has not been met by humanity. Heaven waits for the fulfillment of the cycle. There remain but a few short years of opportunity to become the Christ. And what will happen if mankind do not follow in his footsteps? I have prophesied before at Lourdes and Fátima and I shall prophesy again. For I have come to warn and to chastise and to urge men to pray the Our Father and to daily give the rosary, for those to whom I spake understood the prayers that are necessary to sustain a momentum of light.

Precious hearts, be not afraid; ye believe in me, believe also in him.[74] I am a cosmic mother but this does not exclude yourselves, for you also are cosmic mothers and sons and daughters of God. And Jesus—was he not representing the feminine ray of the Divine Mother when he said, "O Jerusalem, Jerusalem,…how often would I have gathered thy children together, even as a hen gathereth her chickens under her wings, and ye would not."[75] And so in the one who has attained the Christ consciousness, there is the fourfold manifestation of the Father, the Mother, the Son and the Holy Spirit in perfect alignment and in balance.

The energies of this alignment of the four lower bodies with the divinity of the fourfold aspect of God's consciousness—this mastery, this victory we have anchored in the physical octave in Jerusalem, in Bethlehem, in Bethany. Put off thy shoes from thy feet, for the place where thou standest is holy ground.[76] Can you not also consecrate this ground? Can you not also consecrate the ground where you walk—wherever you walk, wherever you are in the world of form? This is your hour and this is your calling—to bring the light and let it shine in the darkness of the streets of the cities of the world. This is the opportunity.

The light is a quickening power; it is electrifying. It leaps from heart to heart and from hearth to hearth. Be not discouraged, but bear a flaming sword that is the tenacity of an archangel to press onward and onward and onward with courage unto the victory. Faint not, for the rainbow of promise is the path of attain-

The Light That Shines in the Dark Streets of Jerusalem

ment, of victory over the seven rays, of victory in the manifestation of the Christ-power, the Christ-love, the Christ-wisdom.

I say to you who have gathered here, there is much to be done. We who were gathered in the upper room, we who heard the teachings of the master for forty days after his resurrection—we know that only a handful of devotees chosen by the Lord were responsible for beginning the cycle of two thousand years of Christendom, of the victory of the light, of the victory of the Christ consciousness and the culture of the Divine Mother.

We know also that it is the intensity of the heart's devotion that determines the victory—not the quantity, not the numbers, not the numbers of people that can be herded into a gathering, into a church or a mosque. No, it is in the simplicity of the heart's devotion, the heart that has surrendered all unto truth, unto victory, that is relentless in the search, in the quest, in the mission of leavening the entire lump of mankind's consciousness as the woman who took the leaven and hid it in three measures of meal[77] and it leavened the entire lump of the mass consciousness.

I say to you, be that woman! Be the Divine Mother! Men and women of the flame, I call to you to give mankind the victory by your individual devotion. Take the thoughts of the Holy Comforter and realize that they are a leaven, a yeast that expands when it is placed in the fertile dough of the minds of mankind. It expands and expands and expands, almost involuntarily. The dough cannot resist the yeast. The yeast takes over and it rises. The dough rises, and so the consciousness of mankind can be raised thusly.

Do you know, precious hearts, the angelic hosts of light who assisted in the releases of the Brotherhood that have come to be known as the Dead Sea Scrolls (the releases to the Essene community)—those angelic hosts have watched with great rejoicing as those same teachings which have now been brought forth in the Everlasting Gospel of God, *Climb the Highest Mountain*, have been spread abroad in the hearts and minds of those who are now reading that precious book. The angelic hosts have watched as people have accepted concepts in spite of themselves, in spite of their resistance to truth. For they have followed the logic of the divine Logos which displaces, replaces, dissipates and consumes the logic of the carnal mind. And so, precious hearts, when the minds and hearts of humanity are placed upon the right track, the track that leads to God, it is a resistless flow, it is an unceasing flow, it is a train that never stops.

You have heard of the car of juggernaut, which represents mankind's karma and its descent at an untimely moment. So I say to you, there is also a car of the Christ-ideation, the action of the ideas of God in the human consciousness which carry the devotee unto the victory by the very nature of the spiral of God's consciousness. And so the angels rejoice that one, two, three, five, ten, one hundred or a thousand souls have been touched; for they become the leaven that shall leaven the whole lump. And so you are a part of that leaven—leaven for the Christ, leaven for the Divine Mother.

Here is where it began two thousand years ago, but it must begin again and again and again. Wherever you stand, wherever you pray, wherever you decree, there it begins again. A coil of light is spun. It whirls around and it widens; and each time it whirls around, it gathers more of the chickens unto the hen of the Divine Mother. Consider, then, the power of the divine Logos as a giant spiral that goes out from you including greater and greater rings of light, rings of humanity climbing upward on the spiral that you have begun by a right thought, a right word, a right deed.

Yes, you can go forward and portray the great drama in your own Jerusalem, in your own Bethlehem, in your own Bethany. For wherever you are, there God has sent you; and you cannot be where he has not called, where he himself has not been.

Be born again. Invoke your own star—the star of your mighty

I AM Presence, which shall become a light which the shepherds and kings follow to the birthplace of the Christ over and over and over again. Fill the firmament of the heavens with stars so that mankind can follow them to the place of their own divinity, the altar where the human consciousness is sacrificed for the divine consciousness and time is no longer and space is no longer, for all is one and eternity is now.

Be of good cheer, it is I.[78] It is the I AM Presence within me, within you, within all that is the Presence of your victory. On behalf of the Essene Brotherhood, a branch of the Great White Brotherhood, on behalf of the angels of Bethlehem, on behalf of the brothers and the sisters of my retreat, I offer to you my gratitude for your pilgrimage to the Holy Land and for your reconsecration of that land to the flame of the Christ. In the name of the living God, who lives in all, I say, thank you.

Mary

Jerusalem, Israel
September 30, 1972

The LORD possessed me in the beginning of his way, before his works of old. I was set up from everlasting, from the beginning, or ever the earth was. When there were no depths, I was brought forth; when there were no fountains abounding with water. Before the mountains were settled, before the hills was I brought forth: while as yet he had not made the earth nor the fields nor the highest part of the dust of the world. —Proverbs

11

Hail, Thou That Art Highly Favored!

How marvelous is the concept that man can at last perceive the reality of God, the reality of finding favor with God. To be highly favored of God is the lot of all who can accept this concept. The conception is an immaculate one, one that belongs to everyone. For he who framed the worlds has not despaired of bringing peace to the centuries, to the millenniums, even to the minutiae of the second.

And so even the tick of a clock can be endowed with the concept of immortality, for immortality swallows up all things into its vastness and man findeth favor with God. And the moment that this favor comes to his consciousness, the moment that awareness that he is breaking the bread of life is his own thought because he has made it so, that moment does he realize the truth that has always been so—that he, man, is also a creator.

Man is a creator of destiny even as God is. The works of his mind and of his heart, when tethered to the darkness of the double standard, the double-eyed vision, produce many harms and much pain. But when the divine concept that man has found favor with God is truly realized, man begins the outworking of the wondrous spiritual nature of God into the appearance world. And the veil of the appearance world no longer becomes the dense enfoldment of his consciousness by all of the mortal dregs that result in pain and suffering, and even shame.

Shame is a state to the mind and consciousness which ought to be wiped away as tears from the eyes. And truly God shall wipe away all tears from the eyes of mankind[79] and establish that Christ-reality which is a veritable fountain of hope to the world—

the fountain of hope that radiates the light of the world to mankind. This is that fountain whose crystal stream, by reason of its purification and of its purity, radiates to man the purity of God, the purity of creative purpose, when creative purpose is perceived. When it trembles as the truth and reality of God upon the shaft of the mind descending into form, it produces the miracles that mankind now sometimes vainly hope for.

For faith is the substance of that which is not seen as yet.[80] And man should recognize his role in calling forth faith from the very heart of God—faith to do the necessary tasks in this day when the light of hope seems to have burned out in so many individuals, when the fears of uncertainty are come upon mankind—for the sins of the world are truly gross and becoming grosser each day.

Perfect love that casts out all fear[81] dwells within man. But man—by reason of his sense of solitude, his separation from his fellowmen and from his God, which makes him feel alone even in a multitude—is separated from the great realization of the oneness of the garment of God, the seamless robe my Son wore.[82]

Let all who can, conceive now of the seamless robe as a garment of light that humanity may wear today and that one day—if they are to end their turmoil and the return of vicious karma they have sent out—they must also universally wear. Within each individual there is posited by angelic hands and the fire of the certainty of the sacred Son of God the awareness that I AM is the name of God, that in the concept of Be-ness, in the concept of universal awareness, man may come, if he wills it so, to that wondrous place where the eyes behold the universal Christ as the spirit of living truth and high adventure who seeks to step through the veil in every man that he might change every man into the glowing fires of the spiritual sun.

The words "Our God is a consuming fire"[83] were majestically inscribed upon a tiny necklace which my Son wore around his neck. Inscribed in the Hebrew tongue and treasured highly, it was lost and never found again by man the night when he was captured and betrayed. But I tell you, the eternality of God has this day brought forth from the memories and treasure of my heart that sacred memory that you may this moment share that moment with me. For the words are true, and the power and principle of light and fire are as one. But so many see all around them the evidences of eternal spheres and know it not. For their consciousness is of a metal which, brittle and shining, produces only glitter and small reflection of reality.

Open the eyes of your consciousness! Open the doors of reality to yourself, and become strong upon the rock of God. For the foundations ought not to be moved. They ought to stand firm in each individual, carrying him from glory unto glory[84] each day. And men ought not to permit their consciousness to go downward into despair, even to the pits of despair, and then mightily rise as an arrow into the air.

Instead they ought to seek to maintain that constancy of the total man that always knows that he is upon the spiral road, rising higher and higher into the universal ethers, deriving from this high adventure of cosmic progress the realization that the purposes of God are being worked out in his own life and that ultimately all that is not of the goal and the shining end will fall from his grasp and be no more. Instead he will joyously leap, as a young child leaps forward in a green and golden meadow to pluck from the grass the flowers that allure him most because they are products of the sun, the earth and the rain. And he perceives in these mortal blossoms the realization of immortal hopes not yet realized.

And so in the lives of all individuals upon the planet there remain many unrealized hopes. But the hope that has most often been dashed to pieces in the world is the hope of the living God that humanity (putting away their toys, their ploys, their darkness and even their human joys) will realize at last that "there is a way that seemeth right unto a man, but the end thereof are the ways of death"[85] and then linger no more upon those strands of darkness and shadow but instead move ahead to the crowning, Christ-victorious victory of each life, a triumph of God-adventure. This is the divine triumph that is made possible in the cathedral of each man's mind where God is enshrined, where hope lives on as a perpetual flame upon an altar to the living God and the principle of immortal life.

Life is worthy when men make it worthy. Life is worthy as the world draws nigh to the high adventure. The world in reality seeks but knoweth not where to find. They are imbued unfortunately from time to time with a sense of boredom, with a sense of purposeless drift. Let them come instead to that point which they have missed in their evolution in the law of cycles. Let them come instead to the pathway where they can, holding the hand of God as a little child, recognize that maturity is being born within them, even in their younger years.

And one day as they attain the pathway of cosmic mastery, each one may find that blessed fulfillment which we also found in the angelic salutation "Hail, thou that art highly favored, the Lord is with thee and with thy Spirit: blessed art thou among women."[86] I pondered much upon this salutation. And in the days since its fulfillment in part,

> I have also perceived
> The glorious illumination of God
> Shining forth in the cathedral
> Of my being and mind,
> A hope that never remains blind
> But always opens consciousness' door
> To see, to perceive,
> And in the perception to be
> Not a bruised reed or smoking flax[87]
> But a strand of hope,
> A rope leading upward to the light

> And the glory and the fire
> Of true cosmic desire.
> A god is born in man,
> For man was born a god.
>
> And now as I stretch forth
> Over you all this day
> The rod of Aaron,[88]
> The rod of cosmic truth,
> The rod of hope—
> No bruised reed
> But the strongest seed,
> The seed of God-perfection—
> I say, let this vine be
> The true vine of immortal life.

And let the great joy bells ring out over the earth as an eternal Easter in the fall. For whereas man has descended into all manner of darkness and destructivity and karmic meanderings, the light of God has not gone out, the hope of God is not extinguished. There is before all the flaming power of victory transcendent. The victory of my Son may be shared by everyone. Remember this, for I speak as a mother of hearts who gathereth her children that they may give homage and honor to the purposes of the immortal Son, the universal Christ shared by all. The giant pall darkening humanity's consciousness lifts, and in its place the pure perfection of eternity shines, not as a vagrant mist but a golden mist of scintillating hope.

"I am the way, the truth, and the life."[89] Let this be in you, let this seed dwell in you, let these words sink down into your hearts; for so do you honor his purpose and you honor my purpose as well. And above all, we bow our knees gratefully toward the living God, the Spirit that has created the sweet vale of earth as a place where man may shed his tears and fears and then come at last with the passing of the years into the eternal dayspring from on high that has visited man[90] in the past and visits him now.

Let those who have ears to hear, hear what the Spirit has to say.[91] For the Spirit of the living God still speaks and the veil stands still, rent in twain.[92] The doorway, the gateway, the shining path to the universal Holy of holies,[93] is before each one. And each one determines the progress he will make by the very actions he does take.

I pledge you my love. I pledge you my hope. I pledge you my faith. Will you give me yours also, that hope may exchange with hope, and upon the rising ladder of cosmic glory we may stand together—mother, son, daughter—all one in the Christ consciousness, the face of God, reflected light of the immortal Presence.

Peace be upon you.

Mary

Colorado Springs, Colorado
October 3, 1971

When he prepared the heavens, I was there: when he set a compass upon the face of the depth: when he established the clouds above: when he strengthened the fountains of the deep: when he gave to the sea his decree that the waters should not pass his commandment: when he appointed the foundations of the earth: then I was by him, as one brought up with him: and I was daily his delight, rejoicing always before him; rejoicing in the habitable part of his earth; and my delights were with the sons of men. —Proverbs

12

Go Forth to Challenge the Night!

Pray therefore that ye enter not into temptation[94] in the final hours of testing and of the battle won. In those hours, when those denizens of darkness rise to stir the dust and create the fray, to opaque the vow, to ride in upon the delicate threads of your consciousness, remember the vow that was made in the Beginning before the world was of the fulfillment of the divinity of God in the humanity of man. Remember that you came forth with great courage, great determination, saying to the Lord of hosts: "Yea, Lord, I will go! Send me also. Send me in the name of the risen Christ." And the Lord answered and said: "As thou wilt. So go forth, sons and daughters of dominion. Go forth to challenge the night, the darkness, the discord and the fray."

I seal within your hearts this day the divine memory of the divine vow. I seal it there so that at the hour of the final testing, of the battle won, the divine memory shall appear as a giant screen of light to play again before your eyes that scene where you stood before the Most High God.

The courage of action, the courage to do battle when all the world is set against thee, must be evoked from the very heart of hearts. And prayer without ceasing must accompany the devotee who would win over the human consciousness with all of its deception, with all of its illusion, with all of its attempts to preserve itself against the day of the appearance of the Christ. For in the hour of the Second Coming, as the thief that cometh in the night,[95] the human consciousness is dissipated, it is scattered, it is no more. That very human consciousness anticipates the coming of the great light of the Son of God. And so it attempts, by devious methods and means, by all sorts of ruses and insanities, to preserve that last straw of identity.

Quicken the heart, quicken the mind, and quicken the determination, beloved ones, to slay the last foe! For the hour is indeed five minutes before twelve. It is the hour when the tail of the great dragon Tiamat swings as a backlash against the sons and daughters of God and against the holy innocents. It is the hour of victory for those who are ready to draw forth the light and challenge the tail of the great dragon—the challenge of the misuse of the sacred fire and the tail of man's own carnality.

Do you not perceive, precious hearts, the warning that was given to you in the thoughtform for the year?* Do you not realize that this is the year of the supreme effort of the darkness to retaliate, to take its revenge upon the Divine Woman and her seed? Do you not realize, then, that the defense of the Mother flame and of the Divine Manchild appearing in all humanity is the supreme watch of the hour? This is the watch of Christ: "Could ye not watch with me one hour?"[96]

And as we are now in the final quadrant of the year, will you summon the vision of the All-Seeing Eye of God to clear the pathway before you unto the victory over all manifestations in the physical plane that are less than the perfection of Almighty God? This is the supreme moment of opportunity to challenge all spirals and cycles initiated by yourselves and by mankind in the first three quadrants in the year. There is still time, still opportunity to say to that proud wave: "Thus far and no farther. Halt! I challenge you in the name of the living God."

You see, until the spiral becomes physical, it can be reversed. That is why Jesus said to Judas, "That which thou doest, do quickly."[97] For until the malice becomes tangible as the physical action, the karmic recompense cannot be meted out and the

---

*A golden clock showing five minutes to twelve with a Maltese cross at the point of the twelve.

return cycles begin and a new day then commence. And so you see, all that has begun at the etheric level of the memory, at the mental plane of thought, at the feeling place of desire—all this can yet be reversed if you challenge it ere it becomes physical. I say, then, it is your moment of triumph or your moment of submission. In the name of Almighty God, you have the authority in the name of Jesus the Christ to challenge every cycle of negation, every spiral of darkness that is released against you like a boomerang, like a tail of a serpent, like the forces of the night.

This is your hour of victory, blessed hearts. And I have come this morning to tell you that there are indeed many cycles that must be challenged by you if the earth is to come to the place on New Year's Eve that it can receive the opportunities and the benedictions that are contemplated by the Lords of Karma. Thus you might say it is an act of divine mercy in advance that I have been permitted to come before you this day to tell you that there are few upon the planetary body who understand the laws of God as you do, who understand the authority of the Sons and Daughters of Dominion, who call in the name of Jesus the Christ for the victory.

I say, then, it is up to this handful of people gathered here and those [throughout the world] who will respond to analyze the year's events beginning January 1, 1972, to see those things which have transpired in every nation upon earth and to call, in the name of my Son and in the name of the Divine Mother, that all activities not in keeping with the divine will or the divine plan for this earth be checked, be consumed, be held in abeyance during this final cycle. For only if you thus systematically follow these trends and untangle the labyrinth of mankind's thoughts and feelings and actions will you be able to prepare the way for the golden-age cycles that are to be released on New Year's Eve.

I have seen in the past the prayers that you have mustered, the long hours you have spent in decrees. I have seen the faith, the worthiness, the response of the student body, and there is not a shadow of doubt in my consciousness that you will respond this day. I know that you shall, for I know that you have done so in the past and I behold the immaculate conception of your divinity.

I place my hand, then, upon your foreheads this morning to seal within the focus there of the All-Seeing Eye of God the immaculate conception of your own divinity. And I say, let that image of the cosmic City Foursquare—the temple beautiful of your own individuality, your own individed identity—appear now for the victory, parting the way, parting the Red Sea of your own human consciousness, and providing the pathway into the Promised Land of the golden age and the new heaven and the new earth.[98]

I, then, will stand with you. And if you will call to me asking in the name of the Christ that I show you what things you ought to call for, how ye ought to pray, I will certainly show you. Heaven is not beyond the methods of research that are pursued by your scientists and scholars today, for heaven also keeps its records and has its libraries. The Keeper of the Scrolls (that great being who sends forth his legions of angels to keep the record of every man, woman and child upon this planet) will draw forth from the Book of Life in your behalf, if you will call to him and to the Lords of Karma, those pages that require seeing and examination if you are to make the proper calls.

I say to you, beloved hearts, be not weary in well doing.[99] If it is necessary to go to your libraries to examine the events of the years, then do so. Then look and listen and learn, for I have spoken. I have shown you this day that it is possible for a dedicated humanity to transmute not only present but past turmoil, past discord, past records of darkness and of death. By transmuting the past before it is able to be written upon the pages of the future, the devotees can spare mankind the holocaust and the cataclysm of their own returning karma.

Do you not see, then, that the mercy of the Great Law is

retroactive—past, present and future? The beacon of mercy turns round and round, circular in motion, in the great lighthouse of the world. Mercy is the beacon, the lamp that is placed there now by the hand of Almighty God. Seize it, then! Withhold not the last measure of devotion.

These are they who love not their lives unto the death.[100] These are they, O Lord: These are they which stand before you this day and plead on behalf of an ignorant and blighted humanity. These are they who are willing to do penance that the Law might be satisfied, that the Law might be fulfilled. These are they who know that the suffering of the human consciousness prepares the way for the glory, the *glow-ray*, of the Christ consciousness to come into manifestation in the planes of Mater, of the Divine Mother.

O Lord, have mercy! O Lord, have mercy! O Lord, have mercy upon their souls! I, Mary, stand before the Most High God this day to intercede on behalf of humanity everywhere—those who call to me, those who spurn me, those who know me not. From the least unto the greatest, all are the children of my heart. And I stand with my heart bleeding, as it were, as the sword of mankind's disobedience pierces the heart of the Mother once again. I, too, am willing to bear the pain of the travail of giving birth to the Divine Manchild, the travail of a planet overcoming the darkness and the night. For I AM a cosmic mother, and I know that when the dawn appears, the dawn of the great golden age, so the Christ Child shall be born in everyone. Every man, woman and child upon this planet shall give birth to the Divine Son, and this shall mark the golden age.

This is the beginning of the new order of the ages. This is the Second Appearing. This is the hour when the capstone is placed upon the pyramid of each man's identity. For the All-Seeing Eye is the eye of the immaculate conception of the Christ. And when he shall appear, we shall see him as he is[101] in manifestation in man, in woman, in all life. By the authority of the Holy Spirit and the Divine Mother, who is the bride of the Holy Spirit, I seal you in my love, in my protection and in the divine memory of the vows you have taken to serve until every last one has the opportunity for the victory and the ascension in the light.

Mary

Colorado Springs, Colorado
October 13, 1972

Now therefore hearken unto me, O ye children: for blessed are they that keep my ways. Hear instruction, and be wise, and refuse it not. Blessed is the man that heareth me, watching daily at my gates, waiting at the posts of my doors. For whoso findeth me findeth life and shall obtain favour of the LORD. —Proverbs

13

The Key to Opportunity

The key to opportunity, beloved ones, is the fulfillment of the law of your own being. Until that law is fulfilled, the next cycle of attainment cannot be opened for you. Therefore consider with me this day, as we approach together the portal of a new year of promise to all mankind—consider what we may do together on behalf of mankind.

They are my children and you also must consider that they are your own. Mankind find it difficult to have a forgiving heart toward those who are grown to maturity, those who are in adulthood, and therefore they sometimes are wont to judge unjustly, whereas toward children their hearts wax tender and forgiving in love. Consider, then, that as you approach your fellowman, each one is still in the childhood of attainment and must be so regarded. By this attitude the ladies of heaven maintain a permanent state of grace in loving understanding and consideration for the evolutions of this planet.

You recall the statement "Never underestimate the power of a woman." I say to you, do not underestimate the power of the divine Feminine, of that ray that is anchored in your heart from the Divine Mother, or the power of the ladies of heaven to effect change in the world of form. You recall the incident this year of those who demonstrated because of high prices in the shopping markets. The ladies of the world, when they mobilize on behalf of a victory, of a cause, can do much good. And so the suffragettes of the early part of this century achieved in America woman's suffrage.

Beloved ones, it is so important that equality not manifest

among mankind as competition. Equality is the opportunity to rise to one's own God Source in the administration and outpicturing of one's own divine plan fulfilled. How important it is, especially for disciples on the pathway of attainment, to understand that they are never competing with one another but only with their own momentums, striving to overcome and to arrive just a little bit ahead of the mark where they perhaps another time had failed.

This is the admonishment which I gave to the disciples after the passing and the ascension of the Lord Jesus. You recall that there was a time of strife among them. And this, of course, was not their intent but was fostered upon them by the brothers of the shadow. Even so, you today must do battle with unseen forces which are arrayed against you and at every hand attempt to make you think that it is your own mind acting within you. Beloved ones, it is never your True Self that is out of harmony with the universe. For your divine identity is the mighty I AM Presence, and in that you must stand and face and conquer every situation that would array itself against you.

The soft voice, the gentle whisper of the Holy Spirit, is the only presence of the creative force of life within you. The holding to and clinging fast to that vine of divinity will work wonders in the world of form for you. And whenever you are amidst the tempest, as beloved Jesus was in the boat[102] and the sea roared without, remember that you can simply say, "Peace, be still, and know that I am God!"[103] And you can call to your mighty I AM Presence, the entire Spirit of the Great White Brotherhood or an individual ascended being and say, "Mighty I AM Presence, take command of that situation!" and know that all will be well.

Then turn your attention to God and go about your daily activities. Do not feel that you must strive with opposition. For the forces of light, the power of Michael's band and of all the archangels stand ready to go forth to do battle for you as you

The Key to Opportunity

continue to press forward toward the mark of the high calling in Christ Jesus.[104]

Remember that, beloved ones. You do not need to struggle. The hosts of the Lord are encamped about you and they indeed go forth. And they are the conquerors. But remember that in this world you must always consider that the manifestation of God is sometimes, of necessity, tempered by the conditions of time and space. At other times, instantaneous precipitation is possible. Therefore expect the immediate, but be willing to wait in patience in the possession of your souls[105] for the fulfilling of the divine within you.

It is true that saints in the past have lost initiations and have failed tests because of impatience. Your patience must be tried, for it is the trying of your faith, the trying of your momentum and your dedication, and this must be tested in all ways. For to give you the full power of the kingdom all at once (as beloved Ray-O-Light explained to you) would mean that with that added power, you would have double the karma or triple the karma or whatever increase that power would mean to you. And so you must be ready to receive the offering that is given to you from on high. Your cup must be expanded—the chalice of your heart flame. And this is an hourly process; it goes on continuously. And you must learn how to meditate while you are about your daily tasks. This is so important.

To feel the attunement with the Holy Spirit at all times is something which was taught to me before I could be given the opportunity to bear the Christ and assist him in his mission. For if you are not in attunement with God at all times, how can he act for you in time of danger or crisis or opposition? It means that in the presence of danger, you must first make your attunement before you can receive assistance. In the life of a disciple there is not time for this, beloved ones. Attunement must be ready as an armour, as a sword of truth. When you are in a battle, you cannot run back to the lines and put on your armour and your sword after the enemy have launched their attack. There you must be ready.

Attunement, therefore, is somewhat of a subconscious quality. It is begun with the outer mind; it is begun by its supplication, by the prayer to the Holy Christ Self to take command and continue the prayers and decrees of your heart throughout the twenty-four hours. This is an important request, and it should be made by you each morning before you even rise from your beds. If you would follow in the pathway of the Mother of the World and of the Christ, you must say to yourself:

"Beloved mighty I AM Presence, Father of all life, act on my behalf this day. Fill my form. Release the light that is necessary for me to go forth to do thy will, and see that at every hand the decisions I make are according to thy holy will. See that my energies are used to magnify the Lord in everyone whom I meet. See to it that thy holy wisdom released to me is used constructively for the expansion of God's kingdom. And above all, beloved heavenly Father, I commend my spirit unto thee and ask that as thy flame is one with my flame, the union of these two flames shall pulsate to effect in my world the continuous alertness and attunement which I need with my holy Presence, with the Holy Spirit and with the World Mother."

And then accept this in full faith, beloved ones, and realize that then the hierarchy of light may take over your form, your world; and you no longer need to feel that at any moment in the day you must first approach God, for you are already one with him. And thus no situation that comes to you will take you off guard, for you will be on guard in the vanguard of light. This is the requirement of the hour. For as K-17 told you at the last class, it is necessary that this group of disciples shall become the fuse that shall trigger the blazing torch of the flame of truth throughout the entire planetary body as a mighty catalyst of light.

Do not underestimate your service to the light, then, and realize that one with God is a majority for the entire planetary body. And this is scientific; for we have proven it, we have demonstrated it. And by the power of this law, the mighty Christian dispensation has come forth and remained to the present hour a mighty bulwark in the world of form. For it has retained the worship of the one God in the West, and it has set to naught those forces of Communism which by now would have long ago taken over the entire planet were it not for the mission and the flame of the Christ and the focuses which we hold in the Western world.

And so you see, never discredit those disciples of truth who have gone before you, for they did all that they could according to the knowledge which was given unto them. Many of them, beloved ones—those who were sincere and truly humble before God—as they knelt in the great cathedrals in the hundreds of years that have gone by, have seen pulsating before them the roaring violet flame. And they have come to know the knowledge of the law as you have been given it in the outer. They have come to know this law in the inner and they have seen it by the dedication of their hearts.

This knowledge, which was known to us as we were the followers of the Christ, has been carried hand to hand through the centuries, and it has not been lost. It has been passed as a mighty torch. And now this torch is given to the many in the outer world as the knowledge of the sacred fire which must be spread abroad, and spread abroad speedily this year by your very decrees, your hearts, your heads, your hands, your dedication, by the published material that is to come forth through this activity, and by all that you can do in the service of the light.

You are the chosen ones, beloved ones. Remember that. Remember that you are chosen because you have chosen. You have chosen to be servants of God, and therefore recognize the meaning of being a servant of God. It demands your total being, your total consciousness—all of your love, all of your life and more!

For the prize is very high, and all that you give to God is given back to you in return. And this is the law of the tithe which comes forth from the very heart of Alpha and Omega. When you give forth your energies in decrees, God must return to you that which you have given. As you give to your fellowman, so it is multiplied unto you. By this very same law, Jesus broke the bread and fed the multitudes, five thousand in number and even more. And there was substance left over.

You, too, can go forth and break the bread of the body of God, of the Holy Spirit, among men. And as you go in the streetcars and on the streets of life and in your own vehicles, as you decree, realize that all within your sight and those whom you cannot see can receive of the body of God, of the Holy Spirit, through your simple call. Remember the simplicity that was taught to you by Saint Germain this evening past. Remember that well—the simple call "O God, help me!" the simple call to God "Break the body of the Lord among these thy children, O Father!" And then return to your tasks.

Realize that you can utter simple prayers all through the day as they are inspired upon your heart by your own Holy Christ Self, who is indeed praying before the Father twenty-four hours a day. The prayers of your Holy Christ Self can be reaped in the world of form only as you appropriate them and ask that they descend into your heart's chalice. For all that occurs in the macrocosm is destined to descend into the microcosm.

The lever of the valve is opened by your decree. And until you make the call, the valve is shut and nothing can come forth to you except the allotment for your embodiment of the pulsation from the mighty I AM Presence. Anything in addition to that—the expansion of your heart flame and all that you need to have and do and be to go forth in the light—must come forth because you *invoke* it, because you *decree* it and because you *accept* it unflinchingly on behalf of the service of the light.

Steel your minds, precious ones, and realize that the discipline of the Law is the saving grace of mankind. The discipline of the Law is mercy. For as you align yourself and your four lower bodies with the being of God, you appreciate that there are vast spheres of power that may be released to you because you are one with the Law. The Law is not bondage. Obedience is never a chain, beloved ones. Because you are one with the Law, you have and are entitled to reap the benefits of the entire cosmos. Do you see how this is the key to your opportunity in the new year as you consider the law of your own being, as this law is set against the law of cosmos?

Do you know that you are lawmakers for your own world just as the congress of this country is the lawmaking body for this nation? Do you know that when you decide that this, that or the other thing is wrong for you or you can't do this or you are too weak or such and such is a requirement for your lifestream, you set up a law which is limiting? And conversely, when you declare, "I AM the full perfection of God! I have the full potential of the seven mighty Elohim to go forth in their name!" that thereby you expand the law of your being and you are permitted, then, to reap the benefits of the law which you create?

The Law is a circumscription of energy; it defines what man can do and what he cannot do. Therefore as you define in your world the sphere of your activity, remember that all law that is based on the infinite conception of God will fulfill in you your victory, the fullness of your service and the mighty ascension in the light. That which, then, circumscribes you to a round of mortal pleasure, of sensation in matter, of the mortal consciousness, will limit you, and you can never tie into the great infinite storehouse of light that is just behind the veil.

If you could but reach out your hand and touch mine! You can almost *feel* that there is very little between us, beloved ones.

Very little is the line between the angelic hosts and mankind. As you give your prayers, as you are in your beds at night, realize that simply by a touch, by a thought, by a point of light, we are in your presence.

And if you will ask, beloved ones, that the Electronic Presence of the master of your choice be superimposed over your form before you go to sleep at night, you will find that throughout the hours of rest, all of the momentums of light of that ascended being can be absorbed into your consciousness, into your four lower bodies by the power of the electrode upon the spine—the ascending and descending currents of God that formulate the magnetic forcefield which is the focus of the great cycles of infinity within your very own Presence.

Realize what this can mean for you, beloved ones! Ere you go to sleep at night, if you say, "Beloved Father, beloved Jesus the Christ, send me the Electronic Presence of yourself, and let that duplicate of your image rest over me and through me and in me while my body sleeps," you will waken, then, with the Spirit of the resurrection flame within you as Christ awakened on Easter morning. And you will find that within you, you have the full pulsation of that mighty flame that is his full-gathered momentum of the victory of the ascension currents.

Do you see what this can mean to you, beloved ones, if systematically you make a list for yourself of all the known members of the hierarchy and then each night call to a different master, make supplication to the flame on which he serves, and then ask that that be imbibed by you? You will find that you will be prepared, then, to go forth as teachers, ministers and preachers of the Word and that you will be given mighty assistance that otherwise might take many generations for you to develop through your own inner training and through simply the application to your own heart flame without the assistance of the momentum of the beings of light.

Will you do this with me this year, each of the three hundred sixty-five days that are to come? Will you do this, beloved ones? Stand and pledge yourselves to the light, and realize that as your Cosmic Mother I will amplify whatever calls you make. For I am pledging myself this year, as part of my dedication unto mankind, that every call that is made in my name shall have the full-gathered momentum of my service and even more. A special dispensation has been given to me by the great Karmic Board whereby I may assist the lifestreams of this earth. And so, beloved ones, those of you who know to make the call in my name, amplify the power of that flame and let it be released through all mankind. For in his Spirit is the victory of the light.

We are determined—the ladies of heaven, the Karmic Board and the angelic hosts—as we stand by mankind, to give every assistance possible before the approach of the time when it may be possible that the Dark Cycle* shall descend upon mankind. This may not be necessary if mankind turn and face the light. But if they do not, we are ready and we are preparing for the time when you individually will be held accountable to hold the balance for this planet. This time is coming soon and, as in the parable of the wise virgins,[106] keep your lamps trimmed, beloved ones. For you will need every erg of energy that is given unto you. You will need it in that time.

Rejoice, then, that the heavenly Father has prepared for you a way of salvation, that mankind can receive the glory. That there is hope in the world is the greatest joy and promise of the Christmas season, of the Eastertide, which we now prepare to receive in the coming weeks prior to the resurrection and the ascension of the Christ within each heart. Look forward, then, to the resurrection of all life.

---

*The Dark Cycle of the return of mankind's karma began on April 23, 1969. It is a period when man's misqualified energy, held in abeyance for many centuries, is being released for balance in order that the golden age can come in.

Go forward in the name of the Christ. Go forward in the name of his flame. And bear within you that Diamond Heart that is my own, that is the heart of beloved El Morya, that is the heart of the will of God. And when your heart becomes the diamond-shining mind of God, the wisdom of that heart will be unmoved, you will be unmoved. And no riptide of emotion, however great or small, will be able to deter you from your course, which is the course of freedom. It is the cause of freedom, the cause of victory.

Develop, then, that courage and determination that says, "I shall not be moved!" And then go forth to conquer. Conquer in his name, beloved ones, for that mighty flame is nigh you alway. And I am with you alway,[107] even as is my Son and the presence of the Holy Spirit. As you receive our radiation this day and the sublimity of the rule of the Holy Family, realize that this Trinity of manifestation is the true meaning of the threefold flame within your heart. For in the balance of the Father, Mother and Son principles, you attain the glory of your victory. Receive it, then. For it is lovingly, freely given from the heart of your own mighty I AM Presence.

Mary

Colorado Springs, Colorado
December 31, 1967

Wisdom hath builded her house, she hath hewn out her seven pillars....Whoso is simple, let him turn in hither: as for him that wanteth understanding, she saith to him, Come, eat of my bread, and drink of the wine which I have mingled. Forsake the foolish, and live; and go in the way of understanding. —Proverbs

14

Come into the Arms of the Divine Mother

Blessed children of my heart, gather now into the folds of my consciousness. Come into the arms of the Divine Mother and feel for a moment the longing of your hearts for the Eternal Bourn assuaged by the love of one who long ago held the Christ in her arms. So I would wrap you in the swaddling clothes of my consciousness, the folds of wisdom carefully placed around your bodies, the folds of love and power, of faith and grace, the unguents of healing. So I take the swaddling garment from my consciousness and I enfold you, each one, in the love of the Divine Mother, whose office it is my opportunity to represent to embodied mankind.

How beautiful it is to behold faces upturned in holy prayer, in supplication unto the Divine One, whom they identify in my person but who is not confined to my person, blessed hearts, but who is all-pervading. For the Divine Mother is the cosmos itself. And it has been my lot to outpicture a fractioned part of it, and in that part was the Whole and is the Whole. And thus, when devotees of the light pray, "Mary," so they receive the effulgence of the *Mother ray*, which is the inner meaning of *Mary*, released from my hands and heart, released from my being.

Faces upturned in adoration always have the ear of the angels. The angels of the Divine Mother tarry with those who pray the rosary each day or who offer decrees and affirmations as they have been taught in their peculiar faiths. For the Divine Mother has no one faith but is universal, blessed hearts. Realize, then, that to her all are children of the Most High. All have come forth from the seed of the Father. And by her nourishment, her tender care and regard, she knows that they shall return unto him.

Therefore, when you pray to the Divine Mother, include in your prayer the supplication for all who know not the meaning of the Mother, for all who have been deprived of the image most holy of the Virgin and Child. For by the acts of darkness and Luciferianism, a plot has been spawned upon a great many in the West as well as in the East. The Mother has been taken from them and their souls cry out as Mary* cried out, "They have taken away my Lord, and I know not where they have laid him."[108] So the souls of men cry inside and say, "They have taken away the Mother, and I know not where to find her."

Precious hearts, until the soul finds the Mother again—the Motherhood of God personified in many heavenly beings and angels—that soul cannot find reunion with the Father. For do you understand that the child goes to the Father through the Mother? It is the Mother that teaches the child the wisdom of the Father. It is the Mother that draws the children into the heart of nature. It is the Mother, above all, that seals the soul with the patterns of individuality, that draws out by the power of her love the magnetization of the God flame, which is as a kernel of light locked in the heart until the warmth of the Mother's love reaches it, as the sun touches the flowers. And so they begin to germinate even beneath the soil, and so the soul germinates within man even before the Christ appears on the surface to transform his entire being and world.

Pray, then, not only for yourselves and your children, ye daughters of Jerusalem who wept at the hour of the crucifixion of Jesus.[109] Pray for your children. Pray for yourselves. Pray for all humanity. Pray that they might also know the Divine Mother.

How will they come to know that Mother? There is one very important way in which you can assist, and I have come to tell it

---

*Mary Magdalene.

to you this day. It is that you become the Divine Mother yourself!—that you receive into your arms those who need succor and healing, and comfort and compassion. You who are strong men and wise, you too must become the Mother, you must outpicture her flame. And women of the sacred fire, you who have borne the children of this generation, understand that all people are your children. And as the babes have sucked at your breast, so understand that all humanity must be fed the milk of the living Word, the true teachings of my Son. These have been imparted to you not to hide beneath a bushel,[110] not to hide the light under the garment of self-righteousness but to bring it forth in humility.

I say, then, be ye representatives of the Virgin, the Holy Virgin of God. Draw forth the consciousness of the Most High in purity and love, and minister unto the needs of my children everywhere. Lo here and lo there, they come. Some know not that their souls yearn for the light of the Divine Mother, for they are surfeited in intellectual pride and arrogance. They have sought her in many ways, but they have been given the chaff instead of the wheat. They have not been given even a morsel of the true consciousness and the true wisdom of the Mother.

Beware, then, that you become not puffed up with the wisdom of the world, with the intellectual meanderings that carry the mind far afield from its attunement with the Christ. Beware also that you use knowledge as a tool. For all that is given in your schools of higher learning, in your universities, is for the edification of man that he might be brought to the feet of the Divine Mother, who teaches her children. Therefore the true wisdom of the ages must be enshrined in the halls of learning. And you must learn to discern that which is real and that which is unreal, that information which binds the soul to a decadent materialism and that divine inspiration which frees the soul in an ascending *Mater*-realization.

The realization of the Mother is the purpose of all study.

Therefore, let Wisdom teach her children. Pray when you are in school, in college and in the universities. Pray that the wisdom of the Mother shall inspire the teachers, the professors, the hearers also, the pupils who come. Why do they come, precious hearts? They come because the Mother flame is enshrined wherever wisdom is spoken, and it is the flame of wisdom from the Divine Mother that draws all people to a desire for higher learning. For deeply embedded within the being of man is the soul that yearns to be free and that knows that his freedom will ultimately come through the knowledge of the sacred Word.

And so it is, "Seek, and ye shall find; knock, and the door shall be opened unto you."[111] It is ever thus that the call compels the answer. Would you have love? Then invoke love. Would you become love? Then invoke love. Would you give love to all the nations? Then I say, invoke love. How can you give that which you do not have, that which you do not know or understand? Except it be given to you of God, it is not everlasting or real or healing or filled with power. If you would be wisdom, invoke it. If you would have it and become it, invoke it, precious hearts.

Invoke! Invoke! Invoke! For the representatives of the Almighty One surround you. And yet they will not touch one hair of your head unless you give them entrée into your world, unless you bid them enter, for this is the law of the planes of consciousness.

Do not forget that God gave man the opportunity to take dominion in the footstool kingdom,[112] and he gave to him free will that he might prove himself worthy to become a co-creator with the Infinite One. Therefore, man must make the fiat "Thy will be done! Thy will be done! Thy will be done in us daily!" With this fiat, man gives the authority back to God, who then enters into his world, into his kingdom, to work the works of the fires of the will of God. This call must be made hourly, momentarily, daily. Not just once but perpetually must you recite the mantra "Not my will, not my will, not my will, but thine be done!"[113] This is the key to the cornucopia of heaven, to the abundance of blessings which shower upon you each time you give that immortal fiat of the Son of man.

Precious ones, if the kingdom of heaven is to become a reality upon earth and if this generation is to be spared the cycles of the return of karma which have been prophesied as cataclysm, as the mountains and the rocks falling upon man,[114] as the weeping and gnashing of teeth,[115] as the travail of the Divine Woman[116]—if this generation is to be spared, then I say, a more than ordinary dedication shall be required of the devotees of the sacred fire for and on behalf of their misguided brethren.

For heaven requires that a remnant of the people shall show forth their devotion. And as the Lord agreed that he would spare the city of Sodom if ten righteous men could be found,[117] so he agrees in this hour of impending doom that if but a handful of righteous men and women are found totally dedicated and consecrated, so the impending karma can be stayed—the hand of man's own self-destruction will be bound.

But do you know what the Lord requires of thee? Do you know what it means to be wholly dedicated, wholly selfless, having surrendered the human personality, no longer engaging in strife and discord, giving yourself to the altar of God each morning when you arise, consecrating your energies—each erg, each erg of energy, each measurement that is pulsated from the heart of God to the heart of man, from the center of being, the heart, the head and the hand—in manifest dominion each day? Dedication is something that must be sought, and when it is found it must be transcended. And dedication must become a greater and greater fervor, a flame that expands to include all who come within its gentle aura and radiance.

The fires of dedication are the fires of love. These are the fires that draw all men into the worship of the one God and cut them free from their idolatry, their self-loves, their rebellion against the law of the Father. I say to you, then, if you consider yourself dedicated, then say: "I must become dedicated tenfold more. I must multiply my dedication!"

You must never be satisfied with dedication. For I tell you that as soon as you are dedicated enough in one plane of consciousness, then you earn the right to rise to the next plane, which is an expanded awareness of God's consciousness, which has greater initiations, greater trials and tests. And therefore immediately the dedication must be multiplied in order to meet the challenges of the next level of God's consciousness. As soon as you have met those, then you earn the right to enter the next plane. And so we hear of the levels of heaven—the third heaven to which Paul rose,[118] and this means the third plane of God's consciousness.

Do you understand, then, that there can never be complacency, there can never be a standing still? For once the cycle of initiation has begun in your life, it is like a giant coil, a spiral. It has exactly thirty-three turns to the coil. Beginning with a wide base, as it rises it becomes narrower, in the shape of the pyramid of life.

And you will find that as you rise upon this coil of initiation as Jesus did in the thirty-three years of his final embodiment, there is less and less room for the human consciousness. For the walls close in and there is only room for the spirit, the soul of man. And if you begin to feel a cramped feeling on the Path, understand that it is because you are rising on the spiral of initiation. And the only thing that is cramped is the human ego, the carnal mind, the human will, the human motive, the human intellect. These, then, must be surrendered if the soul would go on and rise a step higher.

And so I say to you, men and women of the twentieth century, this is the hour when the fate of the planet shall be determined. For mankind have in their hands this day the knowledge and the use of weapons of atomic power, explosives with which they could destroy the very earth that supports their consciousness. Do you think that I speak harshly? You have only to look at the asteroid belt between

Mars and Jupiter to find what a civilization did with the misuse of atomic power. For that was once a mighty and noble planet. The warring factions of that civilization could not come into agreement in the reason of the Lord: "Come let us reason together, saith the LORD."[119] No, they would not, they could not. They refused to surrender their mortal pride, their vilifications of one another.

They understood not that in hating one another, they were hating themselves. And so the hatred they sent forth came back upon them in a mighty surge of explosive power. They actually blew up their home and annihilated themselves with their hatred, blew themselves to smithereens. And all that is left is chunks of clay floating in space, unfit for habitation. Is this the destiny that you desire for your star? I think not.

But, then, I say, there is work to be done, there is much that you must do. You must not be idle, not forgetful that every hour is a countdown and at the end of the hour the judgment is come, the determination is made. Will the energies that mankind have employed during that hour return to him as self-destruction or as self-elevation? You see, the final judgment is meted out to man twenty-four times in each twenty-four-hour cycle. And at the close of the hour, the angels of record write down for every man, woman and child the exact use to which he has put the sacred fire. And one day that energy in its cumulative state shall be released to mankind. They consider that day to be the Final Judgment, but I say that Final Judgment is only the effect of causes which they have set up prior to the end.

Therefore each hour it would be well for you to consider: What have I done with my time, with my thoughts, with my feelings? Have they been cups and chalices whereby the Lord of hosts might deliver into the hands of my people the energies of purity and of healing? Or have I wasted this hour and thus wasted the grains in the hourglass, grains of energy entrusted to me by the Holy Spirit? It is well that you assess your use of time, for time is energy and time is the only gift you have in which to bring the kingdom of heaven into manifestation.

As you consecrate the hours to the threefold flame of love, wisdom and power, so you will set the pattern whereby all humanity who follow after you, walking in your footsteps as they walk in the footsteps of Christ, might also learn the lessons of the law of cycles. Do you understand, precious hearts, that to you is given a tremendous opportunity—an opportunity that can save the planet from self-destruction, that can usher in a golden age of enlightenment, a two-thousand-year reign of the Christ in which all mankind shall have the opportunity to practice the laws of sacred alchemy as Jesus taught them.

This is the hour, precious hearts. And so, as the manifestation of the Mother ray, I, Mary, have come to you this hour to break bread with you, to commune with you, with the Holy Spirit, to draw you into my heart. And do you know, as I have held you in my embrace during these precious moments together, I have renewed the anchoring within my heart flame of the Electronic Presence of your own divinity. And I shall carry that with me as a precious souvenir, as a precious token of this time we have spent together commemorating that moment in cosmic history when the Mother flame returned to the continent of Africa. And because you have been drawn here by the love of your hearts, so I shall give to you, precious hearts, that special dispensation that you might always be with me through the pattern and the blueprint of your divinity, which I shall henceforth carry within my heart.

Will you recognize, then, the mantra "We are one, we are one, we are one, we are one, we are one." [sung by Mary and echoed by the audience] Beloved children, as you sing this song of the sacred fire together, will you remember the prayer of Jesus "Father, make them one even as we are one."[120] In your hearts and in your consciousness, in your thoughts of one another, will you embrace each other each day as you would the Christ that is cradled and aborning within your heart. For only by this great love for your brother, for your sister will you come to know the oneness which we share—the oneness of the Mother and of the Christ, the oneness of the Father.

If you weld yourselves together as a mighty body of God upon earth—inseparable in service, in thought, in prayer, in dedication—you will see a mighty work done upon this continent that has never before been accomplished since the last golden ages of the blue and the violet race. These are the words which I left with the disciples who stayed with me unto the hour of my own ascension. These are the precious words of oneness. For in the union of that oneness, you find the strength, the overcoming victory and the power that enables you to withstand all of the fiery darts of wickedness[121] and all the temptations of the world.

Will you remember, then, in time of stress and strain, when I am no longer with you in a speaking voice and in a tangible manifestation, will you remember these sacred moments together when we renewed our covenant of oneness, even as that covenant was renewed amongst the disciples and myself.

For that will give you the courage to move onward, to follow the three wise men, to follow the Christ and the star of the East that shall come to rest over the continent of Africa, prophesying the birth of a new nation, a new people, a new beginning, a new resurrection, a new opportunity. That is the star Afra! That is the star born from Alpha and Omega! That is the star whose energies shall flow in a mighty release to inspire the hearts of all souls evolving here until they too, walking in His footsteps, mount Bethany's hill and also rise into the cloud of their I AM Presence, as did Jesus.[122] So be it.

By the power of the Divine Mother, I have spoken. And I AM with you alway, even unto the end of the age![123]

Mary

Accra, Ghana
July 23, 1972

The Chart of Your Divine Self

The Chart of Your Divine Self is a portrait of you and of the God within you. It is a diagram of yourself and your potential to become who you really are. It is an outline of your spiritual anatomy.

The upper figure is your "I AM Presence," the Presence of God that is individualized in each one of us. It is your personalized "I AM THAT I AM." Your I AM Presence is surrounded by seven concentric spheres of spiritual energy that make up what is called your "causal body." The spheres of pulsating energy contain the record of the good works you have performed since your very first incarnation on earth. They are like your cosmic bank account.

The middle figure in the chart represents the "Holy Christ Self," who is also called the Higher Self. You can think of your Holy Christ Self as your chief guardian angel and dearest friend, your inner teacher and voice of conscience. Just as the I AM Presence is the Presence of God that is individualized for each of us, so the Holy Christ Self is the presence of the universal Christ that is individualized for each of us.

"The Christ" is actually a title given to those who have attained oneness with their Higher Self, or Christ Self. That's why Jesus was called "Jesus, the Christ." *Christ* comes from the Greek word *christos*, meaning "anointed"—anointed with the light of God.

What the Chart shows is that each of us has a Higher Self, or "inner Christ," and that each of us is destined to become one with that Higher Self—whether we call it the Christ, the Buddha, the Tao or the Atman. This "inner Christ" is what the Christian mystics sometimes refer to as the "inner man of the heart," and what the Upanishads mysteriously describe as a being the "size of a thumb" who "dwells deep within the heart."

The Chart of Your Divine Self

We all have moments when we feel that connection with our Higher Self—when we are creative, loving, joyful. But there are other moments when we feel out of sync with our Higher Self—moments when we become angry, depressed, lost. What the spiritual path is all about is learning to sustain the connection to the higher part of ourselves so that we can make our greatest contribution to humanity.

The ribbon of white light descending from the I AM Presence through the Holy Christ Self to the lower figure in the Chart is the crystal cord (sometimes called the silver cord). It is the "umbilical cord," the lifeline, that ties you to Spirit.

Your crystal cord also nourishes that special, radiant flame of God that is ensconced in the secret chamber of your heart. It is called the threefold flame, or divine spark, because it is literally a spark of sacred fire that God has transmitted from his heart to yours. This flame is called "threefold" because it engenders the primary attributes of Spirit—power, wisdom and love.

The mystics of the world's religions have contacted the divine spark, describing it as the seed of divinity within. Buddhists, for instance, speak of the "germ of Buddhahood" that exists in every living being. In the Hindu tradition, the Katha Upanishad speaks of the "light of the Spirit" that is concealed in the "secret high place of the heart" of all beings.

Likewise, the fourteenth-century Christian theologian and mystic Meister Eckhart teaches of the divine spark when he says, "God's seed is within us." There is a part of us, says Eckhart, that "remains eternally in the Spirit and is divine....Here God glows and flames without ceasing."

When we decree, we meditate on the flame in the secret chamber of our heart. This secret chamber is your own private meditation room, your interior castle, as Teresa of Avila called it. In Hindu tradition, the devotee visualizes a jeweled island in his heart. There he sees himself before a beautiful altar, where he worships his teacher in deep meditation.

Jesus spoke of entering the secret chamber of the heart when he said: "When thou prayest, enter into thy closet, and when thou hast shut thy door, pray to thy Father which is in secret; and thy Father which seeth in secret shall reward thee openly."

The lower figure in the Chart of Your Divine Self represents you as a soul on the spiritual path, surrounded by the violet flame and the protective white light of God, the "tube of light." Your soul is the living potential of God—the part of you that is mortal but that can become immortal. The high-frequency energy of the violet flame can help you reach that goal more quickly.

The purpose of your soul's evolution on earth is to grow in self-mastery, balance your karma and fulfill your mission on earth so that you can return to the spiritual dimensions that are your real home. When your soul at last takes flight and ascends back to God and the heaven-world, you will become an "ascended" master, free from the rounds of karma and rebirth.

Notes

Foreword
1. Matt. 13:33.
2. Rom. 12:4; I Cor. 12:27; Eph. 4:12.
3. Rev. 12:10–11.
4. Acts 2:1.
5. Rev. 21:3.
6. Matt. 24:14.
7. Rev. 11:3, 10.
8. Rev. 12:5.
9. Rom. 8:7.
10. John 1:9.

Introduction
1. I Sam. 16:1.
2. I Sam. 16:11–13.
3. Isa. 11:1–2.
4. Ps. 16:9–11.
5. Ps. 17:15.
6. Ps. 19:14.
7. Deut. 6:4.
8. *The Lost Books of the Bible* (Cleveland and New York: World Publishing Co., 1926), The Gospel of the Birth of Mary I:1–3.
9. Matt. 5:37.
10. John the Beloved, April 19, 1973, "The Body of God upon Earth" in 1973 *Pearls of Wisdom*, vol. 16, no. 25 (Corwin Springs, Mont.: The Summit Lighthouse), p. 108.
11. *Lost Books*, Birth of Mary I:5–6.
12. Exod. 3:14.
13. Saint John Damascene, quoted in *Heavenly Friends* (Boston: The Daughters of Saint Paul, 1958), pp. 312–13.

14. *Lost Books*, Birth of Mary I:9–10, 11.
15. Ibid., II:1–5.
16. Ibid., II:9–12.
17. Ibid., III:1–5, 11.
18. Ibid., IV.
19. Ibid., V:1–3.
20. Ibid., V:4–6.
21. Ibid., V:10–17.
22. Ibid., VI:1–5.
23. *Lost Books*, The Protevangelion IX:7.
24. Ibid., IX:8–17.
25. Ibid., IX:18.
26. Luke 1:39–56; *Lost Books*, Protevangelion IX:20–21.
27. Ibid., XI:8–22.
28. *Lost Books*, The First Gospel of the Infancy of Jesus Christ I:4–21.

PART ONE
Fourteen Letters

1. Gen. 5:18–24.
2. Matt. 15:14.
3. Matt. 23:24.
4. Prov. 4:7.
5. Matt. 28:18.
6. Rom. 8:17.
7. John 16:13.
8. II Tim. 2:15.
9. Matt. 6:10.
10. I Cor. 12:13; Eph. 4:4.
11. Matt. 6:23.
12. Exod. 25:20.
13. I John 4:18.
14. John 8:11.
15. Rev. 12:11.

16. Rev. 3:8.
17. Gal. 5:22-23.
18. James 1:27.
19. John 17:11.
20. II Pet. 3:16.
21. Eph. 6:12.
22. Matt. 19:26.
23. Col. 2:9.
24. II Cor. 3:6.
25. I Sam. 16:7.
26. Gen. 4:9.
27. Gen. 1:28.
28. Matt. 6:34.
29. I Thess. 5:21.
30. I John 2:17.
31. I Cor. 3:13.
32. Ps. 23:6.
33. I Cor. 13:13.
34. Matt. 5:16.
35. Matt. 24:6.
36. John 14:1.
37. I Thess. 5:21.
38. Matt. 5:6.
39. Rev. 16.
40. I Tim. 6:10.
41. Matt. 25:14-30.
42. John 6:1-14.
43. Matt. 15:27.
44. Job 1:21.
45. Luke 12:32.
46. Phil. 4:19.
47. Dan. 11:31; Mark 13:14.
48. St. Athanasius, *On the Incarnation of the Word of God*, 54, 4th cent.

49. Matt. 24:6.
50. Acts 17:24.
51. John 15:17.
52. John 5:17.
53. Gen. 1:27.
54. John 10:30.
55. Phil. 2:10.
56. I Cor. 15:28.
57. John 4:24.
58. I Cor. 8:5–6.
59. Rev. 5:13.
60. Matt. 5:18.
61. Gal. 6:7.
62. Ps. 136.
63. I Cor. 15:50.
64. Exod. 8:15; Matt. 19:8.
65. Luke 2:40.
66. Gen. 1:26.
67. Gal. 6:9.
68. Jer. 31:34.
69. Matt. 13:25.
70. Matt. 24:22.
71. Josh. 24:15.
72. I John 4:1.
73. Luke 21:19.
74. Luke 2:14.
75. II Cor. 3:6.
76. Rev. 21:1.
77. John 16:13.
78. Ps. 23:3.
79. Aesop's Fables, *The Hare and the Tortoise*.
80. John 14:26.
81. II Sam. 6:6–7.

82. Thomas à Kempis, *The Imitation of Christ*, bk. 1, chap. 19, p. 35.
83. Luke 23:46.
84. "God and my right," Richard I.
85. "The state, it is I!" Louis XIV.
86. I Cor. 13:12.
87. Prov. 14:12.
88. The Apostle Paul in a letter to the Galatians.
89. Gal. 6:7.
90. Matt. 5:18.
91. Rev. 3:12.
92. Rev. 21:16, 23.
93. John 10:30.
94. Isa. 65:24.
95. James 4:3.
96. Acts 17:28.
97. Heb. 11:1.
98. Lam. 3:26.

PART TWO
Christian Prayer Forms

1. Matt. 6:6.
2. Isa. 45:11.
3. Gen. 1:28.
4. Isa. 66:1.
5. Luke 22:42.
6. Ps. 91:14–16.
7. Luke 11:2.
8. Job 22:28.
9. Matt. 18:19.
10. John 16:23.
11. Matt. 14:23; Luke 6:12; 9:28; Mark 1:12–13; 4:39; Luke 22:42; John 5:8; Matt. 9:2, 22; John 11:43; Matt. 16:23.

12. John 17:9–10, 20–21.
13. John 21:15–17.
14. Matt. 16:18.
15. Matt. 5:5, 8–10.
16. John 11:25; 8:12; 9:5; 10:10; 14:6; 14:10, 11.
17. Gen. 4:25–26.
18. Rom. 10:18.
19. Rom. 10:13.
20. Luke 1:28.
21. Luke 1:42.
22. *Encyclopaedia Britannica*, 1949, s.v. "Nestorius."
23. John 1:14.
24. Mary, "A Letter from Mother Mary," Keepers of the Flame Lesson 16, p. 9.
25. Rev. 12.
26. Mary, Keepers of the Flame Lesson 16, p. 11.
27. Rev. 12:17.
28. Rev. 1:8.
29. Exod. 3:14.
30. Ps. 82:1–2, 6.
31. Rev. 12:10.
32. John 10:30.
33. John 5:17.
34. John 10:32–38.
35. John 1:12.
36. I John 3:2.
37. Gen. 2:7.
38. Matt. 3:17.
39. William Thomas Walsh, *Our Lady of Fatima*, (Garden City, N.Y.: Doubleday & Co., Image Books, 1954), p. 202.
40. Dictation by El Morya, 12 December 1972.
41. Mother Mary, April 20, 1973, "Communion Feast at the Temple of the Resurrection with Mary, Jesus, and Lanello," in

1973 *Pearls of Wisdom*, vol. 16, no. 30 (Corwin Springs, Mont.: The Summit Lighthouse), pp. 128-29.
42. Ibid.
43. John 17:22.
44. Rev. 21:2.

The Teaching Mysteries

    First Teaching Mystery
    Matt. 5:1-12.
    Second Teaching Mystery
    Matt. 22:2-14.
    Third Teaching Mystery
    Matt. 18:23-35.
    Fourth Teaching Mystery
    Matt. 25:1-13.
    Fifth Teaching Mystery
    Matt. 13:36-43; 18:18-20.

The Masterful Mysteries

    First Masterful Mystery
    Matt. 4:1-11.
    Second Masterful Mystery
    Luke 8:41-54; Mark 5:41; Luke 8:55; Mark 5:42.
    Third Masterful Mystery
    Matt. 14:22-33.
    Fourth Masterful Mystery
    Luke 9:28-29; Matt. 17:2; Luke 9:30-32; Matt. 17:4-8.
    Fifth Masterful Mystery
    John 11:1, 3-4, 6-7, 20-27, 41-44.

The Love Mysteries

> First Love Mystery
> John 3:30; 1:6-9; Matt. 3:1-3; Luke 3:16, 17; Matt. 3:13-17; 11:11.
>
> Second Love Mystery
> John 14:15-31.
>
> Third Love Mystery
> John 15:1-17.
>
> Fourth Love Mystery
> John 21:3-6, 9-12, 15-17.
>
> Fifth Love Mystery
> I John 3:1-11.

The Joyful Mysteries

> First Joyful Mystery
> Luke 1:26-38.
>
> Second Joyful Mystery
> Luke 1:39-55, 57; John 1:6; Luke 1:67, 76-79.
>
> Third Joyful Mystery
> John 1:1-5; Luke 2:4-14, 20, 19; Matt. 2:1-2, 11; John 1:14.
>
> Fourth Joyful Mystery
> Luke 2:22, 25-40.
>
> Fifth Joyful Mystery
> Luke 2:41-49, 51-52.

The Healing Mysteries

> First Healing Mystery
> John 8:12-19, 28, 29, 31, 32.
>
> Second Healing Mystery
> John 5:2-9, 19, 24-25.
>
> Third Healing Mystery
> John 9:1-7, 39-41.

Fourth Healing Mystery
Luke 17:11-21.

Fifth Healing Mystery
Rev. 11:3-13.

The Initiatic Mysteries

First Initiatic Mystery
Matt. 26:26; I Cor. 11:24; Matt. 26:27-29; John 13:4-10, 14-15; 14:12-14.

Second Initiatic Mystery
John 17:1, 4; Luke 22:39-44; Matt. 26:40-41, 45-46; John 18:4-6; Luke 22:50-51; John 18:11; Matt. 26:53-54; Luke 22:52-53.

Third Initiatic Mystery
Matt. 27:1-2; John 18:33, 36-38; Matt. 27:24-26; John 19:2-5.

Fourth Initiatic Mystery
Luke 9:23-24; Matt. 11:28-30; John 19:17, 19; Luke 23:26-28, 31; John 15:20; 16:2, 22-24, 33.

Fifth Initiatic Mystery
John 12:24-25; Luke 23:33-34, 39, 42-43; John 19:26-27; Mark 15:33-34; Luke 23:46; Mark 15:38-39; John 12:31-32.

The Glorious Mysteries

First Glorious Mystery
Matt. 28:1-10; John 20:19-23.

Second Glorious Mystery
Luke 24:46-49; Matt. 28:18-20; Acts 1:8-11; Mark 16:20.

Third Glorious Mystery
Acts 2:1-4, 6-7, 14, 16-18, 21, 38-39, 41.

Fourth Glorious Mystery
Rev. 12:1-11.

Fifth Glorious Mystery
Rev. 12:12–17; 21:1–4, 6, 7; 22:17.

The Miracle Mysteries

First Miracle Mystery
John 2:1–11.

Second Miracle Mystery
Luke 8:22–35.

Third Miracle Mystery
John 6:1–10; Luke 9:14; John 6:11–14.

Fourth Miracle Mystery
John 8:2–11.

Fifth Miracle Mystery
John 6:35, 38–40, 44, 48–51, 53–57.

PART THREE

Fourteen Messages

1. Isa. 6:3.
2. Matt. 22:11–12.
3. John 19:23.
4. Eph. 6:11, 13.
5. Gen. 15:1.
6. John 1:14.
7. Rom. 8:7.
8. Jer. 13:23.
9. Matt. 6:27.
10. Rom. 13:12.
11. II Tim. 3:1.
12. Ps. 24:1.
13. Rev. 1:6; 5:10.
14. Gen. 1:28.
15. Rom. 8:7.
16. Acts 2:1–4.

17. Rev. 18:2.
18. Matt. 24:51.
19. John 21:22.
20. Rev. 12:11.
21. Thomas Jefferson, *Declaration of Independence*.
22. Jer. 8:22.
23. Matt. 28:6.
24. Matt. 22:11–12.
25. John 19:23.
26. Rev. 3:17–18.
27. Col. 3:9.
28. James 4:8.
29. Acts 2:1–4.
30. James 1:17.
31. Gen. 3:24.
32. Matt. 10:42.
33. John 14:2.
34. II Kings 2:14.
35. II Kings 2:11.
36. Alexander Pope, *An Essay on Criticism*, pt. 3, line 66.
37. Gen. 14:18; Heb. 6:20.
38. Jer. 31:33; Heb. 8:10.
39. Gen. 1:28.
40. John 4:35.
41. Isa. 30:20.
42. Heb. 13:2.
43. Matt. 9:20–22.
44. Rev. 1:16.
45. Matt. 15:8.
46. Heb. 6:6.
47. Num. 21:9.
48. Rev. 12:5.
49. Ruth 1:16.

50. Matt. 25:40; 18:6.
51. I Cor. 3:16; 6:19.
52. Matt. 24:35.
53. Matt. 5:18.
54. John 19:23.
55. Matt. 5:5.
56. I Kings 17:17-23.
57. Dan. 3:19-28.
58. John 11:25.
59. Matt. 28:18.
60. William Shakespeare, *Hamlet*, act 1, sc. 3, lines 78-80.
61. Matt. 8:20.
62. Mark 4:39.
63. Rev. 12:11.
64. John 1:9.
65. Luke 2:40.
66. Isa. 9:2; Matt. 4:16.
67. John 8:3-11.
68. Luke 12:32.
69. Matt. 3:17.
70. Phil. 3:14.
71. II Thess. 3:13.
72. Matt. 25:7.
73. John 10:30.
74. John 14:1.
75. Matt. 23:37.
76. Acts 7:33; Exod. 3:5.
77. Matt. 13:33.
78. Matt. 14:27.
79. Rev. 7:17; 21:4.
80. Heb. 11:1.
81. I John 4:18.
82. John 19:23.

83. Heb. 12:29.
84. II Cor. 3:18.
85. Prov. 16:25.
86. Luke 1:28.
87. Isa. 42:3; Matt. 12:20.
88. Num. 17:8.
89. John 14:6.
90. Luke 1:78.
91. Rev. 2:7.
92. Matt. 27:51.
93. Heb. 10:19–20.
94. Matt. 26:41.
95. Matt. 24:43–44.
96. Matt. 26:40.
97. John 13:27.
98. Rev. 21:1.
99. II Thess. 3:13.
100. Rev. 12:11.
101. I John 3:2.
102. Mark 4:39.
103. Ps. 46:10.
104. Phil. 3:14.
105. Luke 21:19.
106. Matt. 25:1–13.
107. Matt. 28:20.
108. John 20:13.
109. Luke 23:27–28.
110. Matt. 5:15.
111. Matt. 7:7.
112. Isa. 66:1.
113. Luke 22:42.
114. Rev. 6:16.
115. Matt. 24:51.

116. Rev. 12:2.
117. Gen. 18:32.
118. II Cor. 12:2.
119. Isa. 1:18.
120. John 17:11.
121. Eph. 6:16.
122. The ascended masters and their messenger Elizabeth Clare Prophet have revealed in later years that Jesus did not take his ascension at the conclusion of his Palestinian ministry, returning to the heart of God, but removed himself from Palestine in the ritual on Bethany's hill. He left in this way because he had fulfilled his Palestinian ministry. After his crucifixion and resurrection he journeyed to Kashmir and at the age of eighty-one ascended from the etheric retreat of Shamballa. See Jesus Christ, June 27, 1993, "The Path of the Builders," 1993 *Pearls of Wisdom*, vol. 36, no. 36 (Corwin Springs, Mont.: The Summit Lighthouse), pp. 522–23.
123. Matt. 28:20.

OTHER TITLES FROM

SUMMIT UNIVERSITY ☙ PRESS

Fallen Angels and the Origins of Evil
Kabbalah: Key to Your Inner Power
Reincarnation: The Missing Link in Christianity
The Lost Years of Jesus
The Lost Teachings of Jesus
The Human Aura
Saint Germain On Alchemy
Saint Germain's Prophecy for the New Millennium
Prayer and Meditation
The Chela and the Path
Lords of the Seven Rays
Quietly Comes the Buddha
Warrior of Light: The Life of Nicholas Roerich
Keys to the Kingdom and New Dimensions of Being
Soul Reflections: Many Lives, Many Journeys
Inner Perspectives: A Guidebook for the Spiritual Journey
Wanting to Live: Overcoming the Seduction of Suicide

CLIMB THE HIGHEST MOUNTAIN SERIES:
The Path of the Higher Self
The Path of Self-Transformation
The Masters and the Spiritual Path
The Path of Brotherhood
The Path of the Universal Christ
The Masters and Their Retreats

POCKET GUIDES TO PRACTICAL SPIRITUALITY:

Karma and Reincarnation*

Your Seven Energy Centers*

Alchemy of the Heart*

Soul Mates and Twin Flames*

The Art of Practical Spirituality*

Creative Abundance*

How to Work with Angels

Access the Power of Your Higher Self

Violet Flame to Heal Body, Mind and Soul

The Creative Power of Sound

TITLES FROM

THE SUMMIT LIGHTHOUSE LIBRARY®

The Opening of the Seventh Seal

Morya I

Community

Walking with the Master: Answering the Call of Jesus

Wanting to Be Born: The Cry of the Soul

Afra: Brother of Light

Books from Summit University Press and The Summit Lighthouse Library are available from fine bookstores everywhere. For a free catalog or to place an order, call 1-800-245-5445 or 406-848-9500.
www.summituniversitypress.com

---

*also available as audiobooks

Mark L. Prophet and Elizabeth Clare Prophet are pioneers of modern spirituality and internationally renowned authors. Among their best-selling titles are *The Lost Years of Jesus, The Lost Teachings of Jesus, The Human Aura, Saint Germain On Alchemy, Fallen Angels and the Origins of Evil* and the Pocket Guides to Practical Spirituality series, which includes *Karma and Reincarnation, Your Seven Energy Centers* and *Soul Mates and Twin Flames*. Their books are translated into more than 20 languages and are sold worldwide.

Printed by Libri Plureos GmbH in Hamburg, Germany